# SHOOTING
# STARS

# SHOOTING STARS

*Heroes and Heroines of Western Film*

EDITED BY
Archie P. McDonald

*Indiana University Press*

BLOOMINGTON & INDIANAPOLIS

Manufactured in the United States of America

**Library of Congress Cataloging-in-Publication Data**

Shooting stars.
1. Western films—History and criticism.
2. Moving-picture actors and actresses—United
States.   I. McDonald, Archie P.
PN1995.9.W4S48   1987        791.43'09'093278        85-45988
ISBN 0-253-36685-2
ISBN 0-253-20415-1 (pbk.)
1 2 3 4 5 91 90 89 88 87

# CONTENTS

# ILLUSTRATIONS

ARCHIE P. McDONALD

# Shooting Stars: An Introduction

IN BEAUMONT, TEXAS, in 1945, the magic of the cinema charged the air-conditioned atmosphere of the Jefferson Theatre on Fannin Street. A boy of ten, I often attended the Jefferson (or the People's, the Rio, the Liberty, or the Tivoli) to participate in the two-dimensional make-believe world of the movies. For a three-cent bus ride "downtown," a nine-cent child's ticket, and a three-cent ride home, or fifteen cents American, I could enjoy one of the few air-conditioned facilities in town, a factor of some importance in that humid, coastal capital of the Texas petroleum industry, and if I had an extra fifteen cents for pop-corn and a coke I would sit through the feature twice.

Saturday mornings found me in line early for the Organ Club. The already irritated ticket lady, for she had been dreading the invasion of exuberant youth that awaited her all night, began to sell tickets to the day's entertainment at 8:30 A.M. By nine o'clock, every seat filled with a squirming, yelling, child of six or sixteen, the place resembled the dwelling of the Old Lady Who Lived in the Shoe.

The Jefferson Theatre, one of those ornate movie-vaudeville show places constructed with such elegance in the 1920s, housed the Organ Club. This profitable Saturday morning entertainment was so named because a man named Al Sacker descended into the organ pit precisely at nine o'clock. Presently the sound of music filled the air from more than 100 pipes, and then Sacker and the whole organ would rise on its hydraulic pedestal from beneath the stage and continue until it reached the maximum height allowed by the limits of the lift. We cheered as if Sacker and the Organ were the only entertainment in town, and we were very nearly correct.

Then the stage curtains parted—the Jefferson never surrendered a proud claim as a legitimate playhouse despite the fact it showed movies most of the time—and then we would sing along as a bouncing ball prompted us through song after song that appeared on the screen.

Warmed up and ready for more, we watched local talent perform live, on stage, while the bald-headed theatre manager, who acted as master of ceremonies, encouraged the audience to support a nine-year-old girl attempting to sing a torch song, a twelve-year-old boy tap dance, or three stairstepped siblings do their best to sound like the Andrews Sisters. When this torture mercifully ended, the stagestruck youngsters lined up on the stage, blinked through the brilliant haze of strong lights, and tried to smile when the manager stepped behind them and placed his hand over their head. If the crowd wanted that performer to win the silver dollar premium that represented first prize at these contests, they screamed as loud as possible. When the winner, usually meaning the candidate with the most friends rather than the most talent, had prevailed and the others received consolation free passes to a new opportunity to win next week, we got down to business.

Next came Episode Six of the Jungle Jim serial, assorted cartoons—the only color film we would see—previews of coming attractions, and the Movie-Tone News, considered the last chance to get more popcorn or go to the john, we finally got to see the feature. It mattered little who acted in the movie, when it had been filmed, or how long it ran: It would be a cowboy picture, and that was all we needed to know.

So with the older kids paired and holding hands in the back seats, and the younger ones anxiously bunched on the front rows to get a better view of the perennial contest between good and evil, we passed our youth enthralled by the images before us. Later, after the tests of puberty and the passing into adulthood, a few of us continued this infatuation with movies.

Twelve of us, the contributors to this tribute, study, and celebration of the Shooting Stars, the heroes and heroines of the silver screen, caught the vision and kept it, however separated we were by geography and time. Later generations found their entertainment and their profession on a smaller screen and perhaps a bigger world.

As for me, though older if not wiser and more experienced if not more sophisticated, things came closer to their rightful order amid the chaos of the Organ Club than when movies are explicit, and good and evil are fuzzy and situational. There was the good feeling, no matter how twisted the plot or how dire the situation, that the movies, and our lives, would have a happy ending. Hollywood knew better than to leave its audience wanting to kick a dog in frustration because the hero died or failed to save the ranch at the end of the movie. And somehow we knew that if we lived like Gene, or Roy, or Hoppy that the rainbow of our life also had a pot of gold waiting for us.

The Jefferson is still there, a monument to its breed. Its kind could be found in every sizable town in America. Now it is surrounded by parking lots instead of drug stores, ladies specialty shops, and the other

services of a bustling downtown shopping area. The curtains are drawn
only for road shows, and this only because some could not let the Jefferson die a clean, quick death. It is the well-meaning way of preserva-
tionists; they kept it alive because no one had the guts to pull the plug.
It is now mostly dark, and a sad thing to see, this place of so much joy.

What happened to the Jefferson theatres of our youth symbolizes
our lives. The reader should note that most of the contributors do not
share the editor's generation. For them, the results of their research on
their subject represents historical and critical scholarship. But for
some, and especially for me, this has been a profound experience of hero
worship and of remembering a time when there were heroes to
worship.

Of course the time came when I knew that my heroes could not be
real. They could not remain as the film captured them forever, for life
let them get old. Some accumulated great wealth—Randolph Scott, for
example—and some did not. A few shifted to other genre of film when
the Westerns died, and some just faded away to an unknown life much
different from our idealized image. While they held center stage,
though, they filled our need for heroes, persons worthy of our faith and
respect.

The American Frontier, the real one, gave us such heroes as soon
as there was a Frontier. John Smith, the argumentative, early co-
governor of Jamestown Plantation in Virginia, became the first
because he said he was a hero in his own book, the very first history of
Virginia. Daniel Boone, David Crockett, George Armstrong Custer,
and a host of others, including some such as Pecos Bill or Paul Bunyan
who were real only in the mind, joined Smith in the hero's line. All
became legends from accounts of their lives that were only partly historical, and each became larger than himself in the telling of his cleverness, his strength, and his intelligence. We needed such heroes because
they represented our ideal of ourselves as Americans.

Then came the movies, and we could see real people represented on
the screen. This helped us visualize and personify our heroes: Wild Bill
Hickok forever in my mind's eye will look like a handsome man I knew
as Gary Cooper, and for my generation Wyatt Earp and Burt Lancaster
are the same.

The movies replaced the printed page in its representation of our
heroes. Owen Wister's *The Virginian* started the twentieth century
with a Western hero, but the origins of the movement began at least as
early as Cooper's *Leatherstocking Tales*, found form in Twain's *Rough-*

*ing It*, and later blossomed and matured in Guthrie's *The Big Sky* or Clark's *Ox-Bow Incident*. Lesser writers—Ernest Haycox, Luke Short, Max Brand, Zane Grey, Frank Slaughter, and the one-and-only Louis L'Amour, writers of hundreds of Western novels—have contributed to the image of the Western hero. Radio played its part, for before television allowed us to see such heroes at will sound alone did the job. Brace Beamer, the voice of the real Lone Ranger, and the gravelly voice of Bill Conrad, the original Matt Dillon, showed us right from wrong and that right prevailed in the end.

The first genuine movie hero, G. M. "Broncho Billy" Anderson, got his start in *The Great Train Robbery* near the turn of the century. Anderson could not ride a horse at the time, but eventually he survived hundreds of one- and two-reel episodes in the early days of commercial film.

Anderson set the format for a Western. The hero comes first. He must be clean of mind and pure of body, and, in the celebrated Ten Commandments attributed to Gene Autry, must not take unfair advantage or go back on his word; he must tell the truth regardless of the cost; he must show gentleness to children and animals and respect for the elderly; he must help those in distress, work hard, and respect women and the law; and he must be patriotic. In Camelot there was such a man, Lancelot by name, but alas, even he got lost in the spell of Guinevere.

Allowing our man this one human trait, the Western plot had to have a "girl." Usually she lacked a mother but loved a father who always needed help. She herself frequently required rescuing, so our hero seemed in perpetual motion saving the heroine or her hapless pappy.

But rescuing from whom? Or what? Indians sometimes, but most likely from "the bad guys," the villains. We knew them on sight: the "dog heavy" who wore scruffy boots, ill-fitting and usually dark clothing and hat, and always seemed shifty and defensive; and the "brains," usually a banker, for they were evil men who duped ranchers out of their land, or saloon owners who cheated their customers, or some other incarnation of evil. Their chastisement, usually reserved for the final reel, required cheers, even when we became too old to let the world hear.

Anderson began it. William Surrey Hart added authenticity during his co-reign with Tom Mix during the 1920s, and then Buck Jones, Ken Maynard, Harry Carey, among others, joined them to

satisfy our insatiable desire for more heroes. In the 1930s a whole corral
of them appeared, some with guitar and comic sidekick. The best by far
was Gene Autry, followed by Roy Rogers, William Boyd as Hopalong
Cassidy, Charles Starrett as the Durango Kid, Lash LaRue and Whip
Wilson—masters with the whip—Sunset Carson, Johnny Mack
Brown, Bob Steele (Bradbury), Rocky Lane, Wild Bill Elliott, Monte
Hale, Don "Red" Barry, Tim McCoy, George O'Brien, Hoot Gibson, and
. . . the list goes on. They rode Champion or Trigger or Tony, and drew
amusement and help from Smiley Burnett, Walter Brennan, "Fuzzy"
Knight, or George "Gabby" Hayes, and they dispensed justice with
fairness, firmness, and inevitability.

Then things changed. John Ford pioneered "social Westerns," and
the rangy frame of John Wayne as the Ringo Kid caught a stagecoach to
Lordsburg. From that moment until his death nearly four decades later
Wayne became THE Western hero. Some preferred Cooper, or Scott, or
James Stewart, distinguished and successful actors all, but for the
majority of moviegoers the world over, John Wayne was simply the ultimate Western hero.

In the shade of World War II, the last era in which all Americans
joined in a common purpose, we entered a Cold War and a cold world
that changed us forever. And our Westerns followed suit. Howard
Hughes introduced Jane Russell's ample and memorable body in *The
Outlaw*, and now our cowboys discovered sex—not just sexuality—but
sex. And Gregory Peck and Jennifer Jones made their *Duel in the Sun*
sultry. Our cowboys also discovered psychology, as in the *Gunfight at
the O.K. Corral*, which explored the curious relationship of Wyatt Earp
(Burt Lancaster) and Doc Holliday (Kirk Douglas), or in *High Noon*,
when the hero is saved by his low-woman and rejected by his high-
woman at the most crucial moment of his life, his defense of his honor
and his town, even though the town is afraid to defend itself. Things
really turned violent in the 1960s when Sergio Leone's Westerns introduced a different kind of hero in the laconic but forceful Clint Eastwood
to those who remembered his less frightening performances in *Rawhide* on television. And television gave us so many cowboys we could
not count them all. And then, partly because of the plenty, Westerns
died.

Eleven colleagues from throughout the United States have joined
me in this examination of Western film heroes. We did not work toward
a central theme; each pursued his or her subject independently and
expressed his or her own interpretations. Michael K. Schoenecke

examines William S. Hart and his insistence upon authenticity in his Westerns; Raymond E. White reminds us of the athletic prowess and genuine cowboy skills of Ken Maynard; John Lenihan, author of *Show-down*, in an examination of the impact upon Westerns by the times in which they were made, tells us of a Randolph Scott surprised by his success; Stephen Tatum writes of the classic Westerner, Gary Cooper; the significant impact of Gene Autry is chronicled by Ray Merlock; the editor contributed a rhapsody (some would call him biased) on his all-time favorite Cowboy Hero, John Wayne; Don Graham remembers a kid from Texas, an absolutely authentic hero named Audie Murphy; Michael Welsh writes of President Ronald Reagan when he rode the range; Richard Robertson tells us about Burt Lancaster; Jim Miller, a writer of Western novels, traces the career of Clint Eastwood; Sandra Kay Schackel tells us about the civilizers and the saloon singers—the women—in the Western; and Gary A. Yoggy concludes the volume with a remembrance of when television wore six-guns. Each has reviewed the literature and the films, each has studied his or her subject as scholar and as student, and each has given us a fresh, informative, and entertaining look at his or her subject.

In the summer of 1985 the corpse of the Western gave a twitch. Perhaps it did not die after all. Perhaps the Western had been there all along, cruising in spaceships instead of riding honest horses, shooting lasers instead of Colts and Winchesters. Could it be that after the *Star Wars* and *Galacticas*, when Rambo and the Ninji go past the possible, and beyond cute comedies, nearly all of them starring the gorgeous and humorous Goldie Hawn, could it be that a *Pale Rider* will return, a *Silverado* will soar, and a COWBOY will reign again?

In July of that resurrection summer, a cartoon appeared in the newspapers. In early frames two young girls talk in front of a movie house. One looks at a playbill advertising *Silverado* and says "Good looks are just not enough for me," to which the other responds, "Yes, I want a man of intelligence." The first responds in the second frame that she wants a man with financial savvy and political astuteness, and they agree on the desirability of computer literacy. In the third frame they are in the movie, silent. In the last frame they exit the theatre and shout in unison, "I WANT A COWBOY."

Many agree. But it can never be the same. Most of the heroes in this book are gone, save for their image on film that quickens less frequently now that they are consigned to film festivals or late shows on television. Only Eastwood is still professionally active. Some are dead,

Wayne among them. That great, heavy figure who fought hard and shot straight, who brought Debbie home from the Comanches, fulfilled Katie Elder's faith in her sons, faced down the evil men in Lordsburg who killed his brother and stole his father's ranch, who nearly even saved the Alamo, is silent forever.

Some day, perhaps, another Wayne or Cooper or Scott or Autry will come along for a new generation. But not for me. My heroes, my ghosts, are still in the Jefferson. I can yet catch the echoes of Al Sacker playing the organ, see the poor kid trip over his foot in the talent contest, feel the self-consciousness of singing along with the bouncing ball, and above all, remember the satisfaction of sitting back and watching the Duke take on the town, knowing that, in the end, everything will be all right.

# ACKNOWLEDGMENTS

SEVERAL PEOPLE deserve special thanks. Dr. Robert Mandel invited the submission of the manuscript after reading my essay on John Wayne in Richard W. Etulain's *Western Film*, a special issue of the *Journal of the West* that appeared in October 1983. For his confidence in the viability of this book, I thank him most kindly. My colleagues—Don B. Graham, University of Texas at Austin; John H. Lenihan, Texas A&M University; Ray Merlock, University of South Carolina at Spartanburg; Jim Miller, Aurora, Colorado; Richard C. Robertson, St. Louis, Missouri; Sandra Schackel, Albuquerque, New Mexico; Michael K. Schoenecke, Texas Tech University; Stephen Tatum, University of Utah; Michael E. Welsh, Albuquerque, New Mexico; Raymond E. White, Ball State University; and Gary A. Yoggy, Corning Community College—contributed far more than I to the scholarship of this book.

I would especially like to acknowledge Drs. William R. Johnson, Edwin W. Gaston, James V. Reese, William J. Brophy, and Robert N. Mathis, my bosses, for their support, and Mrs. Karen Gehring for manuscript preparation.

My admiration also goes to all the Western movie heroes from Broncho Billy to Clint Eastwood, with a special tip of the hat to John Wayne. And I would like to thank Judy McDonald, my heroine for three decades who never needs rescuing, for thinking there was nothing abnormal about a grown man strapping on a toy pistol and outdrawing James Arness at the beginning of each episode of *Gunsmoke*.

# SHOOTING STARS

MICHAEL K. SCHOENECKE

# William S. Hart:
# Authenticity and the West

W<small>ILLIAM</small> S. H<small>ART</small> saw his first Western film in 1914 while traveling with a theatrical troupe in Cleveland, Ohio. Hart complained to the theatre manager, who assured him that the film was one of the best Westerns he had ever shown, that the film was bad because of the historical inaccuracies, the burlesque acting, and the flaws in setting and costume. Spurred by the insensitivity and simpleminded portrayal of this Western experience, Hart believed that he could rescue the Western genre if he could make his way to California. In *My Life East and West*, Hart's autobiography, he recalled the opportunity because

> Rise or fall, sink or swim, I had to bend every endeavor to get a chance to make a Western motion picture. Usually when stirred by ambition I would become afraid. But surely this could not be the valor of ignorance. I had been waiting for years for the right thing, and now the right thing had come! I was a part of the West—it was my boyhood home—it was in my blood. The very love I bore it made me know its ways. I had a thorough training as an actor. I was considerd the outstanding portrayer of Western roles on the American stage.[1]

Hart saw as many pictures as possible in preparation for the move to California to begin work in Western films. When the opportunity for acting in motion pictures presented itself, Hart made good. His films not only helped revive the genre between 1910 and 1920 but also established him as the first true Western hero.

William S. Hart, the son of Nicholas and Rosanna Hart, was born
on December 6, 1870, in Newburgh, New York. Hart's family, who called
themselves "white gold [flour] pioneers,"[2] wandered across Minnesota
and Wisconsin before settling near a Sioux reservation in Dakota Territory, where they began construction of their flour mill. As a youngster
"Willie" Hart played with Sioux children and learned to appreciate and
cherish Indian mores and traditions. He tended to associate Indians,
particularly the Sioux, with the frontier past that produced many
unique and desirable human characteristics: kindness, honesty, and a
straightforward character.

> What clean, healthful lives they lived! A tipi is a poor place to hold
> secrets—so they had none. They were as God intended human beings
> should be; there was no lying, cheating, bickering—no strife. They
> wronged no man or woman either; every custom under which they lived
> was one of trust and fairness. Their tipis all faced the east, from whence
> came the sun.[3]

For Hart the Indian personified the fundamental premises of life. Not
only did he incorporate these values into his personal life, but they became the gist of his film persona. Later, when he built his Horseshoe
Ranch in Newhall, California, he championed the Indian culture and
spirit with paintings, sculptures, and artifacts.[4]

Hard work and danger characterized Hart's early life on the frontier. As a young man he accompanied his father on a cattle drive to
Abilene, Kansas. Later, trapped in the crossfire of Sioux City's sheriff
and two "gambler gun-men," they saw two men die.[5] These experiences,
plus personal contact with men who helped tame the West such as
Wyatt Earp and W. B. (Bat) Masterson, fired Hart's imagination;
because the sheriff and Earp jeopardized their own safety to fight the
enemies of the community, their willingness to sacrifice their lives for
others represented the highest form of heroism to Hart. To endure and
survive in the West required a special breed of men who were tough,
humorless, hard-nosed, and prepared for violence. With this in mind,
Hart began to develop a perspective of life that governed the West:
"that lawless law, 'survival of the fittest,' that disregards ALL law, had
a strangle grip on the cripples and weak doggies that bawled their distress in a pathetic manner."[6] Hart, whose first thirteen years developed
an understanding of the true ways of the West, drew upon these personal observations to define the Western hero he later portrayed on
screen.

Nicholas Hart was a quiet, thoughtful man and William later referred to him as one of the "atoms in the building of an Empire."[7] Although Nicholas never fully realized his dream—a millsite and waterpower of his own, which would mean a lasting home for the family—he symbolized courage, honesty, and manliness to Willie. Twice Nicholas fought and defeated two men who threatened his family; once he captured two horse thieves; once he saved another man from being hanged. Nicholas instilled in Willie the need for direction in life:

> On the plains the foreman of a wagon train, when going into camp, always pointed the tongue of his lead wagon toward the North Star. If it was cloudy the next morning or if he broke camp before sunup, he had his direction. My father's "North Star," to which he always pointed in cloudy weather or sunshine, was a river of rippling water that had power behind it. The scorchings of fate only burnished his desire and made him stick the stronger to this direction. He never wavered.[8]

Willie learned to persevere, and from these recollections of his father, he learned that he could be successful in life if he possessed an indomitable spirit which embodied such traits as simplicity, humility, self-reliance, and moral insight. Interestingly, Hart's film portrayals championed the cowboy who epitomized such characteristics.

Dreams of a western home and life faded for the Harts when their mill failed to produce a profit and when they incurred considerable medical expenses. First, his baby brother died in Dakota Territory and Willie, his sister, and their father buried the infant on a hill overlooking the Mississippi headwaters near Red Wing, Minnesota. Then his mother, who lacked the physical stamina needed to lead a nomadic life, was told that she would have to return to the East for surgery. His father suffered an eye injury while milling when a sliver of steel lodged near one pupil; the inflammation then spread to the other eye. He could not afford to send half of the family East while he and Willie stayed in Dakota Territory. Finally, in 1878, the Harts were forced to return to Newburgh. These hardships exposed the young, impressionable Willie to the harsh realities of establishing a family on the frontier.

Nicholas Hart took a job in a mill in Newburgh. When his hand was caught in a conveyor belt, he had to pull his crushed arm free and, as a result, lost the back of his hand from his wrist down. Now the family needed another breadwinner to pay for Rosanna's hospital bills as well as basic living expenses, so Willie worked as an errand boy, a paper boy, and manual laborer, which ended any hope he had for a formal education. Hart's frontier schooling was erratic, as it was for most. His father taught him "his letters," read several Charles Dickens novels aloud in the evenings to the children, and took them to church. At the age of fifteen Hart worked as a messenger boy for the Everett House and the Clarendon Hotel in New York City and spent his leisure time building a reputation as a fine amateur race-walker at the Manhattan Athletic Club. Track taught Hart the true meaning of sportsmanship and fair play and at the same time reinforced what he had learned from the Sioux and his father.

Poverty and hard work took their toll on Hart, and soon he was forced to seek his fortune through less strenuous means. In his autobiography, Hart reminisced about his dreams as a young man and of his decision to become an actor: "I never had but two ambitions. One, to go to West Point; the other, to go on stage. The desire to become a United States Army officer was probably born of my Western life. Soldiers and forts were a part of the West. The stage idea just came, always remained, and will be with me when the final curtain is rung."⁹ A West Point career was impossible because Hart lacked an adequate academic background to help him prepare for the entrance examinations. An acting career, however, was possible. Although the family was financially unstable, Hart's father encouraged him to pursue his dream. So, under his father's guidance Hart took dancing and fencing lessons to improve his skills of movement, and then traveled to Europe "to have the rough corners . . . rubbed off and smoothed down by education and cultured surroundings . . . rich with the spoils of time."¹⁰ Homesickness brought him back after only two weeks, but the trip was important because he enrolled in acting classes and saw Mary Anderson and Forbes-Robertson perform in *A Winter's Tale* at the Lyceum Theatre in England.

When he returned to New York, Hart studied with F. F. Markey and Daniel E. Bandemann, two of the American theatre's most respected teachers. Bandemann gave Hart his first break in the theatre; at the age of nineteen, he made his professional stage debut in *Romeo and Juliet* for the matinees and *Dr. Jekyll and Mr. Hyde* in the evenings. The plays opened in Hart's native Newburgh. Encouraged by Bandemann, who complimented Hart on his studiousness and raised his salary by two or three dollars, and by success, Hart pursued and won more mature theatrical roles, including the parts of Messala in *Ben Hur*, Orlando in *As You Like It*, Macbeth in *Macbeth*, Iago in

*Othello*, Antony in *Antony and Cleopatra*, and several others. As a result of these roles, some critics may have been making an approving critical comment when they reported that the "S." in Hart's name stood for Shakespeare instead of Surrey.

In 1905 Hart secured the role of Cash Hawkins in Edwin Milton Royle's *The Squaw Man* and created, according to Hart, "the first presentation of a real American cowboy that Broadway had ever seen. The critics and the public loved the devil, drunk or sober, as much as I did."[11] When Hart learned that the cast would wear old rugs and doormats for chaps, he demanded real chaps, quirts, and spurs. Authenticity, which became a trademark of Hart's films, originated in the theatrical melodramas in which he starred. Several Western stage roles followed, including the lead in Owen Wister's *The Virginian* in 1907. Hart respected Wister as a creative writer, for who else, according to Hart, could imagine such wild happenings yet maintain a consistently delightful story? But he told Wister privately that *The Virginian* contained too many improbable situations. Perhaps Hart should have kept quiet, but he chose not to do so because, as he said, "The truth of the West meant more to me than a job and always will!"[12] Hart later played the part of the wily Dan Stark in *The Barrier* and was singled out for an ovation on the opening night. He reveled in the critics' praise, and he cherished most *The Morning Telegraph*'s editorial written by a legend of Western folklore, Mr. W. B. (Bat) Masterson:

> The part of Dan Stark by William S. Hart seems to have been made to the order for that clever impersonator of Western characters. Any one familiar with the character of the cool, calculating, and daring desperado, whose presence was a part of the frontier life a generation ago, will instantly recognize in Mr. Hart a true type of that reckless nomad who flourished on the border when the six-shooter was the final arbiter of all disputes between man and man. Mr. Hart looks the part, dresses the part, and acts as if he were the real Dan Stark and had stepped out of the book upon the stage.[13]

Such praise for realism and primitive energy, coming particularly from "Bat" Masterson, encouraged Hart to pursue other Western roles for stage and screen as well as to reinforce his compulsiveness for authenticity.

Hart's popularity and acclaim as an actor rose for the next twenty years, and many of the conventions of legitimate theatre remained with him throughout his film career. Having studied stage history and worked with Bandemann, who emphasized the importance of emotions when acting, Hart began to theorize about acting. "Acting," according to Hart, "is the art of reproducing human emotions: the face and eyes carry out the wishes of the brain."[14] Simplistic though this analysis may be, it did serve as the impetus for most of Hart's initial inquiries into acting. When he moved into film, he emphasized the face and eyes with full close-up of himself to show mental stress and his facial mobility. Also, the close-up focused the audience's attention on his slightly horse-shaped face, which dominated the screen, and his glowering, silent eyes intimidated the villains as well as caused the film's audiences to squirm in anticipation.

Although Hart had been a successful stage actor, he preferred the limitless arena of the screen to the restriction of the proscenium arch. Later, in a publicity pamphlet published by The William S. Hart Company, Hart listed three reasons why he moved into motion pictures:

First,—because today I am able through the medium of the motion picture screen to play before an average daily world audience of six million people.
Secondly,—because I honestly believe that the motion picture screen gives greater scope for the art of acting than the speaking stage.
Thirdly,—because, naturally, motion pictures have brought me the reward of world-wide fans. On the stage, the actor's reward in applause for a thing well done is practically confined in his own company, or to the race who speaks his tongue; but the silent applause for screen portrayals thunders from all over the world.[15]

Hart's desire to reach the world with his films helped make him the major Western box-office attraction by 1920.

When Hart decided to go to California in 1914 at the age of forty-four, he traveled with *The Trail of the Lonesome Pine* theatrical company. When he arrived in Los Angeles, he called on his old friend Thomas Ince, who was manager of the New York Motion Picture Company, located on the 101 Ranch at Santa Monica. It was later called "Inceville" and finally "Hartsville." This 18,000-acre location contained several open-air stages, Western town sets, a ranch set, and other buildings designed for filming Western movies. Hart, enraptured with the primitiveness of life in California, told Ince of his plans to appear in Western films. Ince informed Hart that the American public was becoming tired of Westerns, but he agreed to cast Hart in supporting roles at seventy-five dollars a week. Although Ince never directed Hart in motion pictures, he did recognize Hart's talent and determination to create authentic Western films.

The movies in which Hart made his first two film appearances starred and were directed by Tom Chatterton with Clara Williams as the heroine and Hart as the villain. These two-reelers were entitled *His Hour of Manhood* (1914) and *Jim Cameron's Wife* (1914). Although the former was financially successful, Hart rebelled because he did not, he felt, get the opportunity to act. His rebellion occurred when Ince proposed a third two-reeler; Hart asked Ince if he could build up the story line. Ince agreed, and when Hart returned the script four days later, Ince discovered that Hart had not only doubled the length of C. Gardner Sullivan's screenplay but that he had expanded the action by including several dramatic scenes. Interestingly, Hart had salvaged *The Hold-Up*, a vaudeville act, by rewriting and starring in it. As a result of Hart's total involvement, Ince rewarded Hart with the lead in *The Bargain* (1914), Hart's first feature film.

As soon as production was completed on *The Bargain*, Hart and Sullivan coauthored *On the Night Stage*, which was released in 1914; later it was released under the "false title" of *The Bandit and the Preacher*. In both pictures Hart rode a coal-black, high-strung animal named Midnight, and the two performed beautifully in several dangerous skyline rides along the tops of ridges. Although Midnight did not appear in other films with Hart, these films introduced the close relationship between the cowboy and his horse that became prominent in later Western films and television shows. Hart's favorite horse, on and off screen, was a 1000-pound pinto named Fritz. During the shooting of *The Passing of Two-Gun Hicks* (1915) Hart and Fritz became inseparable. Fritz, according to Hart, was a horse of remarkable endurance and power who could perform tricks flawlessly. Like many other Western film heroes and their audiences, Hart anthropomorphized the qualities of Fritz, especially in *My Life East and West*. Hart, for example, recalled that while shooting *The Toll Gate* (1920) he and Fritz were wading across a thirty-foot whirlpool when Fritz, who was struggling and "screaming, looked up at him with the eyes of a human being."[16] Hart's fondness for Fritz inspired him to write a poem, which was published in *The Morning Telegraph* and later adapted into a screenplay entitled *Pinto Ben* (1915). Still later, *Narrow Trail* (1916) was conceived and written out of his love for Fritz. *Narrow Trail* is also important because Ince wanted Hart to use another horse in the film. Hart refused, and Fritz became a symbol of Hart's defiance and freedom as well as a co-star in later films. In several films, Hart, playing the villain, would be reformed by his love for his horse. Another Hart trademark, the reformation of the villain by a fair-skinned, blue-eyed heroine, was also introduced in *On the Night Stage*.

As soon as Hart completed work on these films, he asked Ince to give him a year's contract. Ince refused, but he did offer Hart a job as a director for $125 per week. Hart declined and returned to New York. A year later, after *The Bargain* had become a hit, Ince sent Hart the following telegram: "Can offer you one-twenty-five per week as star. One-year contract. You to direct your own pictures. Wire answer, Tom."[17] Hart, knowing that something important had happened but unaware that *The Bargain* had made him a national attraction, accepted Ince's offer and returned to Ocean Park with his invalid sister Mary Ellen and their bulldog Mack in 1915.

Hart once said that his life was ruled by two equations: his professional sense of honor and the public's appreciation of that sense.[18] The public loved Hart's films because they were replete with physical action, a realistic setting, and creative storytelling. Survival and success in the motion picture industry demanded that the star's popularity increase and that the star rank among the top box office attractions. Hart achieved both. Although G. M. "Broncho Billy" Anderson was the first Western film star and still held claim to the title "King of the Cowboys" when Hart arrived in Hollywood, his films, which included nearly 500 one-reelers and two-reelers, were simplistic in plot and lacked the harsh backdrop of Hart's films. Anderson's work contained taut action sequences, authentic Western town sets with dilapidated buildings, naturalistic costumes, and superior cinematography. But he spent too much time making one- and two-reelers; by the time he realized that he needed to be involved in feature films in 1915, William S. Hart and Tom Mix already dominated the screen and controlled audience appeal.

Hart was once described as a man of parts, and the parts all came together in his total involvement with filmmaking, for he wrote, starred in, directed, and produced many of his films. His complete filmic involvement distinguishes Hart from almost every other Western star. His pictures established the American Western as a genre because his films were, as he said, "justice-triumphant stories" designed for "family and church-goers,"[19] and he was successful because he catered to his audience's frontier fantasies. Hart claimed that "My pictures of the West in the early days will make that colorful period of American life live forever. The camera has caught and imprisoned forever for the ages the West of the stage coaches, cowpunchers, gunmen, 'greaser,' chaps and chapparal."[20] Vigorous plots tinged with a Victorian streak of purity that drew on the dramatic conflicts of frontier life catapulted Hart to the forefront of the American motion picture industry.

Hart knew that he was giving the public what it wanted, so his little "horse-opera troupe," as he liked to call his film company, repeated many of the same themes and released them under different titles. Hart demanded that the films be made according to his requirements, so the cast and crew underwent few changes. Although he occasionally worked with another codirector—Cliff Smith or Charles Swickard—Hart was always in control. To maintain what he would call consistency and what others have called repetition, Hart's crew included cinematographer Joseph August, whose superb camera work captured the dusty, unglamorized West of Hart's imagination; C. Gardner Sullivan, who either wrote or coauthored many of the screenplays for Hart; Louise Glaum, who played the passionate, raven-haired vamp; and Alfred Hollingsworth, who portrayed the sly villain. Leading ladies included such notables as Clara Williams, Katherine McDonald, Anna Q. Nilssen, Jane Novak, and Winifred Westover, whose angelic appearance and shy demeanor made them the object of the hero's and audience's adoration.

Hart proposed to almost everyone of his leading ladies while they were on a set. Winifred Westover accepted his proposal and married him on December 7, 1921. They separated on May 10, 1922, and she obtained a divorce on the grounds of desertion on February 11, 1927. She bore him a son, William S. Hart, Jr., on September 6, 1922. Junior later sued for control of the Hart estate; although the court rejected his suit, it did award him $1.00, as specified in Hart's will.

In real life Hart experienced only problems when dealing with women. Besides his brief, unsuccessful marriage to Winifred Westover, Hart was named in two paternity suits. The first, which was not publicized until 1922, occurred in November 1918; the second occurred in 1920. In both cases, Hart was found innocent of the charges made against him: the Hearst newspapers published the first woman's confession which cleared Hart of fathering her child; the second woman stated in court that she and Hart knew one another spiritually not physically. Perhaps his disappointments in love stemmed from his relationship with his sister Mary Ellen, whom he affectionately called "Mamie," because she was his constant roommate and companion in California. In turn, such films as *Hell's Hinges* examined the relationship between brother and sister who move West to establish a new life.

From 1914 to the spring of 1915, Hart appeared in more than

twenty two-reel pictures, including *The Passing of Two Gun Hicks, The Taking of Luke McVane* (false title: *The Fugitive*), *The Scourge of the Desert, The Ruse, Mr. "Silent" Haskins, The Darkening Trail*, and *Pinto Ben*. These films introduced several standard Hart conventions and characterizations such as physical conflict. *The Disciple* (1915) exemplifies what the audience could expect from a Hart production. *The Disciple* was his first film for the newly created Triangle Film Corporation, which absorbed the New York Motion Picture Company, Reliance-Majestic Company, and Keystone Comedies. With Harry E. Aitkin as president and D. W. Griffith, Thomas H. Ince, and Mack Sennett as director generals, Triangle leased the Knickerbocker Theatre in New York as its major film outlet in the East. Following Douglas Fairbank's *The Lamb* (1915), *The Disciple* was Triangle's second release.

Hart tailored *The Disciple* into a blend of action, sentimentality, and his own personal vision of the West. The virtuous Parson Jim Houston (Hart) triumphs over the corrupt ways of the gambler. The Parson and his family come to Barren Gulch to build a church; however, when Mary, his wife, runs away with "Doc" Hardy, a saloon owner and gambler, the Parson blames God for his troubles, quits the church, and takes his daughter Kate with him into the mountains. Then Kate becomes ill, Mary returns to her child's bedside, "Doc" saves Kate's life, and the reunited Houston family returns to their missionary work in Barren Gulch. Reformation occurs out of love for men, women, and children. Hart incorporated his father's advice into filming as when, in the scene, a gunfight breaks out between two cowpunchers while the saloon people crowd around and watch. Drawing upon personal observation, Hart recalled his father telling him in Sioux City that "If near a gun-fight and the weapons are wielded by amateurs, run for your life; if professionals are handling the trigger, *stand still*—they know where they are shooting."[21] Cowpunchers, however, were never noted for their skill with a six-shooter.

Mary illustrates the typical Hart heroine. As in many of his films, the heroine appears physically and emotionally childlike in contrast to the hero. The woman desires love and attention from the man she loves. When she is denied her desires, she occasionally turns to the villain for comfort and admiration; eventually she learns that the villain is simply using her. During the film, the woman grows, matures, and gains a better understanding of life on the frontier. On the other hand, Parson Jim Houston is atypical of a Hart-style hero. Although Jim does show potential strength and character when he disperses a mob that is celebrating the church's opening with a keg of whiskey, Houston is too submissive and weak. His strength is reinforced cinematically only once when Hart employs a close-up to show the silent impressive stranger's determination and self-reliance when he vanquishes the mob.

In 1916 Hart released *Hell's Hinges*, in some ways his most mature and impressive work although it appeared nine years before *Tumbleweeds*, the film most critics consider to be his best. *Hell's Hinges*, a psychological Western, opens in the East. Blaze Tracey (Hart), an outlaw who falls in love with Faith (Clara Williams), the sister of the Reverend Robert Henley (Jack Standing), who has come to the raw frontier town of Hell's Hinges to build a church. Henley is weak-willed, like Houston, and is easily seduced by Dolly (Louise Glaum) the local tart; Tracey leaves Hell's Hinges to get a doctor for Henley, and when he returns he discovers that Silk Miller, a saloonkeeper, has ordered Dolly to seduce and to get Henley drunk while Silk leads a band of outlaws in burning the newly constructed church. Although Tracey initially participates in the melee, he stops as soon as he learns that Miller is trying to dance with Faith. Angered, he proceeds to the saloon where he kills Silk and then torches the saloon. The fire spreads throughout Hell's Hinges. At the end, Tracey and Faith leave the area to realize a better life elsewhere.

*Hell's Hinges* is the most grim and perhaps the most "adult" Western ever filmed in America. It reflects Hart's love of depicting the West as he recalled it—bleak and hard. Several things distinguish this film from others made at the time. For example, Hart integrates the landscape and action. Hell's Hinges is an isolated town with gritty-looking saloons and stores; even the church appears to be covered with the dust that characterizes the harsh and unglamorous life of the West. The town's ruggedly poetic flavor suggests that the conflict of frontier life involves not only man against man but also man against civilization. Tracey, too, evolves as the typical Hart hero. Although he is a villain, he is respected by his peers and enemies. Like the landscape's striking contrasts of destitution and vast grandeur, Tracey is silent and dominating, yet he is chivalrous and attractive to Faith. When he tells her, "I reckon God ain't wantin' me much, Ma'am, but when I look at you I feel I've been ridin' the wrong trail," Tracey demonstrates that he has begun to acquire true values and that Faith, the blue-eyed heroine, symbolizes the ideal in American life. Tracey has also begun to accept

William S. Hart in *The Gunfighter* (1916). *William S. Hart Park*

religion, although it is only a slight acceptance; he begins to read the Bible while he still smokes and drinks. Tracey's transformation, which traditionally occurs to the Hart hero when he falls in love with a woman or when someone blasphemes against God, leads to a synthesis of the respective values of frontier and civilization.

Unlike Tom Mix and other film cowboys who were becoming popular during the 1920s, Hart's picturization of the West lacked color and gloss; instead, Hart chose to portray the West as raw, violent, and somber just as he portrayed the men who tamed it. The frontier code, which he developed as a young man, served as a basis for universal morality.

*The Return of Draw Egan* (1916), which is noted for its cinematic portrayal of the West, involves the reformation of Draw Egan, an outlaw who is "the most sought after man along the border" of New Mexico. Draw's gang, surrounded by the law, escapes through a tunnel;

Robert McKim, the coward/villain, deserts, then is captured and sent to jail. Draw heads for Broken Bow where he defeats the town's bully. When the leaders of Yellow Dog hear of Draw's accomplishment, they ask him to be their marshal. He accepts, and when he arrives in Yellow Dog he meets the fair-skinned Margery Wilson, the girl of his dreams. Draw, who has now changed his name to William Blake, overcomes the Yellow Dog ruffians, reestablishes law and order, and rebuffs the advances of the town's vamp while he courts Miss Wilson. McKim, meanwhile, escapes from jail, arrives in Yellow Dog, becomes the vamp's lover, and threatens to reveal Draw's past. Draw, who is caught in a dilemma, does nothing to control the outlaws out of fear that Wilson will leave him if she learns of his immoral past. Finally, however, the saloon trash taunt the town's religious-minded folk and Draw must assume his paternalistic duty as protector of the people. McKim reveals Draw's background and is killed in a shoot-out with Draw who enforces true justice. The townsfolk ask Draw to remain as their sheriff and he regains Wilson's affections. By foiling McKim's evil, Draw proves that he is worthy of Wilson as well as demonstrating his ability to protect the fledgling frontier community.

The Testing Block (1920), like Three Word Brand (1921), was written, directed, and starred in by Hart. Characteristically, Hart begins both films with an establishing shot of the mountains to show their majesty and beauty. In The Testing Block the hero ironically is named Sierra. Like the mountains that dominate the opening shots, Sierra emits a peaceful yet rugged quality. Although he is the leader of an outlaw band, Sierra stands apart from his men who respect him for his quiet deadliness and his grim, sarcastic tone. He rules by power of his gun, yet he is fundamentally a just leader. Ringo, an insurgent among the gang, is jealous of Sierra's leadership as well as his attraction to Nellie, a motherless daughter of a wandering violinist. Whenever Nellie plays her violin, the plaintive strains evoke unfathomed, romantic emotions within Sierra while the music heightens the lust that Ringo feels for her.

A battle erupts between Sierra and Ringo for control of the gang. Sierra fights and defeats seven men, one at a time; after Sierra defeats Wolf, the catlike Ringo attacks with iron bolts in his fists to give him confidence. Through a stunning series of shots showing the two men fighting toe-to-toe, Hart shows the defeated outlaws marveling at Sierra's strength, determination, and courage. Intercut with these shots are shots of Nellie sleeping comfortably in a hotel room with moonlight streaming across her bed. Sierra, Hart's vision of Western manliness, defeats Ringo as close-ups capture the streaked, cut, and bloody Sierra standing like a defiant colossus before his men. Later, the drunken Sierra sees Nellie, the woman he wants, so he kidnaps her. A cut takes us five years into the future: Sierra and Nellie have built a mountain cabin and Nellie has given birth to a son, Buster, who is preparing for school. Under Nellie's tutelage and soothing touch, the once wild force of Sierra is transformed into a man of quality. Also, Hart presents his vision of the ideal as the hero and the heroine synthesize their visions of life and create a utopian society in the wilderness.

Hart's skill as a director, his on-screen persona, and his integration of landscape to supplement the film's action and dramatic nature steadily improved. *Three Word Brand* (1921) traces a family's western trek to settle on the frontier as well as the West's stages of development. The film opens with Trego (Hart), a widower seeking a home in defiance of the perils of the West. He is taking his twin boys through Indian country. By means of parallel editing, Hart, as director, dramatically shows the boys' flight to safety while Trego drives the wagon and leads the Indians away from his sons. The frequent close-ups of Trego's face, etched with determination to save his boys' lives, dominates the screen and the viewers' thought as he sacrifices himself and kills half the band of marauding Indians when he blows up his wagon.

A cut to a ranch hand shows the passing of time. The scene opens with mountains in the background, but there are no trails, fences, or other signs of human habitation to be seen. After the cut, a title states that "cattle have replaced buffalo and cowboys ride the warpaths of the mighty Cheyennes." Brand (Hart), one of Trego's sons, is the product of the plains. Like the country, he is big, and slow of speech and movement. The other brother, also played by Hart, is Marsden, the stoical Governor of Colorado. Brand and Marsden struggle for control of the plains. Brand, who falls in love with Ethel (Jane Novak), must demonstrate to her that he is not a coward or a quitter. The climactic scene involves the confrontation between the brothers. Brand defeats Marsden and the unjust law that he represents. Again the Hart hero is transformed by a woman. He is able to conquer his fear of women and rise to a new level of manliness and heroism.

Although several of Hart's films reflect his love for the West and for the people who tamed it, *Wild Bill Hickok* (1923) was a faithful biography of a man whom Hart adored. Hart apologized on film, in fact, for not looking enough like the real Wild Bill Hickok. The film opens

William S. Hart in *Wild Bill Hickok* (1923). *William S. Hart Park*

with a fade-in to a quote from Theodore Roosevelt's *The Winning of the West*: "This country will not be a good place for *any* of us to live in unless it is a good place for ALL of us to live in. The whole western movement of our people was the vital part of that great expansion which has been the all-important feature of our history. It was expansion which made us a great power." A dedicatory note from Hart stated: "As one who has shared in the vanishing frontier life of the present—and with all the love and reverence there is in me—I dedicate this picture to those great Americans of the 'Seventies': to William B. (Bat) Masterson, Charles Bassett, William (Bill) Tighlman, Wyatt Earp, Luke Short, 'Chalk' Benson, 'Doc' Holliday, 'Wild Bill' Hickok. They made the West 'a good place for ALL of us to live in.'"

The film, set after the American Civil War, opens with Hickok traveling to Dodge City, where he becomes a gambler. He is branded a coward because he refuses to intercede on behalf of the townsfolk in their battle with the town's outlaws until Jack McQueen (James

Farley), the outlaw leader, escapes from jail. Later, Bill falls in love with a married woman and chooses to leave town rather than ruin her good name. Hickok, as presented here, lives by a code of honor. Although apparently he is corrupt, he responds to truth and beauty when he confronts a division between good and evil. In turn, he is deadly in vengeance as when he kills McQueen; he is also chivalrous in love: Rather than tainting a woman's life, he quietly rides out of town so that she may maintain her respectability.

Although *Wild Bill Hickok* made money, Adolph Zukor and Jesse Lasky told Hart that the public was willing to abandon his West portrayals for the lighter and less realistic interpretations of Tom Mix and Buck Jones. Hart refused to budge. Evolution of public taste had created his opportunity in 1914, but Hart would not agree that a change on his part was necessary to keep him at the top. His stubbornness brought him to Paramount, where he filmed *Singer Jim McKee* (1924), the worst film he ever made. *Singer*'s story line was rambled, the melodrama was handled heavily, and, cinematically, the production was absurd. Although Hart honestly felt that *Singer Jim McKee* was an excellent film, and it did make money, Zukor told Hart that he would have to submit to supervision if he were going to make other pictures.

Hart refused. As with his theatrical productions of *The Squaw Man* and *The Virginian*, Hart's principles were more important to him than a salary check. For a while it seemed as if Hart would revive his classic Westerns when he released his 1925 epic entitled *Tumbleweeds*. With a $312,000 budget, the biggest he had ever worked with, Hart returned to the screen for the last time. Directed by King Bagott, *Tumbleweeds* presents Hart's picturization of "the last of the West," the end of the cattle drives and the Cherokee Strip in Oklahoma, the last frontier. Don Carver (Hart), a cattle drover, is jobless once the cattle drive is over. He meets and falls in love with Molly Lassiter. They decide to make their home in the Cherokee Strip. A minor plot arises when Don is imprisoned by the villain, but he escapes confinement with the aid of his loyal horse Fritz. Thus, Don is able to participate in the land rush, defeat the claim jumpers, win land, and advance his romance with Molly. Despite its land-rush sequence, which is superior to *Cimarron*'s (1932), and tremendous success at the box office in New York, United Artists cut the film to five reels so that they could book it in minor theatres. Although Hart took United Artists to court for breach of contract and won, his victory was a technical one because he lost approximately $500,000 in unrealized profits.

William S. Hart and Fritz taking a break during the shooting
of *Tumbleweeds* (1925). *William S. Hart Park*

Discouraged, Hart left film making. Occasionally he would make a
guest appearance in films such as King Vidor's *Show People* or coach
such newcomers as Johnny Mack Brown and Robert Taylor in their
respective portrayals of Billy the Kid. In 1939 he filmed the prologue to
*Tumbleweeds* in order to introduce the film, in so doing, he demonstrated that he possessed a fine speaking voice. Eventually, however,
he went into a self-imposed exile.

Hart and his sister Mary Ellen established their home at the base
of the San Francisquita Canyon in the Tehachapi foothills at Newhall,
California. Building his Horseshoe Ranch on the Hill of the Winds,
Hart found a new inspiration. While relaxing in a $93,000 mansion of
10,000 square feet located on 300 acres, Hart found time to write. He
published his autobiography, *My Life East and West*, a novelization of
*The Toll Gate*, and sixteen books. Some were novels and some were col-

lections of popular "boy's stories." All of his writing, like his films, maintains a poetic tone and a romantic view of the West. The novels and stories portray the Western adventurer caught in conflict between the savage frontier and the inevitable encroachment of society. When forced to make a choice, the hero sides with "right" or civilization. He is a man of natural nobility who champions good and vanquishes the insidious forces of evil.

The canyon also marked the beginning of a new era in the life of one of America's most successful Western film heroes. Hart's home became an authentic Western museum that exemplified his spirit and vision and love for the West. Several paintings by Charles Russell, Frederick Remington, and James Montgomery Flagg decorated the walls. Hart particularly liked Russell's work because "Charlie Russell never romanticized his subject; never improved on his punchers and Indians; never, except on special order, painted American soldiers killing American Indians."[22] Like Hart's films, Russell's paintings authentically depicted the West.

Hart also acknowledged the spirit of the Indian in his house. Navaho prints appear on every door, column, and beam throughout the house, and Sioux and Navaho artifacts can be found in almost every room. Like the old squaw he mentions in his autobiography, the home became a museum to the proud, indomitable Indian spirit:

> I can only think and live in the past. The white people have taken away all of the Indian's future. The Sioux is the most famous of all Indian nations—a strong and mighty race possessed of a dominant spirit. We are the monarchs of the plains. We once owned all that we could see. Peace is a great thing—if that peace is a good peace; but if that peace is wrong and does not bring honor on our people, our people will always fight. We will die. Our spirit will kill us.[23]

Like the Indian, Hart's proud spirit, the refusal to buckle to studio demands, forced him out of pictures. Sad like the Indian squaw, he seemed to be trapped in the past toward the latter part of his career. Although he was warned that he was too old to play the hero, outdraw the villains, or "streamline" the films' development, he refused to allow another to perform in his stead. Integrity, honesty, and fidelity to the past as he remembered it forced him to leave film making, just as his characters would leave town rather than risk a scandal.

William S. Hart died at the age of 73 on June 23, 1946, of old age.

At the foot of the Hill of the Winds stands a white, two-bedroom home. Appropriately the wooden house seems dominated by the mansion on the hill. Tom Mix lived in that home before he replaced William S. Hart as Hollywood's leading Western film hero.

NOTES

1. William S. Hart, *My Life East and West* (New York: Benjamin Blom, 1929), p. 199.
2. Ibid., p. 12.
3. Ibid., p. 53.
4. I would like to thank the people of the William S. Hart Park of Los Angeles County, Newhall, California, for their help with this project. In particular, Ms. Dorris Reynolds, museum curator, was both helpful and generous with the museums's files on Hart. Researchers should be aware that Hart's scripts, prose writings, letters, and ephemera are on file at the ranch house.
5. Hart, *My Life*, p. 48.
6. Ibid., p. 45.
7. Ibid., p. 38.
8. Ibid., p. 82.
9. Ibid., p. 87.
10. Ibid., pp. 87, 88.
11. Ibid., p. 169.
12. Ibid., p. 175.
13. Ibid., p. 182.
14. William S. Hart papers. William S. Hart Park, Los Angeles County, Newhall, California.
15. William S. Hart, William S. Hart Publicity Pamphlet. Paul Hubert Conlon, Director of Publicity, The William S. Hart Company.
16. Hart, *My Life*, p. 289.
17. Ibid., p. 209.
18. William S. Hart papers, William S. Hart Park.
19. Ibid.
20. Ibid.
21. Hart, *My Life*, p. 48.
22. William S. Hart papers, William S. Hart Park.
23. Hart, *My Life*, p. 15.

RAYMOND E. WHITE

# Ken Maynard:
# Daredevil on Horseback

KEN MAYNARD, a major Western film personality from the 1920s to the 1940s, reached the peak of his Western film career in the early 1930s before sliding into a decline that continued through his last Western film in 1944. Paralleling Maynard's spectacular and action-filled movie career was his stormy and equally eventful private life. He possessed a short temper and a problem with alcohol that antagonized and alienated his professional associates, his friends, and his relatives. Alcohol resulted in the breakup of one marriage, and sometimes even drove him into drunken rages during which he viciously beat his horse Tarzan. Portraying the life of the perfect American male on film and living a reality in which such perfection can never be obtained created uncertainty and doubts for Maynard. On the other hand, his talents, his determination, and his desire to perform made it possible for him to succeed and to make a significant impact upon the development of the Western film genre. The complexity, variety, and inconsistency in Maynard's life affected his approach to film making, and a narrative of that life provides an understanding of both his film career and his contributions to the development of the Western film.

Kenneth Olin Maynard was born July 21, 1895, in Vevay, Indiana, a small town on the Ohio River. The son of William H. and Emma May Maynard, he was the oldest of five children. His father, a carpenter and building superintendent, moved the family several times to different job sites in Kentucky and southern Indiana before settling in Columbus, Indiana, in 1904. It was here that Maynard grew to adolescence, playing with friends, his brother Kermit, and his three sisters Trixie, Willa, and Bessie. Kermit Maynard later followed his older brother to Hollywood and also became a Western film star.[1]

Maynard was an active, energetic, and adventurous boy willing to attempt almost any daredevil feat. One such event occurred when he constructed and attempted to fly a bicycle-powered biplane. One blustery morning with the wind at his back he pedaled swiftly down Columbus's Central Avenue to see if the contraption would work. At Twelfth Street it took off, rose fifteen feet into the air, and remained airborne until it reached Thirteenth Street, where it crashed.[2] On another occasion when a circus came to town its owners offered $25 to anyone who could ride a steer around the ring three times without falling off. Maynard accepted the challenge and made it around the circle twice.[3] This experience may have started him thinking about becoming a circus or Wild West show performer, and when tent shows came to town Maynard hung around them doing odd jobs and talking to workers and performers. A restlessness already existed within him, and at the age of twelve he ran away with Doc Clayton's medicine show. He tended the horses and van and performed fancy roping during the shows.[4] Maynard's father tracked him down in Kentucky and brought him back to Columbus. The urge to perform remained with Maynard, and it may have been in this period of his life when he began practicing trick riding in vacant lots in Columbus. One story maintains that he built makeshift circus rings and performed for his friends on a pony purchased with money earned helping his father. In the summer of 1911, when Maynard reached the age of sixteen, his parents gave their consent and permitted him to join a traveling carnival. Just which carnival Maynard joined is not known. The only one advertised in Columbus newspapers for the 1911 season was that of the Weidner Carnival Company which appeared there in late May.[5]

During the next five years, Maynard worked with at least four carnivals, Wild West shows, or circuses, including Buffalo Bill's Wild West, Kit Carson's Buffalo Ranch Wild West, and the Hagenbeck-Wallace Circus.[6] In these five years of show business experience Maynard acquired the skills that would make him a spectacular action Western movie star. In his screen performances he occasionally concluded a stunt or riding trick with a wave as if he were performing before a live audience. Moreover, he sometimes used his experiences as a basis for the plots of his movies. Maynard suggested the story for *The*

*Wagon Show* (1926), a First National film with a circus background in which Ken showed off his fancy riding.[7] In *Parade of the West* (1930), he played a medicine show entertainer who became a daredevil circus performer who rode killer broncs and twirled ropes. Maynard spliced clips from this movie into *King of the Arena* (1933), a Universal film that featured him as a former Wild West show star turned Texas Ranger. In this film Maynard worked undercover in the circus to catch the villain and his gang. In both films he used the Coleman Brothers Circus because it was playing in the Hollywood area at the time of filming. In his last Western feature, *Harmony Trail* (1944), Maynard played an undercover lawman who posed as a medicine show entertainer doing fancy roping and trick-shooting. He operated his own circus for a short time in the mid-1930s and toured with the Cole Brothers Circus for at least three seasons.

The Wild West show or circus in which Ken first appeared is uncertain, but by 1912 he allegedly was working for Buffalo Bill and claimed to have been with him when creditors closed down the show. Maynard recalled the incident because it was on his eighteenth birthday, and he and Buffalo Bill sat on bales of hay and shared a cake sent by his mother. Within a year Maynard was performing with Kit Carson's Buffalo Ranch Wild West, owned by Thomas F. Wiedemann. The show featured a variety of acts including camel races, Mexican bull riding, and a "Royal Mexican Guard." Probably while performing with the Kit Carson show the famed Mexican rope artist, Oro Peso, helped Maynard to perfect his trick roping. When Kit Carson's Buffalo Ranch Wild West ceased operations, he toured with the Hagenbeck-Wallace Circus for two years.[8] It is interesting to note that while Maynard performed with these shows the Columbus, Indiana, city directory continued to list him as a resident. Also in 1914 he performed in Columbus at a local show sponsored by the Commercial Club but was not given any special recognition as being a professional.[9]

During these years Mexico was involved in political turmoil and revolution. Maynard claimed at various times in his life that he was involved in that political upheaval and was present when Francisco Madero overthrew Porfirio Diaz. He also maintained that he received a commission from a Mexican general and that he participated in at least two battles. The credibility of Maynard's claims is shattered by the fact that the events in which he claimed to have participated occurred when he was a fifteen-year-old boy living in Columbus, Indiana. Like Tom

Mix, Maynard evidently created the story to glamorize his Western movie personality.[10]

Regardless of whether or not Maynard actually participated in the Mexican Revolution, his patriotism caused him to put aside this professional life and join the Army in 1917. He served as an engineer at Camp Knox, Kentucky. His duties are unknown. He apparently found time for romance and reportedly married a young woman from the Kentucky mountains. The marriage, if there was one, lasted only as long as his Army career. When World War I ended Maynard left Kentucky without a wife.[11]

In the postwar period Maynard resumed his career with the Hagenbeck-Wallace Circus. Some biographies incorrectly indicate that Maynard appeared with Pawnee Bill's Wild West Show in 1920. This show, known as Pawnee Bill's Far East, was part of the Buffalo Bill Wild West that went out of business in 1913.[12] It is certain, however, that Ken participated in another form of Western entertainment in 1920 when he entered the rodeo at Pendleton, Oregon. He won $42,000 and became the All-Around Champion Cowboy. He repeated the feat in 1921, and Ringling Brothers' Barnum and Bailey Circus hired him as a star attraction for its Wild West show. Maynard worked with the big circus until it arrived in Los Angeles in 1922, where Western film star Buck Jones encouraged him to give the movies a try.[13]

Lynn Reynolds, one of Tom Mix's directors at Fox Studios, arranged a screen test for Maynard that resulted in a contract and several bit parts in 1923. While earning $100 a week, Ken appeared in five features for Fox during 1923: *Brass Commandments, The Gun Fighter, The Man Who Won, Somebody Lied,* and *Cameo Kirby.* His income from films was substantially below his circus and rodeo income, but within a short period of time he was on the way to making larger sums of money in starring roles in Westerns. While working on these early pictures Maynard met and married Jeanne Knudsen in Los Angeles on February 14, 1923. The marriage lasted less than a year.[14]

*Variety* gave Maynard his first positive recognition as a film actor for his portrayal of Paul Revere in the period feature *Janice Meredith* (1925). He got this part because of his riding skills and earned $1,000 a week. Although it was one of the few non-Westerns in which Maynard appeared, *Janice Meredith* started him on his way to movie stardom. Within three years Ken Maynard would be as prominent as any Western star of the day.[15]

The short road to that prominence resulted from a series of five low-budget Westerns produced by Clifford S. Elfelt, who paid Maynard $1,000 per picture. The first, *$50,000 Reward* (1925), featuring Maynard's stunts and riding skills, showed him as a handsome cowboy with romantic appeal. His flamboyant, daredevil style worked well in this feature and in the four remaining Elfelt pictures. On his big palomino horse Tarzan, Maynard performed tricks acquired during his circus career. Within two years First National, one of Hollywood's leading production and distribution companies, signed Maynard as a contract player and pushed him to a peak of popularity that rivaled even the success of Tom Mix, Hoot Gibson, and Buck Jones.

Between his career with the Elfelt productions and that with First National Maynard fell in love and married again. Mary Leeper of South Bend, Indiana, wed Maynard in vows said on the set of *North Star* (1926), a film Maynard happened to be making at the time. The marriage was stormy because of Maynard's increasing problem with alcoholism.[16]

First National spared little expense on their eighteen films that starred Maynard. Having budgets of $75,000 to $80,000 each they were filmed at a variety of locations in South Dakota, Arizona, Wyoming, Montana, and California, sometimes with a cast and crew of sixty people. An able production and directorial team emphasized production values and capitalized on Maynard's strength, his horsemanship. Charles R. Rogers produced the films with the assistance of Harry Joe Brown. Brown directed five of them, and Sidney Albert Rogel directed the remaining thirteen. These three men paid attention to their budgets, found good locations, and used Maynard's talents to the best advantage. In their eighteen films they established Maynard as a top Western film star and gained an impressive profit for their studio.

Brown and Rogel emphasized action in the First National films but sometimes sacrificed the quality of the acting in the process. Interior scenes were kept to a minimum, and outdoor locations became the background for horses and actors. Maynard's horsemanship was evident in every film. In *Senor Daredevil* (1926) Ken leaped from Tarzan and tackled another rider. He flew over the second horse's head while gripping his antagonist. In another film, *The Unknown Cavalier* (1926), Maynard got possession of the villains' horses by using one of his old circus stunts. First he rode on two horses, then three, and finally four. He gathered up the baddies' horses in this manner, leaving them unmounted. He did a similar trick in *Land Beyond the Law* (1927) when he disconnected a wagon from a pair of galloping horses and rode astride the animals during the chase. Perhaps his most spectacular performance occurred in *Red Raiders* (1927), in which he did hair-raising stunts including retrieving the dragging reins of a runaway stagecoach while galloping at full speed on Tarzan. Not only did he get the reins, but he also stood up on Tarzan and then jumped to the team of horses, momentarily being dragged along on the ground by one of the runaway horses. He quickly flipped himself upon its back and then dropped down between the team to pick up the remaining reins before climbing to the driver's box. In a later sequence of this film he rescued one of his troopers who was hanging off the right side of his running horse. Maynard rode beside the runaway horse, hung upside down on the left side of Tarzan, and lifted the trooper to an upright position. These daredevil stunts became the hallmark of Maynard's First National pictures, and they immediately established him as one of the top Western stars of the 1920s.

Maynard's circus and Wild West show experience laid the ground-work for this dazzling stunt work. Movies, however, provided the opportunity for him to develop his skills further. In films he could do things that could never be accomplished in a circus ring or rodeo arena. An example is the stagecoach scene in *Red Raiders*; another in the same picture is the stunt in which he attempts to ride Tarzan down a steep hillside but the horse trips and tumbles over Maynard and they roll to the bottom of the hill together. Maynard took chances with his life and seemed to thrive on the danger and excitement. His skill and confidence in performing these feats made him appear relaxed and casual on the screen. He may have been the most daring and accomplished Western stunt artist in the 1920s. Film historian Jon Tuska believes that Maynard anticipated the feats that Yakima Canutt and other stuntmen performed in the 1930s and 1940s.[17]

When Maynard made the First National films, he was at the peak of his athletic prowess. The making of films was a fresh and exciting challenge for him. He also may have felt compelled to prove himself and to demonstrate that he was as good or better than the established stars such as Tom Mix, who had set a standard for daredevil riding.

Tarzan was fundamental to Maynard's stunt work. He acquired the horse in 1924 about the time that he made his first film for Elfelt Productions. Some sources claim that Maynard paid $50 for Tarzan but others say he paid $600. Whatever the cost, Tarzan was worth it. He appeared in all but one Maynard film made until 1940 when the horse

Ken Maynard and Tarzan in the early 1930s. *Raymond E.
White*

died. An extraordinary animal, Tarzan received billing as the "wonder
horse" or the "white wonder." Maynard trained Tarzan to do a remarkable number of stunts, including everything from dancing to rolling
over and playing dead. In *Red Raiders* Tarzan even used his sense of
smell to warn Maynard that Indians were near.[18]

Tarzan made Maynard's stunts and action work appear easy,
natural, and often spectacular, and their work together revealed a
special relationship. In *Gun Gospel* (1927) Maynard rode Tarzan over a
sixty-foot cliff into a lake. A special ramp used to get Tarzan out over
the water was slick, and when the horse hit it at full gallop, he slipped
and turned over, hitting the water on his back. The fall may have
frightened Tarzan more than it did Maynard, because the horse tried to
climb on top of his master in the water. The two ended up standing in
the shallow water hugging and nuzzling each other. Of all the movie
cowboys, Maynard seemed to show more genuine affection for his horse

than did any of the other screen heroes. He talked to Tarzan, and at least once in every film he patted him affectionately on the neck.

Reviewers often gave Tarzan better notices than they gave Maynard. For instance, in *Pocatello Kid* (1931), a *Variety* critic commented "That horse Tarzan is a good actor, which helps a lot," and a reviewer of *Lucky Larkin* (1930) noted that "Next to Nora Lane, Tarzan is the best actor in the film. . . ." In 1932 Tarzan starred in his own film, *Come on Tarzan.*[19]

Unlike Tarzan's film critics, reviewers had little good to say about Maynard's thespian skills. If Maynard's career had been based solely on acting ability he would not have been successful. On the other hand, his handsome appearance, flamboyant style, and horsemanship overcame his lack of acting ability. When reviewers commented positively on his acting it was usually in regard to the character roles that he played. This was true in both his silent and sound pictures. In *Gun Gospel*, in which he played three different roles, one reviewer noted that "Maynard demonstrated that he was not only a horseman of ability but an able actor. He handles with equal skill his diversified parts."[20] In his sound features *Cattle Thief* (1936) and *Lightning Strikes West* (1940) Maynard demonstrated the same ability when he portrayed a hobo. In these character parts he often seemed more relaxed.

By 1929, when the last of the First National pictures had been released, Maynard was a star. Within five years, he had risen from a bit-part player to a top box-office draw. He reached that position more quickly than Tom Mix or Hoot Gibson who made their first pictures in 1910, or Buck Jones who began in 1918, or Fred Thompson whose acting career began in 1921. Of these four Western stars, Maynard most resembled Tom Mix in style; both were dazzling trick riders who insisted on doing their own stunts. Maynard, like Mix, put little planning into the stunts which gave them a spontaniety and freshness that they might not otherwise have had. While Thompson's athletic skills, as well as his acting and sense of comedy, made him a more versatile performer than Maynard, Maynard's bold and daredevil style had its own appeal. He was certainly more dashing than Gibson and Jones, but like Thompson, both Gibson and Jones bested Maynard in acting and comedy. His principal strength in the 1920s films was his equestrian skills and his willingness to stretch those skills to achieve unbelievable feats of action.

Maynard's quick rise to stardom benefited from the fact that cowboy movie heroes enjoyed great popularity in the 1920s. At a time of

rapid technological and social change, the Western film hero's innocence and simple codes of justice provided Americans with a link to
their past. Perhaps most important in explaining his meteoric rise to
stardom was the fact that he signed with a studio that knew how to
showcase his talents and had a film distribution system that put his
pictures into the country's better theatres.

Maynard achieved major movie stardom just as sound movies
began to appear. Some studio officials believed that action Westerns
would not be successful as talking pictures because making sound films
outside a closed studio was difficult. This attitude prevailed among the
Warner Brothers executives who bought First National in 1929. They
immediately phased out Western films, but Maynard's success with
First National permitted him to negotiate a contract with Universal to
make a series of eight Westerns that were released in both sound and
silent versions.[21]

The move to Universal proved important to Maynard's career.
Universal gave him control over production and provided him with a
good director, Harry Joe Brown, who had supervised his First National
films. More importantly, this period was the most creative and financially successful in his career. Between 1929 and 1934, he achieved a
popularity that was rivaled only by Buck Jones. He made more than
three dozen films with four different studios, exercised control over production, casting, and story content, and introduced an innovation, the
musical Western, that changed the nature of the low-budget Western.

In these years Maynard not only reached a peak in professional
creativity but also achieved a measure of financial success. Maynard
spent the money he made from his films mainly for his pleasure and his
hobbies. He bought two airplanes, a yacht, a large house, and took
vacations in Mexico, Cuba, Central and South America, and Europe.
Flying was a passion with him, and he often flew his own airplane to
Mexico and Central America to explore for sites of Mayan ruins. This
ancient civilization fascinated Maynard, and the money he made from
pictures let him pursue it as a hobby. In fact, Maynard in his own way
became something of an authority on the Mayans.[22]

Maynard's interest in airplanes first provided the opportunity for
him to demonstrate his literary skill. In 1929 he edited the biography
of an early barnstorming airplane pilot. How much of the actual editing Maynard did is not clear, but he definitely wrote the foreword and is
credited with the editorship of the book on the title page. In a later
magazine article Maynard tells about his own experiences flying a

plane into the Mexican province of Campeche. While not a polished writer, Maynard possessed a flair for story telling, a talent he demonstrated in a 1936 issue of *St. Nicholas Magazine* in which he wrote an obviously fictional story about his boyhood on a Texas ranch. It has been said that Maynard wrote Western novels under a pseudonym, but no evidence of such literary works exists. Maynard did, however, provide the stories for two of his films. As with his musical and equestrian skills, Maynard put all of his talents into his film making.[23]

The eight Westerns that Maynard made for Universal in 1929 and 1930 were quality films with good stories, plenty of action, and music. *Wagon Master* (1929) was the first in the series to be released, and about half of it had a sound track. Music and song were incorporated into these early sound Universal Westerns because Maynard possessed good musical skills. He was a self-taught musician who played at least four instruments. In 1930 he recorded several Western songs with Columbia Records but only one record with two songs, "The Lone Star Trail" and "The Cowboy's Lament," was released at that time.[24]

Music and song were natural extensions of Maynard's talents and were another way to demonstrate technological developments in film making. Except for Bob Steele, none of the other cowboy movie stars who made the transition to sound possessed these talents or dared to do musical interludes in their films. In *Sons of the Saddle* (1930), Maynard and three cowboys sang "Trail Herd Song" and "Down the Home Trail With You." Maynard fit the songs into the story and the amateurish vocalizing gave them a natural quality. He did not sing in any of the Tiffany or KBS/World Wide productions that he made in 1931–1932, but when he returned to Universal in 1933–1934 he once again sang and played his fiddle. In *Fiddlin' Buckaroo* (1933), which Maynard directed, the hero fiddled and the heroine and bandits also performed vocally in separate numbers. He composed both the lyrics and music for *The Trail Drive* (1933) and sang as he sat near a campfire strumming on a banjo. While Maynard did not compose the song for *Strawberry Roan* (1933), the title piece dominated the film when Maynard and his two sidekicks, Charles King and Frank Yaconelli, sang it near the opening and repeated it during the film. *Wheels of Destiny* (1934) was a wagon train story. Maynard wrote the words for the title song while on vacation in Europe and composed the music on the piano when he returned.[25]

In 1934 Maynard moved to Mascot Pictures where he introduced Gene Autry, the singing cowboy who would dominate the low-budget

Western for the next eight years. Autry made his screen debut *In Old Santa Fe* (1934), and Maynard introduced the picture with one of his own compositions, a song that seemed to reflect happenings in his private life. It dealt with "married strife" and how he liked his dog better than women; it also said "my only boss is my Tarzan hoss." Nat Levine, the head of Mascot Pictures, did not think much of Maynard's voice so he had it dubbed, the only time that Maynard's actual voice was not used in his musical Westerns. While Maynard was never as good a singer as Autry, his effort to put music and songs in the early sound pictures started a trend that became the standard for hundreds of future low-budget Westerns.[26]

The musical and action Westerns that Maynard made for Universal in 1929–1930 were popular, but Carl Laemmle, president of the studio, believed that Westerns were too much of a financial risk, so he canceled the series after eight pictures. Within three years Laemmle realized that sound Westerns would make money, and he rehired Maynard as a replacement for Tom Mix. In the interim Maynard had made Westerns for two independent studios, Tiffany and KBS/World Wide. Tiffany released eleven Maynard Westerns between 1930 and 1932; these were considered to be Maynard's first all-talking pictures since the Universal films used only partial dialogue and synchronized sound. The Tiffany films were formula Westerns that featured Maynard's horsemanship but not his acting skill. None of the features possessed any musical interludes because Tiffany production manager Samuel Bischoff placed little value on singing cowboys. The studio released one of the features in 1930, six in 1931, and four in 1932. The Depression made economy a necessity, and all eleven features had minimum budgets of $12,000 to $15,000, with Maynard receiving $8,000 a picture. Despite the economy of these Tiffany features, they added to Maynard's popularity.[27]

Bischoff left Tiffany and launched KBS Productions. Maynard signed a contract with Bischoff for eight Westerns to be released in 1932 and 1933. They continued the action format of the Tiffany releases but enjoyed budgets of $75,000 each. Maynard received $10,000 per picture at KBS. The features were action oriented, but Maynard did not do all the stunts himself. He used his brother Kermit in at least two of the films. In *Dynamite Ranch* (1932) Kermit performed as Ken's double and stuntman, and in *Drum Taps* (1933) a feature with a Boy Scout theme, he had an unbilled speaking part. These are the only features in which the two brothers appeared together. Bischoff actually hired Kermit to keep his brother out of trouble when he drank excessively and misbehaved. When they were on location in Kernville, California, Maynard got drunk and rode his horse through the streets of Kernville shooting out street lights and store windows. Kermit, a teetotaler, detested his brother's drinking and his behavior when drinking. Eventually Maynard's drinking and the way he treated his wife Mary alienated Kermit to the extent that the brothers rarely spoke to each other for the rest of their lives.[28]

Despite Maynard's problems with alcohol he remained hard working, creative, and popular. He continued to have box office appeal. In 1933 Carl Laemmle again gave Maynard his own production unit and control over cast, scripts, and directors and a budget of $100,000 per picture. During this second period with Universal, Maynard seemed to reach the peak of his success and popularity. He worked hard, not only with his acting but also with the details of production. It was the most demanding period of his movie-making career; he developed scripts, hired directors and casts, determined shooting schedules, composed music, and supervised editing. The effort paid off. He produced eight Westerns filled with action, music, and unusual plots. In the first, *King of the Arena* (1933), Maynard returned to the circus theme that he had used in earlier Universal and First National films. Indeed, he spliced in action sequences from his 1930 Universal film *Parade of the West* that demonstrated his horsemanship. In addition to his good equestrian skills, Maynard emphasized chases, gunfights, stampedes, and fistfights to keep the pictures moving at a fast pace. *The Trail Drive* (1933), filmed in part on a ranch in northern California, featured a cattle drive that was confronted by stampedes, river crossings, and other trail hazards. The story concerned ranchers who sold their cattle to a buyer for paper script with the understanding that at the end of the drive the script would be redeemed. The buyer welched and Maynard must right this wrong. *Strawberry Roan* used a horse stampede, two horse fights, and a wild bronc raising havoc in a bunkhouse to maintain a fast pace. A *Variety* reviewer noted that *Strawberry Roan*'s "plot thread [was] too thin to gain great interest, but it abounds in physical action." Actually, the film provided a good representation of cowboy ranch life and humor. In *Gun Justice* (1933), the villains who attempt to steal a ranch by murdering its owner, are foiled by Ranger Ken Maynard who happens to be heir to the property. "A lot of flying hoofs

Ken Maynard. *Raymond E. White*

[and] winded mustangs [make this feature] fast, actionful and to the point." *Fiddlin' Buckaroo* was a "very fair production, with plenty of movement."[29]

While the period from 1929 to 1934 was Maynard's most creative and productive, it was also one of personal and professional turmoil. His responsibilities at Universal involved more than acting and added stress to his life. In his role as producer, director, scriptwriter, and actor, he had definite ideas on how his Westerns should be made. Using all of Universal's facilities he spared no expense and often went over budget. His Westerns were probably the most expensive ones made in the early 1930s, with budgets exceeding $100,000 and some films costing as much as $125,000. His growing disregard for economy got him into trouble with Universal executives, particularly Carl Laemmle, Jr., who ordered Maynard to watch his spending. The result was loud and vociferous arguments between the two men.[30]

In at least one film, *Smoking Guns* (1934), it is questionable if

Maynard knew what he was doing. The film had a bizarre plot with locations set in the swamps and jungles of South America and the western plains of North America. He played a dual role and engaged in fights with alligators as well as standard Western villains. Maynard filmed the tropical scenes himself while on vacation, so he could write off some of the expenses of the trip. When Carl Laemmle, Sr., saw the unreleased version of the film, he recalled Maynard from a vacation trip and demanded to know why he had not made a decent picture. Offended at this reprimand, Maynard quit the studio.[31]

He could afford to do so because he had an offer to work for Nat Levine of Mascot Pictures who had a musical feature and two serials in mind for him. *In Old Santa Fe* started production in September 1934, and the film was released in November. Maynard was unhappy about Mascot's casual production methods, and while filming the serial *Mystery Mountain* (1934), he took control of the production himself. His efforts resulted in a sloppy serial, and he overspent the budget by $15,000. In addition to these problems Maynard drank heavily on location; this kept him in a nasty, angry mood that he vented by viciously beating Tarzan and his other palomino horses. When Levine received word of Maynard's behavior, he put restrictions on his control of the script and told him if he did not change, it would be the end of his career at Mascot. Maynard finished the serial and quit, and Levine starred Gene Autry in the other serial, *Phantom Empire* (1935), that had been scheduled for Maynard.[32]

Maynard continued in his uncooperative attitude with his next producer, Larry Darmour, who provided a contract for eight Westerns to be released by Columbia Pictures. These were the last of Ken Maynard's high-budget Westerns and the last in which he took an active interest in scripting and producing. Maynard wanted to make action-oriented features that displayed his natural skills, but Darmour determined to keep the budgets to a minimum. Compromises had to be made, and Maynard and Darmour argued continuously. The eight pictures were good but lacked the quality of Maynard's earlier work. Spencer Gordon Bennett, who liked Maynard and could get along with him, directed seven of the eight features.[33]

Maynard provided the story for the first and most expensive feature, *Westward Frontier* (1935). It was a wagon train story with a son and daughter of one of the traveling families being separated from each other as a result of an Indian raid in which their parents were killed. The boy (Ken Maynard), raised by settlers, grew to manhood with a spotless and sterling character. His sister (Nora Lane), raised by Indians, became the leader of an outlaw band. They ultimately met, but the sister later died at the hands of one of her own henchmen. Maynard included a medicine show in the story to provide a chance to show off his musical and roping talents.

The other feature for which Maynard was responsible for the story was *Heir to Trouble* (1935) in which he inherited a baby and a mine from an old pal. The villain tried to get the baby and the mine but was foiled. The real star in this film is Tarzan. The horse carried the baby to safety just as the mine is blown up, played nursemaid by rocking the baby in a homemade cradle, and protected the baby from several officious townswomen.

While action in these Columbia releases was restricted, music and song were not. Maynard contributed instrumental and vocal interludes in several of the films. In *Lawless Riders* (1935), he sang one song, and in *The Cattle Thief* (1936), he sang two or three bars of a song. His most interesting performance came in *Heroes of the Range* (1936) in which he impersonated a notorious outlaw, "Lightnin' Smith," who was noted for both his gun handling and his singing. The principal villain (Harry Woods) forced Maynard to prove his identity by playing a violin and singing. Before he finished the tune, several of the other outlaws in the hideout picked up their musical instruments and joined in the singing.

Maynard's continuing troubles with Larry Darmour and his frustration at not being able to control his pictures drained his interest and enthusiasm. Moreover, his personal life deteriorated as his marriage to Mary headed for a breakup. His drinking continued, and he gained weight. Perhaps these things made him yearn for the days when he had direct contact with the public and received instant public adulation. Before he completed the Columbia series Maynard began to make plans to start a circus and Wild West show.

Maynard's Diamond K Ranch Wild West Circus and Indian Congress took shape in 1936. He hired as many as 400 performers and crew. Headquartered on his ranch, the circus operated only on weekends until it could go on tour. The show traveled to the San Diego World's Fair for a three-day stand but did not make a profit and closed after a few performances. Maynard had put all of his financial resources into the enterprise, and its cost required him to keep working in films. In 1937 he signed a contract with Grand National to make eight Westerns at $2400 per picture. The payment was far below what he had received in his peak years, but he needed the money.[34]

Getting back to the circus was important to Maynard, and if he could not succeed with his own circus, he looked for employment with one already established. In 1937, 1938, and 1940 he appeared in the Cole Brothers Circus and enjoyed equal billing with Clyde Beatty. It was a life that Maynard enjoyed. He and Tarzan could perform their tricks, and he did not have to put up with producers and directors and the regimented life of movie making, although he was under contract to make two films a year with Grand National studio. Circus work did not provide as much money as the movie industry, but his Grand National contract was not making him rich either. Making money seemed less important to him now. Moreover, he had fallen in love with Bertha Rowland Denham, a high-wire artist who had some under-standing of his obstreperous nature and tolerated his drinking. His marriage to Mary officially ended in August 1939, and on October 22, 1940, he married Bertha.[35]

Under the contract with Grand National, Maynard made *Boots of Destiny* and *Trailing Trouble* (1937) and *Whirlwind Horsman* and *Six Shootin' Sheriff* (1938). Grand National filmed the pictures on four- or five-day schedules coordinated with Maynard's circus tours. Maynard's increased weight was obvious in the films, and a foot injury restricted his movement and prevented him from performing his daredevil stunts. In *Boots of Destiny* he never took more than two or three steps in each scene and was usually filmed standing still or astride Tarzan. A double performed all the action sequences. In *Trailing Trouble*, the next film released in the series, the scriptwriters wrote the injury into the story by having Maynard fall from Tarzan and hurt his foot. Although Maynard was more mobile in this film than in *Boots of Destiny*, he continued to limp and doubles and stock footage were used for the action scenes. Maynard managed to mix it up with the villains in the remaining two features, but he often slipped and seemed off balance. A *Variety* reviewer noted that a fight between Maynard and Dick Alexander in *Six-Shootin' Sheriff* involved "more than 400 pounds of struggling, wheezing meat."[36] Maynard was only forty-three years old, but he was no longer the dashing daredevil.

Despite Maynard's increased girth, his name still had drawing power. His producers, Max and Arthur Alexander, wanted to make four more Westerns with him and release them through Colony Pictures. One feature, *Flaming Lead*, was released in November 1939, and the other three, *Death Rides the Range, Phantom Rancher,* and *Lightning Strikes West*, appeared between January and June 1940. Produced on low budgets, the films were mediocre in content, acting, and production values. Maynard portrayed a masked hero in *Phantom Rancher*. *Death Rides the Range* reflected the rising war clouds and had Maynard on the trail of foreign agents trying to gain control of helium on a western ranch. Tarzan began to look a bit emaciated, but Maynard still rode him hard. The big animal died shortly after the conclusion of the series, ending a seventeen-year relationship of showmanship and affection.

Tarzan's death and the conclusion of the pictures for Colony brought to a close an important period of Maynard's career. He began the 1930s as one of the most popular and highest paid cowboy stars in Hollywood. He worked hard on his pictures and put his whole effort into every film he made. His action sequences established standards that other B-Western stars and stunt artists sought to emulate. His use of music and song revolutionized the low-budget Western and set the stage for B Western singing stars of the late 1930s and 1940s.

Maynard also made a significant contribution to the B Western films by introducing Gene Autry in *In Old Santa Fe*. While Maynard was not totally responsible for Autry's appearance in the picture, it gave the young country-western singer a start, and Autry rose quickly to stardom. The two men liked and respected each other. Autry idolized Maynard and even was able to exert a calming influence on the star when he flew into a tantrum. In later years Maynard expressed his admiration of Autry's business acumen when he told movie historian Jon Tuska, "I've always liked Gene . . . because he knew how to keep his money. That's more'n the rest of us ever did."[37]

While Gene Autry's movie career was on the rise Ken Maynard's was in decline. After the Colony productions Maynard made no films for two and a half years. He spent that time mainly on the road making public appearances at war bond rallies and defense plants.

In 1943 Monogram Studio decided to duplicate its successful but defunct *Rough Riders* series that had starred Buck Jones, Tim McCoy, and Raymond Hatton with a new series called the *Trail Blazers* featuring Ken Maynard and Hoot Gibson. Producer Robert Tansey put the series together; it proved successful. Maynard at first resisted participation because of low pay, only $800 a picture, but when Tansey told him that his old friend Gibson needed the work, he relented. Low budgets did not provide for much higher compensation. Maynard continued to complain about the low pay and eventually quit the series because of it.

In 1942 Maynard hardly resembled a movie cowboy hero. He was nearing fifty years of age and weighed well over 200 pounds. He thought about losing weight for the *Trail Blazers* series, but when he learned that Gibson had no intention of doing so, neither did he.

Tansey selected Bob Baker, a singing cowboy at Universal to star with Maynard and Gibson in the initial entry, *Wild Horse Stampede* (1943), but Maynard so objected to Baker that he was dropped after the completion of the film. In the fourth feature of the series, *Death Valley Rangers* (1943), Tansey hired Bob Steele, who had just completed Republic's *Three Mesquiteers* series. Maynard had a personal dislike for Steele too, but he made two more features before quitting.[38]

Although Maynard had personal reservations about his pay he liked Gibson and he enjoyed making the six films. Maynard was too heavy to do daredevil stunts or to have the romantic lead. Those responsibilities were left up to Steele. Maynard and Gibson worked well together, putting an emphasis on humor and comedy. Maynard played himself, using his own name for the first time in his career.

Almost as soon as Maynard quit the *Trail Blazer* series Tansey involved him in another film. In 1944 he made *Harmony Trail* with country-western singer Eddie Dean and veteran B-Western comic Max Terhune. In this film Maynard returned to the medicine show theme that he had used so often in the past and demonstrated for the final time on film his roping and marksman skills. The feature was to be the first in a series that never materialized. It was re-released in 1947 as *White Stallion* to capitalize on Eddie Dean's rise to prominence as a B-Western star.

*Harmony Trail* ended Ken Maynard's western film career. He was forty-nine years old and in good health. His weight problem and his drinking were the principal roadblocks to a professional career, but he continued to work in circuses, tent shows, rodeos, and to make other personal appearances. In 1945 he appeared with Biller Brothers and Arthur Brothers circuses. He once again formed the Ken Maynard Circus with headquarters in Van Nuys, California, and when that show closed he performed at Western star Ray Corrigan's guest ranch on weekends. He also traveled the rodeo circuit in the 1950s and early 1960s, living out of a house trailer.[39] In addition to traveling, Maynard in the mid-1950s had a syndicated radio show on which he told stories and hawked Ken Maynard T-shirts.[40]

Tragedy struck Ken Maynard in 1968 when his wife died after twenty-eight years of marriage. Grief-stricken, Maynard continued to drink heavily. Within a year he became involved with Marilyn

Marlowe who used him to promote her own professional career, even claiming that she was married to Maynard. She advertised and sold his movie memorabilia, including his boots, his still-picture collection, an original tinted portrait, and the rope that he used in his pictures.[41]

In 1970 a diversion occurred in Maynard's life when Robert F. Slatzer gave him an opportunity to play a small role in *Bigfoot* (1971). Maynard relished the opportunity to demonstrate the acting skills that he had acquired over the years. After the filming Maynard's life mainly centered on his trailer, his drinking, and visitors who came to see him. The ravages of time and liquor finally had an effect upon Maynard's physical strength. His health deteriorated and his body gradually dehydrated. In January 1973 Maynard was placed in the Motion Picture Country Home, where on March 23 he died of stomach cancer.[42]

Ken Maynard lived in two worlds. One was the world of entertainment in which he promoted and perpetuated the mythic cowboy as an important American symbol. In Wild West shows and circuses and later in films, he romanticized the cowboy and helped to make him larger than life. In this simple fantasy world Maynard absorbed the myth into his own being. But the perfection that Maynard achieved in the circus arena and on the screen could never be duplicated in real life. This reality was his second world, and in it he was subject to the frailties of human beings. The intermeshing of these two worlds made his life complex and uncertain. The stress of the entertainment world intensified these forces within his life, and he sought an escape through alcohol. Instead of escape, liquor brought anger to the surface of his personality, and he often exploded in verbal rage at his wife, his brother, his producers, and his directors. Despite Ken Maynard's human frailties, he was a significant figure in American culture. His life and career perpetuated the mythic cowboy as an important American symbol. His trick riding in Wild West shows and circuses glamorized the cowboy, and his superhuman feats on the screen made the cowboy even more romantic and appealing. The screen cowboy, with his great physical strength, brains, sense of fairness and justice, and his Anglo-Saxon good looks was a personality with which twentieth-century Americans identified. Maynard played the role to perfection and in so doing developed a style that was uniquely his own. This style made him one of the top movie cowboys of the 1920s and 1930s.

NOTES

1. Jon Tuska has written more on Ken Maynard than any other film historian. His three-part retrospective of Maynard's life and career appeared in the Summer, Fall, and Winter (1969–70) issues of *Views & Reviews*. Tuska used these three essays as a basis for two chapters on Maynard in *The Filming of the West* (New York: Doubleday & Company, Inc., 1976) and then recapitulated much of the material in *The Vanishing Legion: History of Mascot Pictures, 1927–1935* (Jefferson, N.C.: McFarland & Company, Inc., 1982). This last work includes a valuable interview with Ken's brother Kermit. For details on Maynard's birth and early years see the Vevay, Indiana, *Reveille-Enterprise*, March 30, 1930, the *Indianapolis Star* January 7, 1934, and the *Indianapolis News*, August 4, 1964. The Cleo Rogers Memorial Library and the Bartholomew County Historical Society, Columbus, Indiana, possess small files of newspaper clippings and articles that relate to the lives and careers of Ken and Kermit Maynard.

2. *Indianapolis Star*, January 7, 1934.

3. Ibid.

4. *The Evening Republican* (Columbus, Indiana), June 6, 1930.

5. Ibid., May 22, 1911.

6. Buck Rainey, "Cinema Cowboys on the Sawdust Trail," pt. 2 *Classic Images* (December, 1983), p. 35; Tuska, *The Vanishing Legion*, p. 121.

7. *The Muncie Star* (Muncie, Indiana), May 6, 1928.

8. Rainey, "Cinema Cowboys on the Sawdust Trail," p. 35.

9. General Service Bureau, *Directory of the City of Columbus and East Columbus, 1913; The Evening Republican*, June 14, 1930.

10. George A. Katchmer in his article "Ken Maynard, Dr. Jeckyll [*sic*] or Mr. Hyde," *Classic Images* (December, 1983), cites this story from a 1926 *Photoplay* interview with Maynard. Maynard's claims are obviously false when one considers his age at the time of the Revolution in 1910–11. Maynard's sister-in-law, Mrs. Kermit Maynard, maintains that Ken was never involved in Mexican revolutionary activity. Letter, Edith Maynard to Ray White, May 22, 1985. On the other hand, Maynard tells a good story, and he has his facts straight on some of the participants involved in the Revolution. For dates and details of the Revolution see Charles Curtis Cumberland, *Mexican Revolution: Genesis Under Madero* (Austin: University of Texas Press, 1952).

11. Tuska, *Filming of the West*, p. 160.

12. Pawnee Bill or Gordon W. Lillie was a partner of William F. Cody in 1913 when creditors took possession of the Buffalo Bill Wild West and Pawnee Bill Far East. See Glenn Shirley, *Pawnee Bill: A Biography of Major Gordon W. Lillie* (Albuquerque: University of New Mexico Press, 1958), pp. 206–11; Don Russell, *The Lives and Legends of Buffalo Bill* (Norman: University of Oklahoma Press, 1958), pp. 446–56. See also Don Russell, *The Wild West: A History of the Wild West Shows* (Ft. Worth: Amon Carter Museum of Western Art, 1970).

13. Tuska, *Filming of the West*, pp. 160–61; Tuska indicates that Tom Mix helped Maynard get his first film-acting job.

14. Ibid., p. 161.

15. Ibid.; *Variety*, August 13, 1924.

16. Tuska, *Filming of the West*, 161.

17. Ibid., p. 166.

18. *The Muncie Star*, October 7, 1928. The only film in which Tarzan did not appear was *Six-Shootin' Sheriff* (1938). At the time the film was being made Tarzan was en route to a circus performance; Tuska, "In Retrospect: Ken Maynard," pt. 3, *Views & Reviews* (Winter, 1970), p. 25.

19. *Variety*, March 12, 1930; February 2, 1932.

20. *The Muncie Star*, January 1, 1928.

21. Tuska, *The Vanishing Legion*, p. 124.

22. Tuska, "In Retrospect: Ken Maynard," pt. 2, *Views & Reviews*, vol. 1 (Fall, 1969), p. 35; *Indianapolis Star*, January 7, 1934; Ken Maynard, "Yucatan Adventure," *Under Western Skies*, No. 13 (March, 1981), pp. 33–36.

23. For the book Maynard edited, see Leslie C. Miller, *Handsprings for Hamburgers: The Life of a Gypsy Flier*, ed. by Ken Maynard (Hollywood: David Graham Fischer, Publisher, 1929); Maynard, "Yucatan Adventure," pp. 33–36; Ken Maynard, "The Three R's of the Range," *St. Nicholas Magazine* (March, 1936), pp. 16 + ; Maynard provided the story for two of his films: *The Trail Drive* (1933) and *Western Frontier* (1935).

24. Columbia Records 2310. These two songs have been re-released on the album *Back in the Saddle Again*, New World Records, NW 314/315 (1983). Other recently released albums that included original Maynard selections are *When I Was a Cowboy: Songs of Cowboy Life*, Morning Star Records 45008 (1984); *Legendary Songs of the Old West*, 4 record set, Columbia Special Products, P4–15542; Michael R. Pitts provided information on the reissues of Maynard's songs. In the 1960s the John Edwards Memorial Foundation of the Folklore and Mythology Center at UCLA obtained the original test pressings of the recordings Maynard made for Columbia. William Koon's "The Songs of Ken Maynard," JEMF *Quarterly*, vol. 9 (1973), pp. 70–75, provides the lyrics and a brief analysis of each of the eight songs Maynard recorded. In the same issue of the JEMF *Quarterly* see also Ken Griffis, "The Ken Maynard Story," pp. 67–70.

25. Tuska, *Filming of the West*, p. 272; Maynard receives some attention as the original movie singing cowboy in Douglas B. Green's long article, "The Singing Cowboy: An American Dream," *Journal of Country Music*, vol. 7 (May, 1978), pp. 4–62.

26. Tuska, *The Vanishing Legion*, pp. 133–34.

27. Ibid., pp. 124–25, 130.

28. Ibid., pp. 126–27; Maynard's misbehavior was not limited to movie locations. In his hometown of Columbus, Indiana, in 1936 he "made a series of unscheduled personal appearances at downtown cafes and presently launched on a loud and abusive tirade, part of it directed at local individuals, and, part at his hometown in general," *Evening Republican*, July 7, 1936. In Memphis, Tennessee, two years later, Maynard was charged with assault and battery on a woman. He pleaded guilty to the charge and was fined $50. He eventually made an out-of-court settlement of $3,000. *The Muncie Star*, March 18, 1938; *New York Times*, March 20, 1938; *Evening Republican*, April 11, 1938.

29. *Variety*, December 12, 1933; January 9, 1934.

30. Tuska, *The Vanishing Legion*, p. 132.

31. Ibid., pp. 132–33.

32. Ibid., pp. 132–36.

33. Tuska, "In Retrospect: Ken Maynard," pt. 2, *Views & Reviews* (Fall, 1969), pp. 28–29.

34. Rainey, "Cinema Cowboys on the Sawdust Trail," p. 36; Undated newspaper clippings in the Ken Maynard file, Bartholomew Country Historical Society, Columbus, Indiana. These clippings describe Maynard's investment and the circus facilities he built in Van Nuys, California.

35. *Evening Republican*, October 23, 1940. Maynard at the time of the marriage in 1940 claimed that he and Bertha had been married the previous year in Mexico. They wanted the second ceremony to eliminate any questions about the legality of their Mexican marriage.

36. *Variety*, August 17, 1938.

37. Tuska, *Filming of the West*, p. 473.

38. Ibid., pp. 422–25.

39. Tuska, "In Retrospect: Ken Maynard," pt. 3, *Views & Reviews* (Winter, 1970), p. 40.

40. The title of this radio show was "Tales from the Diamond K." Just how widely it was syndicated is unknown. At least one program, #5 "The Squaw Man's Fortune," is available on Radiola Records MR-1144, Western Series No. 6, Radiola Release 144 (1983).

41. Marlowe advertised herself and Maynard's memorabilia in *Wild West Stars*, an intermittent periodical published by Jim Ward, Nashville, Tennessee. The publication carried no publication dates.

42. Tuska, *The Vanishing Legion*, pp. 154–55; *Republic* (Columbus, Indiana), March 24, 1973.

JOHN H. LENIHAN

# The Western Heroism

# of Randolph Scott

In HIS CELEBRATED essay on the Western film, Robert Warshow wrote, "The Westerner is the last gentleman, and the movies which over and over again tell his story are probably the last art form in which the concept of honor retains its strength."[1] No other Western movie star so completely reflected Warshow's thesis than Randolph Scott. The term "gentleman" appears frequently in personal recollections of Scott's polite, civil manner in a business where success reputedly breeds intemperance and easily bruised egos. Although Scott had to settle for being Gary Cooper's dialogue coach when Paramount filmed *The Virginian* in 1929, this Virginia-born actor would have been a natural for Owen Wister's prototypical cowboy—the fusion, according to David Brion Davis, of "the Western scout of Cooper and the Dime Novel" and "the golden myth of the antebellum South."[2]

Born in Orange, Virginia, in 1903, George Randolph Scott prepared himself at Georgia Tech and the University of North Carolina for a possible career in textile engineering. After a brief stint with his father's textile firm in Charlotte, North Carolina, Scott moved to Hollywood to try out his budding interest in acting. He worked as an extra on several films and with local theatre groups like the Pasadena Playhouse until Paramount signed him to a seven-year contract.[3] At first consigned to bit parts, including one of Charles Laughton's caged beasts in a mad-scientist creeper *The Island of Lost Souls* (1933), Scott received top billing from 1932 to 1935 in a popular series of nine Westerns based on Zane Grey stories. In seven of these films Scott benefited from the expert direction of Henry Hathaway, whose own illustrious and longtime contribution to the Western genre culminated with his direction of John Wayne's Academy Award-winning performance in *True Grit* (1969).

Along with the Zane Grey films, Paramount used Scott in several non-Westerns and RKO introduced him to musical comedy in *Roberta* (1935) and *Follow the Fleet* (1936), both starring Fred Astaire and Ginger Rogers. Then came an ideal bit of casting for him as James Fenimore Cooper's Leatherstocking hero, Hawkeye, in *The Last of the Mohicans* (1936). Scott seemed born for what generally is considered the literary source of America's mythic frontiersman.

Despite the success of its Zane Grey films with Randolph Scott, Paramount found a presumably more attractive B vehicle in William Boyd's Hopalong Cassidy series, while selecting bigger stars such as Gary Cooper (*The Plainsman* [1937]) and Joel McCrea (*Wells Fargo* [1937] and *Union Pacific* [1939]) for its prestige A Westerns. To finish out Scott's contract, Paramount provided him one of these feature attractions, *The Texans* (1938). Handsomely clad in buckskin, rebel-veteran Scott drives a herd of cattle to Abilene, Kansas, for shipment on the new transcontinental railroad. Scott's is the voice of patriotic wisdom as he talks heroine Joan Bennett out of a land deal with Maximilian ("I'm an American—I don't need an emperor to give me land"), fights off greedy carpetbaggers, and opposes the dangerously naïve Robert Cummings in his scheme to regain the South through a new organization called the Ku Klux Klan. Bennett converts to Scott's plea for unity and democratic justice when she tells Cummings at the end of the film, "This is America. We govern by laws, not by night riding." Nationalist sentiment of this kind became commonplace as Hollywood and America grew concerned about fascist aggression abroad and braced for another world war.

After Scott completed his contract with Paramount in 1938, he signed non-exclusive contracts with both Twentieth Century-Fox and Universal. Fox started him out in the popular Shirley Temple vehicle *Rebecca of Sunnybrook Farm* (1938) before casting him in one of the most financially successful Westerns of all time, *Jesse James* (1939). As he did so often in his career, Scott played the tall, handsome marshal who was dedicated to enforcing law and order. Unlike his role as Wyatt Earp in *Frontier Marshal*, which Fox released the same year, Scott was neither the hero nor the star player of *Jesse James*. That honor went to

Tyrone Power in the title role and Henry Fonda as his brother Frank. It was typical in literature and films made during the Depression decade to sympathize with the downtrodden worker and farmer and to suggest that justice was often undermined by selfish corporate interests. Hence, the James brothers become outlaws in reaction to corrupt railroad capitalists and politicians who exploit the good farmers of post-Civil War Missouri. Scott plays a well-intentioned public official who recognizes the injustices that have provoked the James gang but at the same time cannot abide Jesse's self-centered defiance of the law. The film suggests that Scott's indignation toward Jesse's reckless behavior is fueled by his unrequited love for Jesse's wife, but for the most part he remains the reserved, honest spokesman for the rule of law. Juxtaposed with the outlaw protagonist, Scott's unwavering commitment to salvage a respect for the law provides an ongoing dialectic on the source and meaning of social justice in an unjust political environment. The audience is asked on the one hand to despise the corrupt system that has shattered the James family and other honest people but on the other hand to insist that Jesse's lawlessness not be allowed to undermine legal authority completely. The film thus concludes with Jesse's death—a kind of atonement for his infraction of the law—while a sympathetic journalist (Henry Hull) delivers a memorial to the deceased outlaw's boldness and freedom. The box-office success of *Jesse James* prompted a Fox sequel, *The Return of Frank James* (1940), and a host of other outlaw sagas. *When the Daltons Rode* (1940) and *The Desperadoes* (1943) again have Scott playing the spokesman for law and order while focusing on the colorful exploits of the badmen. In his review of *When the Daltons Rode, New York Times* critic Bosley Crowther faulted "the ineffectual intervention of Mr. Scott" (as a lawyer) in an otherwise rousing tale of the boisterous Daltons.[4]

Given the obvious attractiveness of the outlaw protagonist in these years, it was only fitting that an emerging star like Randolph Scott be afforded such a plum role. Twentieth Century-Fox proved accommodating in two of its prestige Western features of 1941, *Belle Starr* and *Western Union*. The former exploited the popularity of *Gone With the Wind* (1939) as well as the outlaw fad. Gene Tierney stars as the passionate, willful Southern belle who marries the dashing Confederate officer-turned-outlaw, Sam Starr (Randolph Scott), to save Missouri from an oppressive carpetbag government. Fox dredged up all the pro-South stereotypes—the cowardly conniving carpetbaggers, loyal freedmen who prefer planter paternalism to Yankee skullduggery, and the well-meaning Union officer who is duty-bound to enforce a flawed legal order. Dana Andrews performed the same function in the latter role as Scott had done in *Jesse James*, to include falling in love with the outlaw's wife. Like Tyrone Power's Jesse James, Randolph Scott's Sam Starr exhibits a dangerously self-righteous streak in the course of playing Robin Hood to the people, and by the end of the film he must atone. Whereas Jesse is killed, Sam turns himself in after his beloved Belle is killed and he realizes that his lawlessness no longer serves the best interest of the community.

*Western Union* was less an outlaw saga than a patriotic tribute to those who strung telegraph wires across the continent, but the film's dramatic interest rests with badman Randolph Scott's attempts to redeem himself by helping the famed telegraph company. Director Fritz Lang, a German expatriate noted for his fatalistic accounts of doomed individuals, has his protagonist (Scott) struggling to extricate himself from his sordid past before he is shot down by his malicious out-

Randolph Scott. *Theatre Arts Library, Harry Ransom Humanities Research Center, The University of Texas at Austin*

law brother. Critic Bosley Crowther, who had dismissed Scott's intrusive presence in *When the Daltons Rode*, singled out the actor's performance in *Western Union*: "Randolph Scott, who is getting to look and act more and more like William S. Hart, herein shapes one of the truest and most agreeble characters of his career."[5] Likening Scott to William S. Hart was high praise, since Hart was widely considered the ideal movie Westerner—noble, laconic, and most of all, realistic in comparison to the gaudily clad B-Western stars who strummed guitars and sang instead of sticking to the business of riding and shooting.

Having achieved star status by the early 1940s, Randolph Scott was teamed with some of Hollywood's top headliners. Warner Brothers signed him to play opposite its leading male star Errol Flynn in the episodic *Virginia City* (1940). Scott's role as a proud Confederate officer from Virginia seemed tailored for the gentlemanly actor whose own family heritage was deeply rooted in the history of America's first colony. Early in the film, Scott reminisces with Miriam Hopkins about their wonderful childhood days in the antebellum South. Whether courting the lovely heroine in his immaculate uniform or battling courageously to ship gold across the rugged southwest to the embattled Confederacy, Randolph Scott was altogether convincing in comparison to Errol Flynn whose swashbuckling style always seemed more appropriate for movieland's Sherwood Forest than the American frontier. More pathetically out of place was Humphrey Bogart, who played a Mexican bandit with an accent that qualified for instant camp.

Universal teamed Scott with another promising star, John Wayne, whose image as a Westerner had become well established in numerous B films of the 1930s and in the John Ford classic *Stagecoach* in 1939. In both an Alaskan adventure *The Spoilers* (1942) and a modern-day melodrama *Pittsburgh* (1943), Scott and Wayne are brawling competitors for the attention of Marlene Dietrich. *The Spoilers* was one of several remakes of Rex Beach's gold rush saga, and Scott's one opportunity to play a thoroughly villainous character. Moreover, Scott is entirely persuasive as the unscrupulous, smooth-talking gold commissioner who cheats prospectors, including Wayne, out of their hard-earned claims. Not accustomed to losing the heroine or a fight on the big screen, Scott at least goes down swinging against a no less virile action star in perhaps the grandest brawl in American movies.

Scott and Wayne again fight over Marlene Dietrich in *Pittsburgh*, but this time Scott is the hero who defeats Wayne and wins Dietrich. *Pittsburgh* also happened to be an unabashed appeal for wartime mobilization. Throughout the war years Scott and Wayne battled the Germans and Japanese on the screen. Scott especially treasured his performance as a Marine sergeant in *To the Shores of Tripoli* (1942) and the feeling it gave him of contributing to the war effort.[6] None of his war films were particularly distinguished, but they were superior to what are considered his two worst feature movies, *Belle of the Yukon* (1944) and *Captain Kidd* (1945). He had proved adept at handling any number of different roles and film formulas, but *Captain Kidd* severely taxed his versatility. In this cheaply made showcase for Charles Laughton's histrionics as the notorious pirate, Scott looked awkward as the sword-wielding son of an English nobleman.

After the war years and the embarrassing *Captain Kidd*, Randolph Scott settled comfortably into the genre that suited him best and with which he became identified by an appreciative public. Except for three forgettable films (*Home, Sweet Homicide* [1946], *Christmas Eve* [1947], and a guest appearance in *Starlift* [1951]), Scott's forty-two postwar movies were all Westerns. For the next fifteen years audiences could count on an average of five Randolph Scott Westerns every two years, with as many as four Scott Westerns released in 1949, 1951, and 1955. His total of thirty-eight Westerns from 1946 to 1960, compared with twenty-two for Joel McCrea, twenty for Audie Murphy, and eleven for John Wayne during the same period, made Scott the most prolific star of feature Westerns at a time when Hollywood was turning out more, and arguably better, films in this genre than before or since.

Most of Scott's postwar Westerns were medium-budgeted A features that Hollywood turned out in greater numbers to replace its B-series films that could no longer hold their own in the face of competition from televison. Scott survived the fate of B stars such as Gene Autry and Roy Rogers, who abandoned the movies for half-hour television series in the early 1950s. Audiences would pay to see a Randolph Scott Western that offered technicolor (or on occasion 3-D) and a more elaborate story than could be found on television.

Unlike John Wayne and *Red River* (1948), Gary Cooper and *High Noon* (1952), or Alan Ladd and *Shane* (1953), Randolph Scott was never able to capitalize on a major critical or box-office hit. Instead he relied on a steady stream of solid, action-filled, entertaining movies. Scott told Hollywood reporter Bob Thomas in 1951 that he looked "for a strong believable story with 75 percent outdoor action and 25 percent indoor. If you get any more of your picture indoors, you're in trouble."[7] Whatever script he chose, and they were of varying quality, one could

Randolph Scott in *The Cariboo Trail*. *Theatre Arts Library, Harry Ransom Humanities Research Center, The University of Texas at Austin*

always depend on the actor's credible performance. Already in his mid-forties by the end of the war, Scott's face bore the weathered creases and leathery tan that endeared him to fans who preferred toughness and realism in their frontier heroes. His name on the marquee was the producer's chief drawing card, and for four consecutive years (1950–53) Scott was listed among the top ten money-making stars.[8]

For most of his postwar Westerns, Scott was in the capable hands of veteran producers Nat Holt and especially Harry Joe Brown. Holt's productions in the late forties played fast and loose with the conventional format of a lawman bringing civilization to a wild town. *Badman's Territory* (1946) and *Return of the Badmen* (1948) were fanciful concoctions in which Scott encountered a veritable army of notorious desperadoes, including the James, Dalton, and Younger brothers, Billy the Kid, Belle and Sam Starr, and the Sundance Kid. The idea that more is better may have originated with RKO's executive producer Jack Gross who had orchestrated a comparable gathering of famous characters from the horror genre for Universal's *House of Frankenstein* (1945).[9] Except for Robert Ryan's murderous Sundance Kid in *Return of the Badmen*, the famous outlaws in these films were depicted as likable types who had gotten off to a bad start in life. In both *Badman's Territory* and *Fighting Man of the Plains* (1949), Jesse James actually befriends the hero against the real villainy of a crooked lawman or citizen. Many of these outlaws seemed to be Hollywood's frontier counterparts to the uprooted veterans of World War II and misunderstood juvenile delinquents who troubled American consciences in the postwar years.

Harry Joe Brown, Scott's most important collaborator, produced nearly half of the actor's postwar Westerns at Columbia Pictures with Scott as associate producer. The two had worked together on *Western Union* and *The Desperadoes* and from 1947 to 1960 they generated Scott's best work in the genre, including the RANOWN series directed by Budd Boetticher.

By contrast with the upbeat, rousing style of the Nat Holt productions, the Brown-Scott films were decidedly more violent and somber. In *Coroner Creek* (1948) Scott is nearly consumed with hatred as he sets out to avenge his fiancée's abduction and subsequent suicide, a theme that often reoccurred in the better known RANOWN-Boetticher films. The traditional gentlemanly code of fair play always associated with a Randolph Scott hero gave way in this film to a grim, determined "eye for an eye" philosophy. Hence after winning an unusually brutal fistfight with Forrest Tucker, Scott crushes Tucker's hand with his foot as Tucker had done to him. Scott follows this unsavory deed by threatening to scald another badman with a hot frying pan. Such violent "realism" was becoming commonplace in the postwar Western.

With *Coroner Creek*, Randolph Scott embraced the emotionally torturous realm of betrayal, revenge, and alienation that distinguished the so-called "adult" Western in the postwar years. Far from the confident spokesman for law and civilization seen in Nat Holt films, Scott's character in the Brown Westerns was vulnerable, sometimes flawed, and always subject to a harsh, perpetually turbulent frontier environment. Physical and emotional survival, let alone triumph, becomes more problematic, and in one case at least, impossible. Throughout *The Doolins of Oklahoma* (1949) there was an atmosphere of doom characteristic of 1940s *noir* films. Scott becomes a wanted man after shooting, in self-defense, a scoundrel who had informed on his outlaw friends, the Daltons. Periodically a narrator reminds us that Scott is a man "alone ... with the doors of freedom closed against him ... forced to seek friends outside the law." When Scott marries a church deacon's daughter and settles down to farming, a former gang member reveals a wanted poster so Scott will be forced to leave the respectable life. He retains little taste for the criminal world, however, and plans to accompany his wife in search of a new life in the far West. When a posse shows up, Scott decides to spare himself and his wife further unhappiness. He draws his gun on the posse and is shot down.

Subsequent Scott-Brown Westerns concluded on a happier note, but not without anxiety and grueling brushes with an uncertain world. Similar to *The Doolins of Oklahoma*, in *The Stranger Wore a Gun* (1953) Scott struggles to escape an unsavory past, in this case his association with William Quantrill's butchery in Kansas. A strange twist of fate in *Hangman's Knot* (1952) besets Scott when he captures a Union Army payroll in the course of his duty as a Confederate officer and then discovers that the war ended a month earlier. His hopes of returning home are dashed as he and his patrol are pursued by a malicious posse that wants the stolen payroll more than justice. In *Man in the Saddle* (1951), Scott's promising future as a small rancher is nearly destroyed when his girl deserts him to marry a cattle baron who is out to ruin Scott and his neighbors. He is immersed in treachery and bloody chaos before he is able to reach the point in life from which he started.

*Santa Fe* (1951) was the one Brown-Scott production to emphasize America's expanding civilization as a context in which the hero works out his personal difficulties, this time the loss of his Virginia home and a war-related killing that has made him a fugitive. Scott relishes his newfound job as foreman of the Santa Fe Railroad but his efforts at respectability are jeopardized by feelings of loyalty toward his two outlaw brothers. All ends well and Scott is commended for putting the railroad above self so that "as the railroad grows, so will America." Scott also played the stalwart railroad builder in Nat Holt's *Canadian Pacific* (1949) and Warner Brothers' *Carson City*, but his dedication in these films is uncluttered by the inner conflicts he faces in *Santa Fe* and other Brown Westerns.

*Carson City* was one of a dozen rather standard Westerns that Scott made for Warner Brothers in the 1950s. The only standout was

*Seven Men From Now* (1956), Scott's first film with director Budd Boetticher before the two joined with Harry Joe Brown and Columbia Pictures. Edwin Marin, who directed several of the Holt Westerns, delivered the first three Warner Brothers films before he died in 1951. Marin showed little interest in character development or thematic complications and settled for healthy doses of hard riding, extensive shoot-outs, and handsome technicolored scenery. Audiences were not disappointed. *Colt .45* (1950) turned out to be one of the biggest movie hits of 1950 and Scott's most profitable Western in the postwar period. Bosley Crowther of the New York Times called it "a monumental sanction of the Western formula . . . a whoop-de-do horse opera . . . such a hackneyed picture that it actually is a lot of fun."[10] Like *Winchester 73* (1950), the popular James Stewart-Anthony Mann Western released two months later, the premise of keeping a newly developed weapon out of the wrong hands had a timely appeal given America's current preoccupation with the leakage of atomic secrets to the Russians. In a news story to publicize the release of *Colt .45*, Warners highlighted the theme of keeping a new weapon "out of the hands of the wrong element—Indians and bandits in the Colt days, Russians and the Iron Curtain now."[11]

A related postwar issue that struck close to home in Hollywood in these years was McCarthyism. The major studios blacklisted uncooperative witnesses or those named as Communists and fellow travelers in the congressional investigations of Communism in Hollywood. Another way of demonstrating movieland's patriotism was to produce anticommunist message films. Warner Brothers contributed its share of espionage stories, most notably *I Was a Communist For the FBI* (1951), with Frank Lovejoy, and *Big Jim McClain* (1952), in which John Wayne and James Arness smash a Communist cell in Hawaii. Aside from his name appearing on a list of Hollywood supporters for the reelection of Senator Joseph McCarthy in 1952, Scott stayed relatively clear of active politicking and appearances in the anticommunist message films.[12] He did, however, make one Western for Warner Brothers that focused on treason. In *Man Behind the Gun* (1952), Scott plays an army officer on a secret mission in pre-Civil War Los Angeles to uncover a nest of separatist conspirators. Despite the nineteenth-century setting and Western trappings, the plot was practically interchangeable with any number of modern spy dramas. For the quick eye, the name "Joe Stalin" allegedly appears on a grave marker designed half-jokingly by Warner's property man Eddie Edwards.[13] Scott is unusually grim and uncompromising in the execution of his mission even though it may implicate those with whom he feels some personal attachment. He recalls at one point in the film how he had once killed a close friend for desertion rather than see him branded "a traitor." Off-screen Scott narrates that it is "difficult to believe that the city of Angels also had its share of unholy activities." By 1952 it was not hard for audiences to believe at all.

The onus of being labeled a deserter emerges in Scott's next film for Warner Brothers, *Thunder Over the Plains* (1953). Corrupt carpetbaggers are exploiting the Army's enforcement of Reconstruction in Texas to swindle and oppress the people. Army officer Scott has the unenviable duty of enforcing martial law which in turn brings public derision upon himself and his status-conscious wife. When Scott sheds his uniform for civilian attire to ride out and make peace with a popularly supported guerrilla leader, he faces charges of desertion by his superiors. Eventually he saves his good name and in the process makes way for the readmission of Texas into the Union.

By creating dramatic tension around the hero's personal difficulties in confronting a hostile environment of divided loyalties, *Thunder Over the Plains* was closer to the Brown films than Scott's previous efforts at Warner Brothers. Director Andre DeToth had also filmed two of the better Scott-Brown Westerns, *Man in the Saddle* and *The Stranger Wore a Gun* and in 1954 he delivered two more relatively somber Scott Westerns for Warner Brothers, *Riding Shotgun* and *The Bounty Hunter.*

By the mid-1950s, Randolph Scott's screen persona was no longer that of the confident, amiable representative of a progressive civilization. Nearly all his films incorporated elements of the "adult" Western, which was also making its way to television with the introduction of CBS's *Gunsmoke* series in 1955. Following the lead of Harry Joe Brown's productions of the late 1940s, there is a sad, hard edge to Scott's otherwise stalwart character owing to some tragic or disillusioning experience in a violent and humanly complex environment. Society becomes increasingly discordant, and distinctions between good and evil are less obvious. Even when Scott rejoined producer Nat Holt in 1955 for *Rage at Dawn* an otherwise routine plot took an unusually grim twist. As in most of his previous Holt Westerns, Scott again is a lawman confronting a notorious gang of desperadoes. However, once Scott captures and jails the famous Reno Brothers, he is helpless to protect his captives from being lynched by an angry mob.

The audience is jarred into witnessing an act of social injustice that makes the Renos' lawlessness seem honorable by comparison.

Scott's obsession for revenge in Warner Brothers' *Tall Man Riding* (1953) recalls Harry Joe Brown's *Coroner Creek*, except here Scott learns almost too late that his vengeance is misplaced. The cattle baron he is about to kill for having him beaten and run him out of the area is now helplessly blind. Moreover, the cattle baron is the only authority figure who has been able to prevent a villainous saloon boss from grabbing up the entire territory. Of course Scott sets things right, but only after coming perilously close to killing a helpless man and in the process removing the one obstacle to conniving profiteers.

The image of civilization on the brink of chaos, such as mob violence in *Rage at Dawn*, or scheming land grabbers unwittingly assisted by a wrongheaded hero in *Tall Man Riding*, is also at the heart of the next three Scott-Brown productions, *A Lawless Street* (1955), *Ten Wanted Men* (1955), and *7th Cavalry* (1956). In each film Scott is a beleaguered authority figure who stands alone to prevent the unraveling of a tenuous social order. *A Lawless Street* opens with marshal Scott about to start a new day in his long and harrowing career as a lawman. The years have taken their toll and in his mind he hears the snarling of a beast which is the town. He counts the days on a calendar, wondering how long he can manage to beat the odds and survive hired killers and drunken troublemakers. Although killing sickens him, he must keep up the appearance of toughness and confidence in order to retain his credibility. To compound the psychological burden of his thankless job, his ex-wife (Angela Lansbury) comes to town to sing in the saloon and perhaps to marry its owner who longs for Scott's demise; she had left Scott years earlier because she could not bear the prospect of seeing him killed. When a gunfighter outdraws him and gets off the first shot, Scott plays dead and soon all hell breaks loose. The streets are overrun with riffraff, the snarling beast unchained. Scott reappears once the townspeople have been scared into respecting the importance of law enforcement, and together they restore order. Scott can then retire, knowing that the townspeople will preserve what he nearly died to maintain.

*Ten Wanted Men*, like *Tall Man Riding*, operates on the premise that only the strong entrepreneur—the local cattle baron—stands between order and lawlessness. Scott plays the proud success figure who has earned the community's respect but whose monopolistic power is resented and challenged by a jealous rival (Richard Boone). When Scott

cannot legally prove that Boone is rustling his cattle, he must reluctantly resort to arbitrary force. He almost single-handedly defeats
Boone's hired gunmen and restores his own privileged position which
in turn safeguards the community. This unabashed apology for a
strong propertied elite presages John Wayne's more self-conscious
philosophizing as the righteous cattle baron of *McLintock* (1963) and
*Chisum* (1970).

Respect for authority as the only alternative to defeat and disorder
is the central issue of *7th Cavalry*, one of the last sympathetic Hollywood interpretations of the Custer legend. Scott is a cavalry officer who
suffers official reprimand and hostility from fellow officers for having
been Custer's favorite subordinate and who had been awarded leave at
the time of the Little Big Horn defeat. At an official inquiry Scott defends Custer against charges of glory-seeking and tactical errors, adding that "General Custer was a great human being, Sir." The fault, it
turns out, was not with Custer but the junior officers who did not give
him adequate support. Following the inquiry, Scott leads a patrol of
drunken, disorderly troopers on a dangerous mission to find the bodies
of Custer's defeated troops. Interestingly the bodies of enlisted men are
to be buried and the officers returned home for a special ceremonial
tribute. Paralleling what Custer presumably faced in the way of contempt from his officers, Scott's own authority is challenged during the
mission. He is nearly knifed in his sleep by one enlisted man and has to
use his fists against another who constantly criticizes him. When Scott
refuses to be intimidated by a horde of Indians into leaving the bodies
in place at the Little Big Horn, he faces mutiny by his panicked troopers. Scott's sergeant threatens to take command until Scott makes him
realize that he and the others are helpless without Scott's wisdom and
leadership. Even the Indians, the film suggests, respect the importance
of enlightened leadership and authority: Upon finding an Indian
chief's spear near the spot where Custer lies, Scott declares that this
"is the tribute of one great leader to another."

These decidedly argumentative sanctions of official authority and
entrepreneurial paternalism in Scott's mid-1950s films all but disappeared in the series of exceptional B Westerns he made for director
Budd Boetticher. Along with Sam Peckinpah's *Ride the High County*
(1962), the Boetticher films rank as Scott's finest work in the genre.
Except for *Seven Men From Now* (1956) and *Westbound* (1959), produced
for Warner Brothers, Boetticher worked with Scott's producing
partner, Harry Joe Brown, at Columbia Pictures. The talented Burt

Kennedy contributed four of the better screenplays before trying his own hand at directing in the 1960s and 1970s. The one failure in the series was *Westbound*, a routine "oater" that Boetticher later acknowledged was a lost cause from the start.[14]

Randolph Scott brought to the Boetticher Westerns his bronzed sinewy presence of courageous dignity, practical wisdom, and physical assurance. Boetticher also capitalized on Scott's age, now in his fifties, to shape a protagonist whose strict adherence to a personal code of justice makes him poignantly archaic and sometimes impervious to human frailty, his own as well as others. With the exception of *Westbound*, in which Scott dutifully contributes to a Union victory in the Civil War, Boetticher's protagonist is a man alone acting from a strong sense of moral rectitude as he avenges a personal injury or simply confronts a dangerous encounter by chance. His triumph over the villain(s) or Indians assures his own physical survival and that of a lady in distress but is usually of little consequence to the protection or welfare of a frontier community.

In *Seven Men From Now* (1956), *Decision at Sundown* (1957), *Ride Lonesome* (1959) and *Comanche Station* (1960), Scott's laconic stoicism belies an almost neurotic impulse to redress a personal tragedy. In the first three films he is obsessed with avenging the death of his wife, a quest that is emotionally self-defeating and, in the case of *Decision at Sundown*, unwarranted. His wife, as it turns out, was a tramp. *Comanche Station* begins and ends with Scott's lonely and hopeless search for his wife who was captured years earlier by Comanches. Only in *Seven Men From Now* is there some promise of building a new relationship to compensate for his lost loved one.

In contrast with these disillusioned sardonic characters, in *The Tall T* (1957) and *Buchanan Rides Alone* (1958) Scott is an amiable, good-humored loner who is suddenly plunged into a violent situation. The first third of *The Tall T* and most of *Buchanan Rides Alone* are comical in mood with Scott casually drifting his way through life minding his own business. The latter film bears some structural resemblance to Sergio Leone's first Italian Western with Clint Eastwood, *A Fistful of Dollars* (1967), in that Scott is a free-lance gunman who happens to ride into a corrupt town and becomes entangled in its internal rivalries. Scott manages to break up the ruling Agry family by shrewdly manipulating one greedy brother against another. After a lighthearted opening, *The Tall T* becomes a somber variation of the *Stagecoach* theme of passengers revealing their true colors while under siege, in this case by three deadly outlaws in place of John Ford's marauding Apaches.

In each of his films, Boetticher concentrates on a handful of individuals reacting under stress, with Scott and a worthy adversary edging ever closer to a showdown. The most memorable and fully drawn character in a Boetticher film is often the villain who, like Scott, lives by a personal code of honor, albeit one that is morally perverted. Thus Richard Boone in *The Tall T* and Claude Akins in *Comanche Station* are personable if deadly scoundrels who are respectful toward the distressed heroine and share Scott's attitude of "a man's got to do what a man's got to do"—to the point of suicidally engaging Scott in an otherwise avoidable showdown. At the end of *The Tall T* Scott is willing to let the defeated Boone ride off; but, with his self-respect at stake, Boone reels his horse about and charges into Scott's blazing gun. Similarly in *Comanche Station* Akins refuses Scott's plea to surrender even though Scott, standing behind him, is able to get off the first shot. In keeping with the lighter, more cynical carryings-on of *Buchanan Rides Alone*, Scott and the Agry brothers' shrewd gunman (Craig Stevens) merely part company, Scott riding off to leave his worthy opponent in control of Agrytown. It also seems fitting, given the psychotic wrong-headedness of Scott's vengeance in *Decision at Sundown*, that he is denied the privilege of shooting his villainous quarry played by John Carroll. As the two men are about to draw on one another, Carroll's girl friend shoots her lover in the shoulder to spare his life. Typically Boetticher allows his colorful badmen an honorable way out—dead or alive.

Like prizefighters, movie stars seldom retire in the wake of a crowning achievement. Their finest hour is often obscured by a string of lesser performances late in their careers. This was not to be the case for Randolph Scott. The Boetticher films would have sufficed as a triumphant end to a respectable film career, but Scott went one better when he costarred with Joel McCrea in Sam Peckinpah's *Ride the High Country* (1962). MGM declined to market this gem of a Western much beyond the level of a B product, but leading film critics fortunately took notice. *Newsweek* listed it first among its ten best films for the year, and in Europe, where it was titled *Guns in the Afternoon*, *Ride the High Country* became one of MGM's biggest hits.

Much like Scott's last two Westerns (*Ride Lonesome* and *Comanche Station*) for Budd Boetticher, *Ride the High Country* focuses on a handful of individuals on a dangerous journey highlighted by a contest of guile and will between a stalwart man of principle and an engaging adversary. McCrea was cast as the poor but honest ex-marshal who is hired to bring in a gold shipment from a mining camp. Scott played his longtime friend, also a former lawman with little to show for it, who hires on to help escort the gold shipment but who intends to steal it.

The presence of Randolph Scott and Joel McCrea, who between them had starred in eighty-seven Westerns since the early 1930s, made all the more touching this story of friendship strained by opposing notions of how a man should confront an indifferent, uncaring world that no longer wants or needs his services. The glory days of proud individuals bringing law and order to the West have passed. All McCrea wants now is to live the rest of his days in quiet dignity and "to enter my house justified." Scott on the other hand is willing to cheat and steal, fair compensation in his mind for the rewards that an ungrateful society has denied him for past sacrifices. This conflict between moral rectitude and unprincipled expedience is resolved when Scott, his plan to steal the gold foiled by the uncompromising McCrea, charges to the rescue of his old friend who is pinned down under fire by the thieving Hammond brothers. One anticipates a conventional denouement with Scott laying down his life to amend for his trespasses. Instead, it is McCrea who is fatally shot. In a beautiful final exchange of friendship and forgiveness, Scott promises he will do the right thing and return the gold. McCrea replies, "Hell, I know that, I always did. You just forgot it for a while, that's all." "I'll see you later," Scott says as he leaves McCrea to die amidst the autumnal colors of a fading frontier.

The displacement of aging frontier individualists by an encroaching civilization became a recurrent theme in films of the 1960s and early 1970s. There is ample precedent in literature and film that dates back at least to James Fenimore Cooper's first Leatherstocking tale, *The Pioneers*, in 1823. More than a few Western films, including some of Scott's, had contrasted the dignity and honor of the protagonist, however flawed, with the less attractive features of a community. But as America entered the Vietnam era, Peckinpah and other filmmakers elaborated an even more despairing vision of a corrupt, violent, and repressive modern world that made little allowance for individual worth. Randolph Scott's long career in Westerns, that began with Paramount's Zane Grey series in the early 1930s and spanned the major developments and changes in the genre, ended with his finest performance in what was to be Sam Peckinpah's gentlest lament for the passing of the Old West.

Scott told a reporter in 1975, "I'm not a good person to ask about today's movies because I don't go to them."[15] He added that he was content tending to his business investments, which were considerable. According to a recent biographical notice, Scott's "personal wealth, in oil wells, real estate, and securities, is estimated at anywhere between 50 and 100 million dollars."[16] Lee Marvin recalled that on the set of one of the Westerns he made with Scott in the 1950s that the star sat reading the *Wall Street Journal* as his stuntman passed by on a burning stagecoach.[17]

In 1952 Hedda Hopper wrote of her visit to the Scott residence in Beverly Hills: "There was not one item about his place to suggest he'd ever appeared in a western, or that he even knew what a pair of chaps or a spur looked like."[18] Scott has seldom shown much inclination to discuss his films or acting career, except to express gratitude and wonderment at his good fortune. What Hollywood columnists found over the years was a proud homeowner, avid golfer, shrewd investor, faithful Sunday worshiper, and devoted family man with wife Patricia and their two children. He has been married to Marie Patricia Stillman since 1944, his first marriage in 1936 to wealthy heiress Marianna du Pont Somerville having ended in divorce after two years.

His private life may seem far removed from the frontier exploits he performed on screen, but Randolph Scott is remembered as a symbol for rugged individualism and unwavering honesty, qualities that for some Americans were endangered amidst the turbulence and frustrations of Vietnam, Watergate, oil embargoes, and runaway inflation. "Whatever happened to Randolph Scott?" queried the Statler Brothers in their cheerfully nostalgic song of the 1970s. Mel Brooks singled out Randolph Scott in his lampoon of the Western in *Blazing Saddles*: After denying Sheriff Cleavon Little an additional twenty-four hours to clean up the town, the townspeople bow their heads in reverence when Little reminds them, "You would have given Randolph Scott 24 hours." Indeed they would have, just as Americans in this century allowed Randolph Scott nearly three decades in which to reenact his own inimitable brand of movie heroism.

NOTES

1. Robert Warshow, "Movie Chronicle: The Westerner," *Focus on the Western*, ed. Jack Nachbar (Englewood Cliffs, N.J.: Prentice-Hall, 1974), p. 48.

2. David Brion Davis, "Ten-Gallon Hero," *Myth and the American Experience*, ed. Nicholas Cords and Patrick Gerster (Encino, Calif.: Glencoe, 1978), p. 77.

3. Gene Ringgold, "Randolph Scott: Embodied Everyone's Idea of a Southern Gentleman," *Films in Review*, 23 (December, 1972), pp. 605–08.

4. *New York Times*, August 23, 1940, p. 13.

5. *New York Times*, February 7, 1941, p. 23.

6. *Saturday Evening Post*, December 11, 1948, p. 114.

7. *Austin Statesman*, January 30, 1951, p. 11.

8. Richard Gertner ed., *International Motion Picture Almanac* (New York: Quigley, 1985), p. 241.

9. Fred Stanley, "Diplomatic Hollywood," *New York Times*, Oct. 7, 1945, sec. 2, p. 3X.

10. *New York Times*, May 6, 1950, p. 8.

11. Production file, "Colt .45," University of Southern California, Special Collections, Warner Brothers' Collection.

12. English author Graham Greene named Randolph Scott as one of several members of the "Hollywood Committee for Senator McCarthy" in *Variety*, October 10, 1952, University of California, Los Angeles, Special Collections, Harold Leonard Collection, folder "Moving Pictures—Political Aspects."

13. Production file "Man Behind the Gun," University of Southern California, Special Collections, Warner Brothers' Collection.

14. Budd Boetticher, Seminar Transcript, June 1, 1970, p. 52, American Film Institute Center for Advanced Film Studies.

15. *National Enquirer*, March 11, 1975, University of Texas at Austin, Harry Ransom Humanities Research Center, folder "Randolph Scott."

16. Ephraim Katz, *The Film Encyclopedia* (New York: Crowell, 1979), p. 1030.

17. Michael Parkinson and Clyde Jeavons, *A Pictorial History of Westerns* (London: Hamlyn, 1973), p. 112.

18. Hopper, Hedda, "This Young Man Went Western," *Chicago Sunday Tribune*, August 31, 1952, p. 12.

STEPHEN TATUM

# The Classic Westerner: Gary Cooper

U<small>NLIKE</small> R<small>ANDOLPH</small> S<small>COTT</small>, a Western star who only occasionally appeared in other movie genres, Gary Cooper may be regarded best as an actor of great subtlety and depth who only occasionally appeared in Westerns. So fixed is our image of Cooper as the beleaguered yet triumphant Will Kane in *High Noon* (1952) that we forget his Western roles comprise only about one-third of his total screen performances during his thirty-six years in Hollywood. As much as Western fans identify Cooper as the Plainsman or the Westerner, many moviegoers remember him as Longfellow Deeds (*Mr. Deeds Goes to Town*, 1936), John Doe (*Meet John Doe*, 1940), Sergeant Alvin York (*Sergeant York*, 1941), Lou Gehrig (*The Pride of the Yankees*, 1942), and Robert Jordan (*For Whom the Bell Tolls*, 1943). Although he apparently provided the model for Robert Warshow's celebrated definition of the Western hero in his 1954 essay, Cooper was also named by other observers as the American Everyman and the embodiment of the ideal American male.[1]

After recognizing his larger career perspective, this point should be made: The figure that Gary Cooper projected in his twenty or so feature Westerns between 1926 and 1959 is the fullest expression of the Western hero's aesthetic significance—and therefore remains the *greatest* instance of the Westerner in the genre. Unlike other stars, his career spans the birth, growth to maturity, and the death of the classic Western formula. His early role as the Virginian illustrates the essential traits of the classic Westerner, and his last role in *They Came to*

*Cordura* (1959) marks the genre's emerging professional plot.[2] Beginning his career as an extra and a stuntman in silent Westerns based primarily on Zane Grey stories, Cooper starred in such classics as *The Virginian* (1929), *The Westerner* (1940), and *High Noon*, and such Westerns distinguished by his presence as *The Plainsman* (1939), *Garden of Evil* (1954), and *The Hanging Tree* (1959). While he appeared in only four or five Westerns during the middle two decades of his career, during his last decade in Hollywood he appeared in several excellent Westerns. His most famous performance as Marshal Will Kane in *High Noon* gained him his second Oscar. Cooper is also associated with the Western because in 1961, the year he succumbed to cancer, Cooper narrated an NBC television documentary entitled "The Real West."

It cannot be denied that other stars are important to understanding the history and appeal of the genre. John Wayne, Randolph Scott, and Clint Eastwood, to name a few, provide exemplary instances of the Westerner's striking singularity. Wayne's towering presence coupled with his unwavering confidence in the rightness of his actions; Scott's honeyed drawl and firm, open face promising unyielding courage and, when needed, compassion; Eastwood's baleful stare and studied indifference bordering on narcissistic self-aggrandizement—these and other types of heroic stances outline aspects of the composite Western hero. Even so, Cooper's screen presence is the most captivating. It consistently reveals the fullest dimensions of the Westerner's heroic image, ultimately defining a paradoxical combination of opposing traits that engages rapt attention rather than exacting, as Wayne's presence does, full complicity with his already determined righteous sense of purpose. Whether as the handsome, nearly beautiful, innocent or the stooped, anxious adult whose creased face dramatizes a faltering moral code, Cooper's Westerner appears to be both complete and yet capable of more growth, stoic and yet capable of profound emotion, calm and yet intensely preoccupied, skilled and yet vulnerable, a transcendent, magical figure and yet also thoroughly human.

Consider the opening sequence to *The Westerner*. As the credits proceed, Cooper on horseback is silhouetted, riding slowly yet steadily from the right rear of the frame toward, and eventually beyond, the frame's left foreground. The stationary camera is tilted slightly upward, so that we look up at the advancing figure on horseback who begins to dominate the frame's spatial composition. As the credit reads "Gary Cooper as 'The Westerner'" he is centered in the foreground, his compelling figure occupying about half of the frame's vertical space and contrasting with the light-colored, impressively huge cumulus cloud pattern behind him. While on one level this opening shot repeats a conventional Western opening, on another level it self-consciously illustrates the transcendent quality of the Western hero that Cooper embodied. Cooper rides across the screen during the credit sequence to other movies—*Vera Cruz* (1954) is one example—but the elements here endow his mounted figure with mythic grandeur. James Fenimore Cooper's rendering of Natty Bumppo's initial appearance in *The Prairie* is recalled, and the opening to *Shane* (1953) is anticipated. Rather than being juxtaposed to sagebrush or confined by a social group, Cooper appears unmolested, free of constraints, and dependent on no one else, an image that confirms the hero's presumed exceptional ability and special status. Rather than positioning the camera so that we look down on this figure, this sequence requires us to look up at the emergent outlines of a shadowy figure who is defined by his proximity to the heavens and whose origins and destination are open to interpretation. Seemingly free of history and the environment, Cooper's mounted figure in this paradigmatic moment is born before our privileged gaze, rising fully armed and capable out of the Western earth.

Both this image and Cooper's entire performance as Cole Hardin in *The Westerner* illustrate the classic Western hero's features and function. Alone against the sky, here is a figure of heroic privacy. His chivalrous manners, innate dignity, at times confounding naïveté, and intuitive moral sense command respect and curiosity. Further distinguished by his unwearying trust, his honorable intentions, and by his keen awareness that, in time, all actions have *consequence*, Cooper's Hardin is an original within a set of conventional figures. Walter Brennan's Judge Roy Bean rivals Cooper's prominence, but his garrulous behavior reveals his essential superficiality. There are no mysteries hovering around Judge Roy Bean. By contrast, Cooper's Hardin possesses a hidden depth, a reserved strength of will that translates into awesome courage when the inevitable moment comes for him to defend both his virtuous sense of honor and justice and an endangered community that shares his values.

With slight variations, this heroic figure performing this kind of action to accomplish the destruction of the old, wild West and the establishment of a settled society defines the Gary Cooper Westerner at least until *High Noon*, and reveals his kinship to a long line of other Western stars in both programmer and feature movies. After depicting a perilous time when the forces of wilderness and civilization are in balance, the classic narrative pattern that we see in Cooper's Westerns celebrates, as a result of his violent, yet socially responsible, deeds, the triumph of order and justice over anarchy and vengeance and of democratic principles over autocratic ambitions. It also reaffirms the traditional middle-class virtues associated with an idealized pastoral tradition. In this sense, the classic Western reaffirms the culture's dominant ideology, since an audience's preoccupation with current problems, conflicts, and anxieties are basically displaced into the Western story and resolved in a special territory where hard work, native intelligence, physical skills, and inner resourcefulness are rewarded. Such clarity in the Western's orientation to morality, reinforced by the genre's use of open landscapes and of figures who wear exposed weapons, has led Robert Warshow to suggest that the Western is *without mystery*. Since its viewers, unlike its screen characters, are privileged to know the Western's entire universe, the pleasure of solving mysteries is replaced by the simple suspense concerning how and when the sagebrush savior will recognize and then defeat the true evil stalking the land. Warshow might well have added that there is in the classic Western pattern no irony or ambiguity either.

The pleasures to be discovered in the Western's spectacular action sequences, in its stunning use of the landscape, and in its repetitive dramatization of Good defeating Evil are not the most profound ones the genre can offer. There may well be no mystery inherent in the genre, as Warshow says, but what should be considered is how the Western creates *wonder*. The most accomplished Westerns dramatize not only the moment(s) when the forces of civilized progress establish legitimate authority. Such Westerns also provide those pivotal moments when the hero pauses to consider, question, or wonder just why the pattern of action unfolds this way time after time. The point is that during such fleeting moments the Westerner confronts the wondrous questions inherent in the genre's classic pattern: Just *why* is it that Fate elevates the Good? that Evil triumphs only in the short run? that the Good always attracts the allegiance of the Strong? that violence is necessary to ensure the Good's survival? that one must often choose between loyalty to friendship and defense of justice?[3]

Occasioned by some principle of confusion (mistaken identity, misinterpreted intentions, ambiguous language, failed alliances), such heightened moments occur throughout Cooper's Westerns. Consider the moments both prior to and during the hanging of his friend Steve in

*The Virginian*, when Cooper's drawn face and searching eyes convey the agony his character feels at negotiating the gap between the claims of friendship and those of an unwritten but clearly accepted legal code demanding the hanging of rustlers; the worn-down yet resolute Hickok's confrontation with Cody in the Black Hills during *The Plainsman*; Cole Hardin's impromptu, yet inventive, storytelling about Lily Langtry that succeeds in persuading Judge Roy Bean to overturn the saloon jury's verdict and keep him alive long enough to retrieve a lock of hair from Langtry; Cooper's grim deliberateness as he works through the inescapable burden of the past and the question of generational conflict in *The Man of the West* (1958); of his probing questioning after the essence of courage in *They Came to Cordura* and in almost the whole of *High Noon*. Other scenes from his other movies may have lighter or darker touches, but what they all essentially reveal is a circumspect hero at a point when he seemingly becomes aware or he is ruefully reminded that knowledge is born of experience rather than being imposed upon experience, that shadings rather than clarity define life.

What can be observed in the best Cooper Westerns is a man often caught up in, sometimes stopped cold by, the process of thought. He is overseen reacting to the exigencies of the moment, reducing previous prior emphases or adding new elements, playing for time so as to come to terms with situations challenging the already worked out ratios between restraint and readiness, privacy and social involvement, action and contemplation. He enacts these moments with great subtlety. Just as the supposedly transparent Western drama actually contains hidden truths, so too Cooper's marked shyness, hesitancy, or bewilderment barely conceals a hero attempting to suppress his chagrined awareness that the world, at bottom, is not clean. Such consideration does not debilitate Cooper's Westerner. Rather, it reveals the moments when the hero realizes pragmatically the costs of maturity: that once having constituted an identity one can lose that identity; that more than one viewpoint is possible at any given time; that individuals' avowals do not always correspond to their real intentions. Thus leavening the Western's stress on self-sufficient, certain actions, the implicit or explicit assessing of realities by Cooper's hero suggests two truths: that the world is customarily seen as through a glass darkly; and that the deepest anxieties affecting the Western hero surface because he must act not only out of a true sense of self but act out of one's best self. That one's true self is not necessarily one's best self occasions, along with the deep-seated questions the classic Western pattern raises, a mature sense of wonder.

Thus Cooper's Westerner, while no Hamlet, is not merely a stylized, transcendent figure with hidden powers and passions but one also thoroughly human and vulnerable, one whom we consistently oversee in the process of adjusting ideals to experience. He is not just sincere (pure, sound, sure, uncorrupted) but also is deliberate (weighs, ponders, settles). The apparently calm, reserved demeanor he projects is belied by eyes and body language that must entertain the melancholy fact that virtue is not always equated with power, and that time and morality are not always retrievable. Some will prefer those Western stars whose determined action, graceful physicality, and relentless energy triumph over any introspection. But after the projector has stopped and the real world once again dominates time, many memories will center on the Cooper Westerner whose deliberate action is occasioned by an implicit self-evaluation that is entirely real and human and accessible. In Cooper's Westerns freedom is not just something one fights for but what one realizes as one tries out different ratios of quietude, negotiation, action.

Montana-born and, for a short time, educated in England, Frank James Cooper arrived in Los Angeles on Thanksgiving Day in 1923 after leaving Grinnell College in Grinnell, Iowa, where he had spent the better part of the two previous years taking classes with the intention of going into the advertising field. His plan was to visit his parents, who had recently moved there from Montana, and then head East to land a job. Instead, he tried unsuccessfully to work in the Los Angeles area as either an advertising man or as an artist for local newspapers. Failing in these ventures, he worked for a short while as a door-to-door solicitor for a family photographer, and then tried selling real estate. Neither of these jobs interested him or paid him well, but he eventually found work selling advertising space for and drawing advertisements on the curtains of vaudeville houses. Since this form of entertainment was declining in popularity, the work did not last. He was able to save about $400 and planned to use his savings to finance coursework in a Chicago professional art school.[4]

Cooper, who never made it to Chicago, used up his savings because he kept delaying the date of his departure. Even though he was out of work, Cooper was not poverty-stricken and hungry, since he was living with his parents. In December 1924, while wondering what to do with himself and what career to pursue, Cooper, as the story goes, was walking along Vine Street in Hollywood when he met two cowboys whom he knew from his Montana days. These cowboys were working as movie extras and stuntmen. They urged him to join them since another Montanan, Slim Talbot (who would eventually serve for years as Cooper's double), was hiring men at Gower's Gulch in Burbank. Later that day he was hired as a cowboy extra and was paid $5 a day to fall off horses. Through the rest of 1925 and into the early part of 1926 he played a cowboy or an Indian or an outlaw, usually in Tom Mix movies. It is unclear exactly which movie he first worked in, but it probably was *Dick Turpin, The Thundering Herd*, or perhaps *The Vanishing American*, all 1925 releases.

While independent producers were making fairly shoddy programmers on shoestring budgets, the major Hollywood studios were producing several high-class Western series with competent scripts, capable direction, and good production values. Fox's Tom Mix series was paralleled by Universal's Hoot Gibson series. At Paramount a fine series of Zane Grey Westerns was made throughout the 1920s. Except for his work in Fox's *The Lucky Horseshoe* (1925), a Tom Mix vehicle, Frank Cooper's work as an extra prior to his breakthrough in *The Winning of Barbara Worth* (1926) was mainly in this Zane Grey series. In 1925, Cooper worked in three of these films: *The Thundering Herd, Wild Horse Mesa*, and *The Vanishing American*.

By 1926 Cooper was earning $10 a day and somehow surviving the stunt work required by the movie studios. Having learned that Tom Mix was earning around $1,700 a week for what Cooper thought was minimal acting duty, he worked to improve his lot in the movie business. He learned how to apply makeup to take advantage of the kinds of light and film being used in those days; he posed for still photos—some in western garb, others in the Valentino style. He used some of his earnings to make a short audition film to show or send to producers. During his work as a villain in actress Marilyn Mills's two-reeler feature *Tricks*, Cooper acted on her suggestion and talked to Nan Collins, a studio casting director (and later Cooper's first agent). Collins recommended Cooper change his first name so as to distinguish himself from other Frank Coopers of the day (one of whom was accused of murdering his wife). She suggested he adopt the name "Gary," as she was from Gary, Indiana. On her further recommendation, *Gary* Cooper made new still photos without the Valentino look, and routinely began to make the studio rounds with his list of screen credits, his photos, and his audition film.

Having heard that director Henry King and producer Samuel Goldwyn were looking for riders to appear in their film of Harold Bell Wright's popular novel *The Winning of Barbara Worth*, Collins recommended Cooper go to Goldwyn's office with his credentials. What happened next can be described as Cooper's first break in the business, yet different versions of his discovery exist. Goldwyn himself claimed to have discovered Cooper waiting in his outer office, while Henry King thought he first saw Cooper in the office and immediately asked to see the audition film. After seeing the short sequence of Cooper riding toward the camera, dismounting, taking off his hat and, in a medium shot, saying "Hello," King immediately offered Cooper a job at $65 a week. However, Frances Marion, screenwriter for the movie, claims that Cooper was dating Goldwyn's secretary and on that day was visiting her at work. Seeing him outside the office window, Marion claims that her immediate recommendation to Goldwyn and King got them to view his short audition. Still, according to her, they did not like the film. Marion then suggested that all the studio secretaries view the screen tests, and when Cooper's presence elicited the most positive response from the women, he was hired.

That is, he was hired to ride well and look like a "natural" Western character, which was not too difficult, given his Montana ranch background. When the actor designated to play the part of Abe Lee was delayed because of work on another film, King expedited the filming by using Cooper as a stand-in for shots in which his face would not show. When the company had to move to Nevada for the outdoor location sequences and the actor had still not appeared, King elevated Cooper to the role of Abe Lee. His role was that of a native western mining engineer who aids the eastern engineer, Ronald Coleman, in building a dam so as to impound water for irrigation. Cooper and Coleman both vie for the affections of Vilma Banky's Barbara Worth, but the movie's primary drama centers on the dam's safety. In Cooper's major scene, he drags himself up a series of hotel stairs, this after riding for an entire day through the desert, knocks on Coleman's door and then collapses in exhaustion at the feet of his rival, warning Coleman of the dam's faulty construction. The catastrophe is averted, but Cooper's character dies.

During the filming of *Barbara Worth*, Samuel Goldwyn tried to sign Cooper to a long-term contract, but he demurred, acting on the advice of Nan Collins and the cast members who urged him to wait until the reviews of the movie came out and, hopefully, increased his worth. Still, he could not pass up Paramount's offer of $125 a week, and he went to work with director John Waters on two Westerns, *Arizona Bound* and *Nevada* (both 1927 releases). Shot on location in Bryce Canyon, Utah, *Arizona Bound* was Cooper's first starring role. Although he had some trouble with his acting during the romantic scenes with his co-star Thelma Todd, Cooper performed admirably enough, and director Waters constructed his part with few long-take scenes so as to lessen any sense of awkwardness or stage fright.[5] Cooper plays a cowboy who appears in a typical frontier town just as a gold shipment is leaving by stagecoach. His character is eventually accused of robbing the coach's shipment, and he narrowly avoids being lynched. But in the end he gets the gold, establishes his innocence, and wins the girl. In *Nevada*, another Zane Grey story, Cooper plays a cowboy who wants to reform his reputation as a troublemaker. He helps a friend break out of jail and then seeks a new life in a new setting where he meets a young woman whose cattle are being rustled. In the process of protecting her and her brother, Cooper unmasks the leader of the rustlers, who turns out to be a prominent rancher (played by William Powell). And he gets the girl.

While these movies were being filmed the reviews for the box-office hit *Barbara Worth* began appearing. More than one critic commented favorably on Cooper's performance, one even mentioning that Coleman nearly had his scenes stolen from him by the neophyte Cooper. Capitalizing on Cooper's obvious screen appeal, Paramount moved him quickly from movie to movie throughout 1927 and 1928. Although modestly praised for his acting in another 1927 Western, *The Last Outlaw*, Cooper began appearing as an aviator, a foreign legionnaire, a farmer, and a society man in movies that starred such notables as Clara Bow, Fay Wray, and Colleen Moore. His affair with Clara Bow and his walk-on role in her major film *It* (1927) gained him notoriety as the "It" boy, and led to his brief appearance in the highly successful *Wings* (1927). Cooper's one-minute performance as a cadet pilot who dies during training generated a tremendous amount of fan mail and proved to be a shrewd follow-up to his performance in *Barbara Worth*.

That the Western was going through some hard times can be seen by the nearly two-year delay between Cooper's 1927 Westerns and the appearance in 1929 of *Wolf Song*. His offscreen relationship with Lupe Velez, his *Wolf Song* co-star, generated intensive publicity and helped ensure that movie's commercial success. It was a part-talkie Western, for the couple had brief dialogue scenes prior to Velez's singing of two songs. The sound alone probably guaranteed the movie's success, but a film story centered on the passionate, stormy love between an Anglo mountain man and a Mexican beauty no doubt attracted audiences wanting to escape from a monotonous round of darkening economic news. Cooper was soon signed to star in Paramount's talking version of Owen Wister's *The Virginian*, and the studio's publicity agents began a campaign comparing him to one of the screen's great Westerners, William S. Hart. As part of this publicity drive, Cooper sat for Norman Rockwell, whose portrait of the actor appeared in the *Saturday Evening Post* for May 24, 1930.

By 1929, on the eve of the Depression, Gary Cooper was a star of the silent screen, known as much for his flyboy roles as for his cowboy roles. By the end of 1929, when the Depression had settled in, Cooper not only had become an even bigger star but also, as evidenced by his work in *The Virginian*, had become an actor. Although Cooper never gained extreme self-confidence in his acting ability, due to his occasional stage fright during romantic scenes or crowd scenes, his performance here contains several long-take scenes in which his distinctive excellence in reacting to the scene and the other actors emerges. His often evasive yet penetrating glances, his casual lean in the saddle, his slight eyebrow movement or pursing of the lips, his calculated shift in weight, his at times halting vocal delivery suddenly exuding firm confidence— these and other aspects of Cooper's subtle performance command the camera's attention and solidify his special status.

This third film version of Wister's novel centers on two conflicts: that between West and East, objectified in the romantic plot between Cooper's Virginian and Mary Brian's Molly Wood; and that between the New West and the Old West, represented by the conflict between the Virginian and Walter Huston's Trampas. As the movie begins, the Virginian enters town driving a herd of cattle to market, already established as the foreman of his outfit. His rising status is confirmed in the next few scenes which contrast his superior talents and practical intelligence to his friend Steve's failed ambition and his enemy Trampas's boorish behavior. Still, the Virginian is not yet completely accepted by the community. His humorous pranks, his lack of education, and his workingman status show he still has some growth to accomplish before being worthy of his new love interest, Molly Wood. At this time there is a crisis in authority, for rustlers are harassing the ranchers. Eventually, the Virginian leads a posse which captures and then hangs his friend Steve, who had been swayed into the rustling venture by Trampas. The Virginian's dilemma is quite involved, since duty, loyalty, honor, and love are at stake. If he remains loyal to Steve and helps him escape, he betrays his own sense of moral rightness associated with socially responsible action; if he sacrifices Steve, his moral code is stained by the necessity of extralegal action. As a consequence of his actions, he very nearly loses Molly's love. But she senses his innate civility and intrinsic worth as she nurses him back to health after he is wounded by Trampas. Over her objections, the Virginian in the end stalks Trampas in the town streets and kills him, thus satisfying his vengeance and ushering in the New West. As was the case in his previous Paramount Westerns, the fitting reward for the heroic individual who has ferreted out the baddies posing as respectable citizens is marriage to the most desirable woman in the territory.

Unlike Cooper's later movie *Vera Cruz*, the dramatic force of the hero's commitment to society's cause is not communicated, since as early as the movie's opening the Virginian's foreman status and his love for Molly clearly indicate his acceptance of society's standards for success. Even so, *The Virginian* remains a distinguished classic Western, highlighted by its fine tone and texture, deliberate pacing of scenes, and its cinematography. The movie is not by any means a tragedy, but its tone suggests anything but a mindless celebration of the nation's epic achievement in settling the frontier. There is a harder, at times elegaic, appraisal of the costs necessary to preserve society and ensure historical progress. Hardened by the confrontations with Steve and Trampas, his boyishness cracking apart as the movie proceeds— his hat pulled down farther, his gaze less evasive, his bearing firmer— Cooper's Virginian experiences a Western version of the fall from innocence as he ponders the necessity of breaking the law in order to preserve the law.

In general, Cooper's 1920s' Westerns dramatize moments in which individuals standing for social division, violent actions, primitive behavior, and selfish materialism lose the future to those working to establish a coherent, peaceful, civilized, and cooperative society based on the principles of freedom, equality, love, and friendship. In a time when traditional heroes were debunked and traditional rural Protestant American values were deemed outdated, Cooper's Westerner demonstrated that an independent, self-sufficient hero could act freely and in support of what should properly be seen as the middle-class American fantasy of a classless, church-centered, participatory democracy. Seen in this light, the Western performed a vital service for those audiences nostalgic for a frontier past which privileged the individual hero and his redemptive heroic moment, and which balanced the claims of the autonomous self and the society which requires, and receives, his loyalty. In a postwar era beset by the record of Prohibition's failure, by extensive judicial and legislative corruption, and by the rise of the gangster to prominence, such narratives reaffirmed that some portion of the nation's historical and cultural past could survive and shape the present world.[6] As Will Wright has persuasively argued in his *Sixguns and Society,* such narratives move audiences because the Western's central tension is internalized by individual viewers caught between the ideals of a market capitalism that celebrate the autonomous, self-sufficient individual and the ideals of institutions that celebrate cooperation, self-sacrifice, social responsibility.[7]

*The Virginian* was a fine commercial and critical success, and helped prove, along with the parallel hit *In Old Arizona,* that the talking Western could be made—and could attract audiences. During the filming of *The Virginian,* Cooper predicted to reporters that the Western would have a great future. "The talkies," Cooper believed, "will give the Westerns new life; that is, if they're good and there aren't too many of them."[8] Between 1929 and 1932, at a time when the Hollywood musical and the gangster sagas were enjoying great popular success, the Western did enjoy a modest, though short-lived, revival. *Billy the Kid* (1930) and *The Big Trail* (1930), while not box-office successes, inaugurated a brief cycle of sound Westerns in the epic mode, the best of them being the Oscar-award winner *Cimarron* (1931).

Cooper himself starred in three undistinguished Westerns within two years of his performance as the Virginian. He played a good-badman in *The Texan* (1930), an Alaskan miner in the third film version of Rex Beach's *The Spoilers* (1930), and a wagon train guide in Zane Grey's *Fighting Caravans* (1931). After his work in *Fighting Caravans,* Cooper did not star in a Western until *The Plainsman* (1936). In this five-year absence from the genre he had taken on more highly demanding roles, including that of The Kid in director Rouben Mamoulian's acclaimed ganster movie *City Heat* (1931) and that of Frederick Henry in *A Farewell to Arms* (1932). After enduring a brief box-office slump, Cooper recovered his popularity with his role in the hit action movie *The Lives of a Bengal Lancer* (1935) and in director Frank Capra's wonderful *Mr. Deeds Goes to Town* (1936).

The *Plainsman* was the first box-office hit Western since the 1931 *Cimarron*. Derived from both Courtney Cooper and Grover Jones's *The Prince of Pistoleers* and tales about Wild Bill Hickok written by Frank Wistach, *The Plainsman*, like its contemporary B-Western counterparts, stressed the virtues of cooperative action and self-sacrifice in the face of danger, and it provided Anglo audiences living in an uncertain present an epic image of historical progress as the frontier is made safe for settlement. As directed by Cecil B. De Mille, the film opens with Abe Lincoln stressing to his advisors that the West must be made safe so that the soon-to-be unemployed Civil War soldiers will have a place to begin their lives anew. However, Lincoln is on his way to Ford's Theatre. As news of his assassination that evening reaches his associates in Washington, the movie switches to the unscrupulous munitions manufacturers who intend to sell rifles illegally to the Plains Indians in order to maintain high profit margins after the Civil War ends. Then the movie cuts to a medium shot of Cooper as Bill Hickok, a discharged Union soldier lounging on a cotton bale waiting for the steamboat to leave St. Louis for the western settlements. He meets a recently married Buffalo Bill Cody (played by James Ellison), on his way west with his new wife to start a hotel. The rest of the film focuses on the pair's efforts to defuse Indian threats and catch the white ringleader of the munitions ring, and on Hickok's love-hate relationship with Calamity Jane (Jean Arthur). De Mille follows history in that the movie ends with Hickok's death at the hand of Jack McCall, but the movie's final image is of Cooper alone on horseback, amidst an expansive vista, riding toward the camera, dead in history but alive in our minds as the legendary gunfighter whose exploits furthered Manifest Destiny.

De Mille, like directors before and after him who worked with Cooper, worried at first that Cooper's characterization was so wooden that the film would never succeed. However, when the director saw the rushes in the evening it was clear that Cooper was playing masterfully to the camera which, unlike the eyes on the sound stage, caught every subtle, purposeful movement of eye, mouth, hand, hips. He fully develops the type of brooding, sardonic, lonely figure that glimmered occasionally in *The Virginian* and *A Farewell to Arms*. Late in the film, when he reaches the Black Hills—on the trail of the villain (Charles

Bickford); being pursued by Cody since he's been charged (falsely) with killing a U.S. soldier—Cooper's Hickok is a somber and determined, yet coolly objective, figure seemingly aware of his doomed fate. In a world of false intentions, deceiving appearances, and selfish passivity, Hickok trusts no one, his eyes questioning everyone's movements and suggesting to us what he has known since his idle chat with a young boy on the St. Louis wharf: that he alone possesses the skills and the necessary freedom from attachments to fulfill his role as protector; and, just as disheartening, that such skills and such complete independence will not thrive in the society his actions help found or preserve. Whereas the Virginian's efforts on behalf of society were framed by his individual vengeance quest to kill Trampas, thus making the picture more of a romantic initiation film, Cooper's Hickok marshals his skills and painfully represses his love for Calamity Jane in order to promote the common welfare. Such stoic, selfless actions, however, do not make him a sacrificial victim: His Hickok resolutely plays out his string with little complaint or self-conscious pity. As he says firmly as the film draws to a close, "What room is there gonna be for a two-gun plainsman?"

The Plainsman remains a discordant yet optimistic manifesto exalting the historical progress of the common white American and denigrating those big business exploiters of laws and finances.[9] In De Mille's supposed epic, civilization's true enemies are the crooked shysters who defraud innocent farmers, pliable townspeople, and—occasionally—unwary Indians, rather than solitary outlaw figures like Billy the Kid. Significantly, it is not so much that the symbols of the state are evil as that evil men are in control of the state and threaten society's very existence. The Plainsman thus discloses the conservative impulse at the core of the classic Western, for Cooper's status as a skilled enforcer unrestrained by an inefficient or corrupt judicial system defines him as a transcendent figure whose virtues are aligned with the dominant social and institutional ideology. In effect, Cooper defeats such evil men on the basis of his individual prowess, rather than uniting with others to reform an economic system that perennially produces such evil exploiters. Rather than emerging finally as an anarchic or autocratic figure who will enjoy the power his skills bring him, this figure dies (or, in other films of the era, returns to the farm, becomes one of the boys, marries, or wears the black mask in order to flush out the real baddies). Just why this reassuring alignment occurs time after time, just why such figures must exist alone on the outskirts of the settlements, and just how long such capable figures will continue to be produced are questions eventually foregrounded in the √Westerns of the 1950s. But here in *The Plainsman*, due to Cooper's magnificent portrayal, we glimpse the future direction of the genre and also, due to the loss of such valiant individualism, realize the deep-seated concern audiences in this era must have felt about the course of historical decisions that lead from Deadwood to the Depression, from the farm or ranch to the idle factory. Although framed by the inexorable advance of civilization into the wilderness and sentimentalized by the closing image, Cooper's moving performance almost transforms the movie into a distinguished Western version of Greek tragedy.

By the end of 1936, with his superlative performances in *Mr. Deeds Goes to Town* and *The Plainsman* behind him, Cooper became one of the top ten money-making stars in Hollywood. Before the Depression decade was over he would be recognized as the highest-paid entertainer in America, and the U.S. Treasury Department would name him the country's largest individual taxpayer—a somewhat dubious distinction for the man who was to play John Doe. Between *The Plainsman* and America's entry into World War II Cooper starred in only one true Western, *The Westerner* (1940), one rodeo-chic Florida Western, *The Cowboy and the Lady* (1938), and a mountie Western, *North West Mounted Police* (1940), that is about as interesting as a Victor Mature muscle epic. In early 1939, apparently acting upon his wife's advice, he turned down the role of the Ringo Kid in *Stagecoach*, thus helping (although he was unaware of this at the time) John Wayne elude a permanent B-Western status as actor.

*The Westerner*, directed by William Wyler, remains a movie distinguished by the deft characterizations supplied by Walter Brennan as the garrulous, autocratic Judge Roy Bean and by Cooper as the droll saddle tramp Cole Hardin. The movie was not the box-office success of *The Plainsman* or of Cooper's later *Along Came Jones* (1945), but Brennan did win his third Oscar for Best Supporting Actor. For his part, Cooper beautifully develops his character from that of an irresponsible, sardonic, drifting cowboy to that of a humorous yet responsibly committed cowboy who helps the homesteaders overthrow the reign of Bean's capricious and cruel sense of justice. Falsely accused of horse stealing, Hardin avoids being hanged by his peers in Bean's Vinegarroon saloon-courtroom when he realizes the depth of Bean's love for Lily Langtry. He invents a story about having once got a lock of Lily's hair, which moves Bean to overturn the jury's verdict of guilty.

After tying on a drunk with the Judge, Hardin leaves for California the next morning, but is forced to fight off Bean's demands that Hardin give him the lock of hair. As he continues on his way, Hardin meets a group of homesteaders who've seen their fences cut and their numbers thinned by Bean's cattle cohorts. Hardin joins up with the "nesters," in large part because of a growing affection for a daughter of one of the farmers. He later tries to negotiate a truce between Bean and the farmers. After making some hollow promises to clean up the rangeland and leave the farmers alone, Bean receives the lock of hair, which Hardin had harvested from his love's head. Bean's men soon begin burning the farmers' crops and homes, in the process killing Hardin's prospective father-in-law. Hardin tracks Bean down to the Fort Davis concert hall where the Judge, having bought every ticket, sits alone, waiting for Lily Langtry to appear in concert. When the curtain rises, Hardin appears instead, and after a shootout in the darkened auditorium, kills Bean, who stays alive long enough to kiss Langtry's hand before he dies.

Cooper's character reenacts here the same dilemma faced by the Virginian eleven years earlier. Conflicting with what Hardin senses is right and just, the bonds of friendship are severed by a violent act that ushers in the new West. Like Steve in *The Virginian*, the Judge represents an outmoded vision of the West, one doomed by the influx of settlers and culture into the once open rangelands—and one finalized by the closing scene in which the dying Bean, archaically dressed in a Confederate Army uniform, pays homage to the feminine bearer of the new cultural order. Like the Virginian, Hardin stands as a man-in-the-middle, attracted to the values each side of the conflict represents, torn between his developing affection for the magnificently childish Bean and his need to defend his honorable code. Neither so totally pure as to refrain from a violent defense of his moral code nor so totally depraved as to relish wielding his power, the Cooper Westerner defines the traditional status of the Western hero whose moment of violent action resolves in fantasy the apparently insoluble conflict between self and society.

*The Westerner* is yet a more satisfying movie than *The Virginian*. It demonstrates superior pacing (slow, but fraught with tension) of scenes, a dramatically compressed statement of the thematic conflict (since both Trampas and Steve's qualities are combined in one major character), and compelling black-and-white cinematography. The movie also works better simply because Cooper has by now reached a beautifully appropriate age. Hardened by experience and yet young enough to hope for a progressive future, his face and figure define perfectly that sought-after moment of poised maturity when one exudes neither boyish exuberance and childish digressions nor an older man's tired cynicism.

After appearing in De Mille's tedious *North West Mounted Police* (1940) as a Texas Ranger who travels to Canada in search of an outlaw and while there becomes embroiled in the Mounties' efforts to crush Louis Riel's second revolt, Cooper's next Western was not until *Along Came Jones* was released in 1945. By this time he had won his first Oscar, for *Sergeant York* (1941), and had been nominated twice for his work in *The Pride of the Yankees* (1942) and *For Whom the Bell Tolls* (1943). A box-office success, *Along Came Jones* is of interest because it represents Cooper's first attempt at producing a movie, and because it succeeds in parodying the Cooper Western persona which had been established since the late 1920s. As played by Cooper, Melody Jones is a common, ordinary, useless broncstomper who can't handle a gun or the strong woman named Cherry (Loretta Young) who manipulates him, at first, in order to save her love, the notorious gunslinger Monte Jarrad (Dan Duryea). Because of Jones's and Jarrad's similar physiques, identical initials, and shared romantic interest in Young's character, the movie develops as a Western screwball comedy dependent upon an outlandish series of coincidences, mistaken identities, and humorous misinterpretations. In the end, Jones gets the girl and feels "high-regarded," for at the moment when Jarrad is fixing to kill Jones, Cherry kills Jarrad, not Jones (who is also in her line of fire), with a shot between the eyes.

Few observers now would call this a major film for Cooper. Even so, considering the parts Cooper played between 1935 and 1945, one finds it easier to understand why the movie was a popular success. Melody Jones's ineptness gains humorous force because his fumbling efforts play off audience expectations against their knowledge of previous Cooper roles. He is a Western version of Longfellow Deeds, and the movie's fine sense of play and use of surprise, evident in both the script and the performances, creates the light-hearted tone that was no doubt appealing to audiences during this last year of the war. In this movie the woman is always called upon to save the man, thus inverting the classical Western's sense of gender roles. However much it inverts the Cooper hero, though, the movie recapitulates the classical Western pattern of action as the unknown stranger rides into town, gains special status, fights the villains, and saves both himself and society. The movie prepares us for Cooper's comic performance as Tex in *It's A Big Country* (1951) and recalls the comic Western tradition established by such films as Buster Keaton's *Go West* (1925), by *Destry Rides Again* (1939), and by Abbott and Costello's *Ride 'Em Cowboy* (1942). Moreover, this film, as much as any other Cooper effort, reminds one of the classic Western's foundation in the romance archetype. In the medieval romance narratives the hero, rather than appearing simply as a towering figure of strength, is also typically naïve and proud—and humbled by the fact that he is always having to be helped out by magical figures (both animal and human) and savvy, concerned females.

Between 1930 and 1950, Cooper appeared in approximately 46 films, only seven of them calling on him to play a recognizable Western figure. Between 1950 and 1960, however, he appeared in some twenty films, including eight starring roles as a Westerner and two brief cameo appearances in other features as a cowboy. He was awarded another Best Actor Oscar for his role as Will Kane in *High Noon* (1952), and he also worked in several of the decade's most underrated Westerns: *Garden of Evil* (1954), *The Hanging Tree* (1959), and *They Came to Cordura* (1959).

*Dallas* (1950), his first Western since *Along Came Jones*, was one of the decade's many Westerns set in or immediately after the Civil War, thus effectively foregrounding the recognizably relevant concerns over ways to heal war wounds and deal with returning veterans. In this movie Cooper plays an ex-Confederate officer bent on killing the three brothers who during the war killed his family and robbed his land. Although the vengeance plot is but a slight twist on the classic Western's pattern, *Dallas* reveals several of the elements stressed in the 1950s' Westerns: Much of it is shot in interiors or at night; there is more violence throughout the movie; thematically, harmony and unity result from the alliance forged by the Union and Confederate war veterans; and the motif of the false identity to gain superior ends appears, a strategy that dominates Cooper's later *Springfield Rifle* (1954) and reveals the movie's Cold War context.

While *Dallas* was being filmed, Cooper was preoccupied with both marital and health problems. By the time he began filming *High Noon* he had recently undergone a hernia operation and was still troubled by an ulcer, back problems, and a hip ailment. These physical problems, plus the fact that the movie's director Fred Zinneman requested little

facial makeup to disguise Cooper's haggard appearance, visually enhanced the dramatic situation facing Cooper's character in *High Noon*.
Will Kane, fighting both the clock and the villains, strives to defend his
concept of honor and courage, nervously pacing the increasingly
deserted town streets in search of allies, discovering instead that he
alone must finish the job that the Northern politicians and complacent,
cowardly townspeople refuse to recognize.

*High Noon*, of course, is one of the most acclaimed Westerns. It won
four Academy Awards and was nominated for two more, it was a smash
box-office hit, and—as all genre classics do—it spawned imitations.
Charlton Heston, not Cooper, was producer Stanley Kramer's first
choice for the part of Will Kane, but the movie's major financial backer
wanted Cooper, who responded with a superlative performance comprised of images that stand now as icons of the so-called "adult" Western. Carl Foreman, the movie's screenwriter, was blacklisted soon

Gary Cooper in *High Noon* (1952). *Stephen Tatum*

after the film's release as a result of his testimony in 1951 before the House Un-American Activities Committee investigating Communist infiltration in Hollywood. Foreman himself later claimed he wrote the script about nothing else but the contemporary Hollywood scene. He and others found the Hollywood community divided, complacent, and indifferent to the plight of those who refused to accede, on constitutional grounds, to the Committee's requests for information.

Such evidence of intentionality, as well as the topical nature of the movie's depiction of the townspeople, has resulted in several critical readings of the movie as a Cold War parable about McCarthyism and Korea, about the relationship between dissent and conformity, and about the proper response to a violent threat that erupts during peacetime. The movie's popularity perhaps can be traced to the fact that the movie can be read as conveying either pro- or anti-McCarthy ideology, depending upon how one codes Cooper's embattled character. What should also be recognized, though, is the movie's emphatic attack on the community. *High Noon* attacks those in Hadleyville concerned for their own skins or for the negative impact on future investments should the gunfight take place, and it attacks the Northern bureaucratic judicial and penal system which has freed Frank Miller. Here the hero and ultimately his wife, who helps him during the climactic gunfight, no longer commit themselves to society because they discover that their personal and social values (love, honor, courage, conviction, sincerity) exist outside the social group. At the end, rather than urging the hero's entry into society so as to reaffirm its progressive direction, as was the case in *The Virginian* and *The Westerner, High Noon* argues that strong individuals must refuse any negotiations with a society whose authority, whether originating from a distant federal bureaucracy or from a nearby popular consensus, is illegitimate.[10]

After completing *High Noon*, Cooper recovered from some of his physical problems by going on hunting and fishing trips in Idaho. He then starred in another Western, *Springfield Rifle* (1952), which pales by comparison to his other Westerns in this decade. In this movie Cooper plays a Union officer charged with finding out why horses intended for the Union cavalry are being stolen and sold to the Confederacy. Cooper's character must pose as an undercover agent to infiltrate the suspected gang of horse thieves, which causes problems for his wife and son who know nothing of his activities and assume that his dishonorable discharge was warranted. Cooper discovers the real villain is the chief Union officer in the area, and after some skirmishing and gunfire, the traitors are flushed out and the horse ring is stopped, and Cooper's character is restored to his rank and his family's good graces. *Springfield Rifle*, an unremarkable, often tedious movie, is also a conventional patriotic movie illustrating some of the chief 1950s' concerns: counterintelligence, subversive activities, superior armaments (it is one of several Westerns named after weaponry), and stresses on family unity.

In 1953 Cooper traveled to Europe to speak against Communism on behalf of the Screen Actors Guild. While in Paris he underwent another hernia operation, yet he felt well enough upon his return home to journey to Mexico where his next three films, two of them Westerns, were filmed. In *Garden of Evil* (1954), Cooper plays a cynical, laconic adventurer who signs on, for monetary reasons, with three others to help Susan Hayward rescue her husband, trapped in a gold mine in a sacred area called "The Garden of Evil." Harassed by bandits and Indians and by the greed and rivalries within the group, they eventually rescue the husband. But, on the return trip the group is killed one by one, with only Cooper and Hayward surviving—because Richard Widmark's character sacrifices himself by staying behind to hold off their attackers. While the movie does not demonstrate the more enlightened attitude toward racial minorities that other Westerns were beginning to reveal, *Garden of Evil* successfully integrates action with introspection, is suspenseful, boasts fine performances, and effectively uses the naturalistic Mexican setting to heighten the characters' probing of their motivations.

Cooper's other 1954 Western, *Vera Cruz*, continues this trend, pairing Cooper's Benjamin Trane, who appears initially riding alone toward Mexico in 1866, with Burt Lancaster's Joe Erin and his cohorts. Having lost everything in the Civil War, Trane hopes to regain his fortune during the Mexican Revolution. After nearly killing each other in the opening scenes, Trane and Erin join forces and hire on for the Emperor Maximilian, promising to escort an aristocratic lady from Mexico City to Vera Cruz. Along the way they learn they are also guarding a shipment of gold; the movie details their various attempts to defraud each other in order to possess the gold and reveals Trane's growing sympathy for the Juaristas' cause. Trane and Erin in the end join up with the rebels and help them storm the fort at Vera Cruz and rout the soldiers. In the confusion of battle Erin tries to steal away with the gold but is killed, reluctantly, by Trane, who believes the gold should go to the rebels.

In a sense, the Lancaster-Cooper character opposition extends the earlier opposition of Brennan-Cooper; thus, *Vera Cruz* retells *The Westerner* in an action-oriented, overly complicated way. However, a shift in the coding of the characters should be recognized. Here it is the older man whose initial selfishness evolves into support for the right cause, while the younger man dies with his selfish materialism intact. Since the Western is always about the relationship between generations, with the classical Western ultimately positing the continuity of history, *Vera Cruz* disrupts this pattern. It rather suggests a disjuncture between the old and the new as the father figure is forced to kill his surrogate son who refuses to be transformed by an appeal to higher ethical values. On this thematic level, the movie is one of the first to question the kind of ending we see in *Shane*, and Lancaster's histrionic acting and toothy grin serve as perfect emblems for a youthful subculture interested in matters of form and the pleasures of immediate gratification rather than the supposed wisdom of his socially conscious mentor.

In his last three Western starring roles, Cooper played Link Jones

Gary Cooper in *Man of the West* (1958). *Stephen Tatum*

in director Anthony Mann's *Man of the West* (1958), Doc Joe Frail in director Delmar Daves's (with Karl Malden) *The Hanging Tree* (1959), and Major Thomas Thorn in director Robert Rossen's *They Came to Cordura* (1959). Although not the most challenging movie, *The Hanging Tree* is the most aesthetically pleasing of the three, a superbly understated, engrossing film whose simple story leaves much room for the actors to explore the nuances of love, friendship, and loyalty. Suffering from a past personal tragedy, Doc Frail enters a Montana mining camp bent on wasting away his last years, but soon saves an accused thief from a lynch mob and then aids a young Swiss woman suffering from shock and blindness as a result of exposure following a stage holdup. He gives her money to get a mine started, and when it yields gold one of her partners makes advances to her. Doc, however, arrives in time and kills the man. He is then taken by a lynch mob who are about to hang him when the Swiss woman offers her mine in exchange for his life. They accept her offer, and the two are reunited.

Besides being entangled in the group situations that appear in *Garden of Evil* and *Vera Cruz*, Cooper's characters in his last few Westerns are also haunted by the burden of the past. The plot complications in both *The Man of the West* and *They Came to Cordura* share this trait. In the former film, Cooper's Link Jones appears in an unnamed town one day to catch a train. Nervous, evasive, and awkward, Link Jones has been sent by his townspeople to recruit a schoolteacher. The train is later held up by bandits, and Jones and two others, a singer and her manager, are stranded on the tracks as the sun goes down. They walk to a darkened cabin that Jones remembers is nearby, and are surprised there by Doc Tobin's gang, who have just robbed the train. In the lengthy scene that follows, we learn that Jones is a reformed bandit, but that he used to be a member of the gang—and capable of cruel violence. To save his two companions, Jones pretends to have come back to the gang, thus rejoining his uncle Doc (Lee J. Cobb) who is saddled with a fine bunch of slimy saddlemates. No one knows whether to believe his story, thus creating the high-pitched, nearly hysterical tension throughout the movie, but the mad Tobin wants to make one last grand robbery in the mining town of Lassoo. As the movie proceeds, Link kills each of his kinsmen in or around the now-deserted ghost town of Lassoo, and finally kills Tobin himself, the human counterpart of the ghost town he wanted to rob. *The Man of the West* is an eccentric, compelling film that runs great risks in pursuing its grand themes, occasionally achieving a quirky grandeur because of its visual brilliance and its engrossing use of Lee J. Cobb's and Cooper's opposing styles.

In *They Came to Cordura*, Cooper plays an Army major in Mexico in 1915 who, as punishment for a past act of cowardice, is given the assignment of "Awards Officer" during the American campaign against Villa. He selects five men whom he had seen perform heroic acts during an American victory as candidates for the Congressional Medal of Honor. Since the War Department wants "heroes" to help their recruiting effort on the eve of World War I, Cooper is charged with writing their commendations and bringing the five men, and the woman (Rita Hayworth) they have captured for aiding the rebels, through enemy country to Cordura, from which location they will then be sent on an American public relations tour. As both the journey's events and Cooper's probing of each soldier's motivations for performing courageous actions proceed, each character's true self emerges. The five soldiers reveal their baseness, while the "cowardly" major demonstrates and discovers the true nature of courage during his unrelenting effort to carry out his mission. The effort brings the others, finally, over to his side, for a once-meaningless concept has now been personified before their eyes, serving to redeem the entire flawed, human group.

In the Westerns of his last decade, the classic Western formula becomes subject to intensive revision as a different postwar cultural context places an immense strain on its basic conventions. The Westerns' previous emphases on a usable past, on national achievement, on the traditional virtues associated with heroic morality, and on group cooperation give way to other topical Cold War themes associated with the problems of returning war veterans, of racial conflicts, of disaffiliated youth, of defense technology, and of subversive activity. A major focus on the triumph of civilization over savagery changes to that of the individual striving to retain his/her integrity in the midst of a materialistic, conformist, and complacent society, or warding off the base claims of a small group that lacks a coherent purpose.

In movie after movie in this decade Western heroes walk or crawl as much as they ride, and they are often entangled in a web of events, usually the consequence of a past action, that puts a lie to the prospect of living an autonomous existence. Often photographed in the interiors of houses or framed by the town's architecture, the hero's uncertain existence is magnified by the typical casting of an aging actor whose face is cracked and posture stooped—or of an orphaned, beautiful youth wracked with the pain of growing up. Whereas the western landscape once tested the hero's deepest resources, thus engaging the viewer who watched the birth or rediscovery of a true identity, the western landscape portrayed in the 1950s forces the once self-confident hero to reassess his identity and his moral code, as well as his commitment to a society which is already established, not in the process of being founded.

There are exceptions to the above generalizations, the most important one being *Shane* (1953). Yet these remarks aptly illustrate the prevailing conventions of Cooper's last Westerns. These last Westerns dramatize a crisis of authority in a world where ethical and moral values lack consensus. Such indeterminacy unleashes a power vacuum in which individuals and groups battle for control. Such battles lack an epic tone: They are more circumscribed, bound by the past, by the environment, by local, family conflicts. The past haunts some of the characters, leading them on monetary quests devoid, initially, of moral concerns, or causing them to adopt attitudes of cynical indifference to meaningful action. As is the case for his post-*High Noon* Westerns, Cooper's character is a less transcendent, more human figure constrained by the imperatives of setting and group personalities—and by his own internal debates. The characters seem dwarfed by imposing father figures (*The Man of the West*), by the landscapes strewn with large boulders (*Garden of Evil*), by violent, strong, crude youths (*Vera Cruz*).

Nevertheless, in the course of the movies, if circumstances force Cooper's characters to question whatever values they have inherited from the past, they still manage in the end to construct pragmatically a relevant moral sense and to rediscover the rightness of their being. Whereas the early Cooper persona was always ready to act in defense of his honor and moral code, even if he was not sure of his ability to succeed, Cooper's later Westerner is not always ready to act, for his characters eventually become preoccupied with the larger problems that inhere in their various experiences. That they do act—that their initial monetary or vengeance motivations evolve into higher ethical choices or at least recognitions; that their violent actions are not casual or arbitrary—and that their actions result in positive consequences affirms a final point. However much his late Westerns reveal the different emphases and strains which will destroy the classic Western formula in the years immediately after his death, his aging, vulnerable Westerner remains in spirit a true father to the Virginian, whether slumped over his desk in near despair in *High Noon* or wearily striding down the sand dune toward Cordura, the rest of the group naturally falling into his wake, striving to emulate his hardened magnificence. Western stars since 1961 have faced the same difficult task.[12]

NOTES

1. Robert Warshow, "Movie Chronicle: The Westerner," in his *The Immediate Experience* (New York: Atheneum, 1970), pp. 135–54.
2. Will Wright, *Sixguns and Society: A Structural Study of the Western* (Berkeley: University of California Press, 1975), chapter three.
3. See Stanley Cavell, "The Dandy," in his *The World Viewed* (New York: Viking, 1971), pp. 55–60.
4. For biographical information I have consulted Stuart Kaminsky, *Coop: The Life and Legend of Gary Cooper* (New York: St. Martin's Press, 1980), and Larry Swindell, *The Last Hero: A Biography of Gary Cooper* (Garden City, N.Y.: Doubleday, 1980). Also extremely helpful is Homer Dickens, *The Films of Gary Cooper* (New York: Citadel Press, 1970).
5. Kaminsky, *Coop*, p. 29.
6. For more on this point see Stephen Tatum, *Inventing Billy the Kid* (Albuquerque: University of New Mexico Press, 1982), pp. 83–94; John Cawelti, *Adventure, Mystery and Romance* (Chicago: University of Chicago Press, 1976), pp. 230–41; Michael T. Marsden, "The Rise of the Western Movie: From Sagebrush to Screen," in *Journal of the West*, 22 (October 1983), pp. 17–23. Useful sources on the history and development of the genre include George N. Fenin and William K. Everson, *The Western: From Silents to Seventies*, rev. ed. (New York: Penguin, 1977); Jon Tuska, *The Filming of the West* (New York: Doubleday, 1976); Brian Garfield, *Western Films* (New York: Rawson Associates, 1982); William R. Meyer, *The Making of the Great Westerns* (New Rochelle, N.Y.: Arlington House, 1979); Jack Nachbar, ed., *Focus on the Western* (Englewood Cliffs, N.J.: Prentice-Hall, 1974); Kevin Brownlow, *The War, the West, and the Wilderness* (New York: Knopf, 1979); and a special issue on Western Films in *Journal of the West*, 22 (October 1983).
7. Wright, *Sixguns and Society*, chapter five.
8. As quoted in Kaminsky, *Coop*, p. 43.
9. Besides the previously noted histories of the genre, particularly useful here are Andrew Bergman, *We're in the Money: Depression America and Its Films* (New York: New York University Press, 1971); various essays in *American History/American Film*, ed. John O'Conner and Martin A. Jackson (New York: Ungar, 1979); Jack Nachbar, "Horses, Harmony, Hope, and Hormones: Western Movies, 1930–1946" *Journal of the West*, 22 (October 1983), pp. 24–33.
10. Peter Biskind's *Seeing is Believing: How Hollywood Taught Us to Stop Worrying and Love the Fifties* (New York: Pantheon Books, 1983) is instructive on *High Noon*. Will Wright's discussion in *Sixguns and Society* of the evolution of the classic Western into the professional Western (e.g., *The Magnificent*

*Seven; The Wild Bunch*) focuses on transition films such as *High Noon*. Gary Cooper's later Westerns such as *Vera Cruz* and *They Came to Cordura* certainly anticipate, if not include, the conventions of the professional Western. Yet Cooper's figures continue to function in a manner similar to his earlier roles in the classic Western.

11. See John H. Lenihan, *Showdown: Confronting Modern America in the Western Film* (Urbana: University of Illinois Press, 1980); Thomas H. Pauly, "The Cold War Western," *Western Humanities Review*, 33 (1973), 258; Jim Kitses, *Horizons West: Studies in Authorship Within the Western* (Bloomington: Indiana University Press, 1970); Cawelti, *Adventure*, pp. 252–59; Philip French, *Westerns: Aspects of a Movie Genre* (New York: Viking, 1973).

12. Completion of this essay was aided by a research leave awarded by the University of Utah Research Committee.

RAY MERLOCK

# Gene Autry and the
# Coming of Civilization

GUITARIST, SONGWRITER, and longtime employee Johnny Bond delighted in telling the story of Gene Autry's encounter with an obnoxious drunk one evening as he was leaving the studio. "Autry," the
drunk declared, "you can't act, and you can't ride, and you can't sing."
According to Bond, Autry smiled and replied, "Friend, you're right. I
can't act and I can't ride and I can't sing. And I have three million dollars to prove it."

The dollar figure suggests Bond's story is an early one for recent
estimates of Autry's holdings are in the $70–$130 million range,[1] but
the point of the episode is Autry's tendency not to take himself seriously. This is a tendency shared by a majority of film, music, and popular culture critics. Neither of the two cornerstone analyses of the
Western, Robert Warshow's essay "The Westerner" (1962) and John
Cawelti's *The Six-Gun Mystique* (1971), devotes much attention or
time to Autry's B Westerns. Warshow writes, "We need only look at
William S. Hart or Tom Mix, who in the wooden absoluteness of their
virtue, represented little that an adult could take seriously; and doubtless such figures as Gene Autry or Roy Rogers are no better, though I
confess I have seen none of their movies."[2] Cawelti's book, although it
makes several good points, is marked with a similar lack of familiarity
and respect. Even Jack Nachbar, editor of *Focus on the Western* (1974)
and an important voice in popular culture criticism, has called B Westerns "the McDonald's hamburgers of the genre."[3] Some attention has

been given to Autry's place in the development and acceptance of country and western music, but neither in this area nor in the realm of the
singing cowboy's importance in the evolution and rejuvenation of the
Western film have Autry's contributions been examined and appreci-
ated sufficiently.

No "Palm Springs Cowboy"[4]—the phrase is Joel McCrea's—
Autry's heritage is legitimately Western. He states with pride in his
autobiography, *Back in the Saddle Again*, "Grandpa's family had
crossed the plains in covered wagons, coming to Texas with the early
settlers (and adventurers) from Tennessee, the Houstons and the
Crocketts. An Autry died at the Alamo."[5] The early life of Autry is the
stuff to delight studio publicists and fans who fail to realize or accept
that most of the perpetrators of the Western mythos, such as Owen
Wister, Zane Grey, and Roy Rogers, have been Easterners. Orvon
"Gene" Autry, who was born in Tioga, Texas, on September 29, 1907,
was one of four children of Delbert Autry, a horse trader and cattle
dealer, and his wife Elnora Ozmont Autry. After high school, Autry
moved with his family to Achille, Oklahoma, about fifty miles from
Berwyn, Oklahoma (a town where Autry later bought a ranch and the
town which became, through a citizen petition and a courthouse resolution, Gene Autry, Oklahoma in 1941). An early job involved serving as
projectionist at the Dark Feather Theatre where William S. Hart, Tom
Mix, and Harry Carey movies ran frequently.

Autry's grandfather, Baptist preacher William T. Autry, was a
major influence, "a practical man who taught me to sing when I was five
in order to use me in his church choir. He was short a soprano."[6] At
twelve, Autry ordered his first guitar from a Sears, Roebuck catalogue,
using $8 he had earned baling and stacking hay on his uncle's farm.
Besides farm and projectionist work, Autry traveled for three months
with a medicine show, his ballads serving as a preamble to Professor
Fields's huckstering his Pain Annihilator. Autry's first feature film,
the 1935 *Tumbling Tumbleweeds*, involves a medicine show with
Gabby Hayes playing a figure like Fields named Dr. Parker.

Autry's most lucrative early job was as a telegraph operator, pro-
gressing from $35 a month as an apprentice to $150 a month as a
proven professional. One of the best-known Autry stories involves
Autry passing the time singing and accompanying himself on the
guitar while working at the Chelsea, Oklahoma, office one morning. A
stranger dropped in to send a message and suggested to the young man,

"I think you have something. Work hard at it and you may get somewhere."[7] The stranger, of course, was Will Rogers, certainly a man
whose advice was to be taken seriously.

A trip to New York City to begin a show business career in 1928
proved disappointing, but back in Oklahoma Autry secured a singing
job on radio station KVOO in Tulsa and became known as "Oklahoma's
Yodeling Cowboy." "That Silver-Haired Daddy of Mine" was released in
1930. It sold 30,000 copies the first month and several million over the
years. Sears, Roebuck was the principal outlet for the Okeh label on
which the song written by Autry and Jimmy Long had been recorded,
and for four years, Sears was the sponsor for "The Gene Autry Program" on WLS in Chicago. Besides hosting his own program Autry also
appeared regularly on "The National Barn Dance" where he first
teamed with Smiley Burnette, the rotund, button-eyed comic, songwriter, and musician who later accompanied Autry to Hollywood.

From the very beginning of the American motion picture industry
in the early years of the twentieth century, the Western film had been a
mainstay, a form popular with both rural and urban audiences. As
with any genre, however, if it is to endure it must be renewed contin-
ually, given new life, be able to move in related but distinctly unique
directions. Not to do so is to invite staleness and, after a time, loss of
audience interest and producers' support. Tom Mix, for example, with
his flashier clothing and more thrilling stunt work, proved more in
keeping with 1920s Jazz Age sensibilities than the older, more somber,
and more Puritan William S. Hart. In the 1930s, established Western
stars, such as Mix, Hoot Gibson, Tim McCoy, Ken Maynard, and Buck
Jones, all carry-overs from the Silent Era, were beginning to show
their age as were the often-used B-Western plots and milieu. What the
Autry persona and the singing cowboy did was bring a freshness and a
new perspective and slant to the genre.

The same principle of resurgence occurs later in the Western film's
history. John Ford's *Stagecoach* (1939) proved that bigger budgeted,
more psychologically and thematically complex Westerns with major
stars and topflight directors could be profitable. In the late 1940s
Howard Hughes's *The Outlaw* and David O. Selznick's *Duel in the Sun*
introduced sex and passion to the genre, and other "oaters" with similar impulses followed. The Italian or "spaghetti" Westerns of the 1960s
turned familiar iconography in new directions, adding European concerns and motifs. The Sergio Leone-Clint Eastwood trilogy, *A Fistful of*

*Dollars, For a Few Dollars More,* and *The Good, the Bad, and the Ugly,* proved profitable and also served as influences for both European- and American-made products.

There were several reasons why, in the 1930s, the addition of musical numbers to the Western seemed to be a logical step. Music, of course, was a commodity rightfully and traditionally associated with the cowboy or Westerner. Wranglers and drovers sang to help settle or pacify herds, and a legacy of Western songs from the 1870s to the 1900s existed. What the singing cowboy in films managed to do, according to Douglas B. Green's *Country Roots: The Origins of Country Music,* was lend "dignity and respect" to country music that "had been condescendingly known as 'hillbilly' for years. Country music's contact with the singing Western gave it the prestige and respectability it needed to enter the mainstream of American consciousness and to rise eventually to its current popularity."[8]

The coming of sound into movie technology in 1927, beginning with Al Jolson and *The Jazz Singer,* opened the way for the inclusion of songs in the storyline soundtrack and, of course, for the creation of the musical genre. As early as 1930, Western star Ken Maynard, a country music enthusiast who, for all his prowess as a horseman, was nowhere near the polished performer or songster Autry was, occasionally sang and strummed in his films. Another predecessor to Autry was Singin' Sandy, played by John Wayne with a singing voice probably dubbed by Smith Ballew. The premise in the film *Riders of Destiny* (1933) involved a steely-eyed Wayne walking toward a gunman and mouthing an eerie ballad while the onlooking townspeople gasped and exclaimed, "Lord, that's Singin' Sandy," as the outlaw enemy at the end of the street turned pale and fearful.

Including professional musical numbers in B Westerns had two benefits: It allowed for a different ingredient in the formula-ridden, horse-opera programmer, and as veteran B-Western and serial director William Witney once explained, musical sequences were less expensive than brawls or scenes entailing stunt work. The idea for the singing cowboy stemmed from filmmakers' awareness of the success certain performers such as Autry were having on radio and supposedly was explored initially in a meeting involving the president of the American Record Corporation, Moe Siegal, and film producers Nat Levine (Mascot Pictures) and Herbert Yates (Republic). Autry's first screen appearance for Mascot involved singing in a party scene with Smiley Burnette in the 1934 Ken Maynard film *In Old Santa Fe.* The same year Autry was given star billing in the Mascot serial *The Phantom Empire*, in which he played a Western radio performer, a role he was to repeat often, who discovers an underground city Murania peopled with sinister invaders. His first B-Western programmer was *Tumbling Tumbleweeds* (1933); ninety-two other films and ninety-one television episodes followed, as did the long running *Melody Ranch* radio series and a lengthy list of hit records.

Autry's success as a singing cowboy involved a number of elements, not all of which were connected directly with musical numbers. A grimness, a two-fisted, hard-edged determination characterized previous B-Western leads, Tim McCoy and Buck Jones being the best examples. Autry was much younger and more easygoing. Closer to the age of the kids in the audience, he seemed more of an amiable, slightly older brother type, always needing to prove himself, likable but still in need of winning parental approval. In one particularly nice scene from *The Phantom Empire*, a contemporary Western/science fiction serial, Autry shields a group of boys who have banded together to protect the land from the menacing invaders with his body when a bomb explodes. The matter of the Autry hero's needing to win parental approval lent to what might be termed "the obligatory Autry rejection scene" in his early films.

This concerns Autry being wrongly shunned or rejected by his father, the community, or the girl. In *Tumbling Tumbleweeds*, Gene quarrels with his father, returns home years later with a medicine show, and learns too late that his father has been murdered. As a homage, he sings "That Silver-Haired Daddy of Mine." In *Ride, Ranger, Ride* (1936), the cavalry refuses to believe Autry about the danger from the Indians who are being enslaved by a corrupt Indian agent. *Yodelin' Kid from Pine Ridge* (1937) has an exceptionally fine Autry rejection scene. His father, played by Charles Middleton of Ming the Merciless fame from *Flash Gordon*, exclaims, "I have no son," when fellow ranchers insist Gene has fled from a skirmish with moonshiners accused of stealing cattle. In actuality, Gene has saved his unconscious father's life and was only riding away to find water for the wounded man. The rest of the film involves Gene's earning his father's respect and demonstrating that the two factions, once the real rustlers are revealed, need not be at odds with each other. In *The Old Barn Dance* (1938), Autry is accused of duping farmers into buying tractors from a crooked firm with his radio commercials; initially shaken and repentant, Gene is finally able to demonstrate that tractors are superior to horses and mules for plowing and to save the farmers and the pretty girl from the scoundrels' schemes.

The "obligatory Autry rejection scene" was successful in these and other early films for a number of reasons. Young viewers easily identified with being misunderstood and wrongly accused by their elders. Autry was at his best as an actor or re-actor in these scenes. Producer Levine's initial thinking about Autry was, "The fact that he couldn't act was at first considered a negligible flaw and later an asset. Like Gary Cooper and Jimmy Stewart, Autry had a kind of awkwardness and embarrassment that audiences like."[9] Seemingly vulnerable and unsure of himself in films in these scenes proved advantageous and drew possibly on Autry's own doubts about himself and his career. His mother, who died without seeing her son's films, asked him, "Was he sure he ought to give up his job with the railroad?"[10] The momentary rejection and the assured hope of the audience, especially youngsters, that Gene would prove his worth, vision, ability, and integrity endeared the songster to the public.

Complementing this was the decision that Gene Autry would play a character, basically himself, named Gene Autry. This further enhanced Autry's appeal. The name naturally and fortunately has a nice ring to it: "Gene" is likable, and "Autry," a possible first name in its own right, has a somewhat harder, more menacing sound. Friendly characters would call him "Gene," enemies "Autry."

A primary element of B Westerns is obviously not acting excellence but rather the presentation of personality. Although similar, the leading men of B Westerns are not interchangeable: Lash LaRue (dressed in black, possessing a brooding, Bogart-like look, appearing in films utilizing more violence, traces of blood, sadism, and numbers of dead) differs from Rocky Lane or Rex Allen or Sunset Carson. The latter's films seem to be more aware of the star's sexual dimension. The decision in 1935 to have Autry use his own name was original. Previously, the names derived for the star's characters were close to his own but not identical. Mix, for example, played Tom Destry as well as other characters whose first name might be Tom but whose last name was not Mix. After Autry, the practice was used for Roy Rogers (although not in his earliest starring films), Rex Allen, Sunset Carson, LaRue, Eddie Dean, and others—generally those in the Republic Studios stable.

The genius of having Autry play Autry was that it dispensed with one of the veils of the fantasy and built on Autry's reputation as a country and western musical performer. The characters Autry would portray constitute the Autry persona, and audiences felt closer to that persona because, in one way, the story was given the underpinnings of a real adventure, an actual happening. Building on this allowed for some of the most interesting Autry films when the plot revolved around a performer making good or had a show business background.

More needs to be noted about the use and value of songs in Autry productions. Initially, the music was a novelty, an addition to what was typically found in B Westerns. But there was a fierceness and almost a sense of pride in how it was presented. *Tumbling Tumbleweeds* has a key scene in which Autry is interrupted by two jeering, music-hating badmen while singing "That Silver-Haired Daddy of Mine" before a gathering of townspeople during the medicine show. "You like this?" one asks of a spectator. "Sure, it's good," is the response. When he is interrupted, Autry brawls with and bests the intruders, signaling the singing cowboy's right to be respected and heard and affirming that he lacked none of the fighting ability traditionally associated with the B-Western leading man. Throughout Autry films villains are characterized as unable to sing or as individuals not in sympathy with music. Audiences, of course, side with Autry and against the unfriendly foes, whose great mistake is consistently to underestimate the amiable, rather bashful singing cowboy.

Another fantasy element connected with Autry's songs involves the winning of the girl. As is often the case in youthful romantic interlude, Autry's character often makes a dismal first impression or has to contend with a seemingly more refined or capable rival for the woman's affections. When he sings, however, the often tongue-tied cowboy hero takes on an aura of confidence, poise, and ease, and his manner and the sincerity of his song are sufficient to win the lady's heart. For male adolescents in the theatre, the concept of romantic conquest, of seeing the girl smile and flash signals of respect, admiration, and even love during a simple serenade, seemed a simple and foolproof, though obviously fantasy-ridden, way of avoiding the usual disappointment and rejection associated with initial courtship contact with members of the opposite sex. Wouldn't it be swell to sing like that (Autry's singing voice is distinctive but not threateningly good or overpowering as were the voices of some later, less successful singing cowboys) and win the girl?

Another reason for the success of the Autry films and an element that infused itself into both B Westerns and the Western in general was the solidification of the comic sidekick character. One of Autry's later sidekicks, Pat Buttram, credits Smiley Burnette and his Frog Milhouse character with perfecting the sidekick role and making it a mainstay of the genre. Certainly the comic sidekick is part of a long-standing literary tradition including Don Quixote and Sancho Panza, Don Giovanni and Leperello, and less comic-oriented pairs such as Hawkeye and Chingachgook, Ishmael and Queequeg, and Huckle-berry Finn and Jim. In earlier Western fiction, however, Deadeye Dick of the dime novels has no sidekick, and the O. Henry story "The Caballero's Way" that introduced the Cisco Kid is devoid of Pancho. The cast of William S. Hart's 1925 classic *Tumbleweeds* does include a sidekick character "Kentucky Rose," played by Lucien Littlefield, but comic sidekicks were not necessary ingredients in Hart or Mix films nor were they so fixed and prominent in B Westerns prior to the Autry-Burnette collaboration.

Prior to being set in film, Smiley Burnette's comic personality drew from sources and roots in country and western humor. The tradition of merging country music with comedy can be traced to medicine shows, vaudeville, rodeo clowns, and country western/barn dance radio shows. Autry and Burnette had a successful association in radio prior to their move to Hollywood and brought a well-developed gag music and give-and-take dialogue interchange act with them. There were a number of other advantages to continuing their partnership in films. Frog Milhouse's allegiance to and esteem for Autry—unlike other characters who rejected or doubted Autry during the plot, Frog is always loyal—aided the storylines and further mirrored the audience's amiable feelings for the star. Autry and Burnette worked well together both on screen and in songwriting ventures. The comic sidekick character in general also enhances and defines the hero's stature. In keeping with the literary heritage, the all-too-human sidekick serves as a counterpart to the hero's idealism, to his questing integrity. Because the sidekick is present, always looking to the hero for guidance, the star has an increased believability and frame of reference. Autry's "soft voice, shy smile, and peaceful looks"[11] were in contrast with the toughness of past Western stars, and the sidekick's antics allowed Autry to enjoy himself, demonstrate his tolerance and capacity for friendship, issue a pleasing smile, and, in doing so, display his pearly, even teeth.

Burnette's Frog Milhouse character also steadfastly defined the characteristics of the sidekick. First, the sidekick serves as a companion to the hero, traveling with him on horseback and sharing his adventures. Second, he is, as is everyone else, a lesser man than the hero, not as handsome or as accomplished with his guns, fists, or crime-solving abilities. Third, the sidekick realizes his own absurdity, enabling the audience most often to laugh with him rather than just at him. This is of interest when one considers how many comic sidekicks had physical limitations—stutters, stammers, strange voices (Smiley's plunging into a deep bass), a lack of teeth, a weight problem, even sub-human intelligence and coordination. Yet instead of emitting bitterness, the sidekick realizes his defect makes him lovable and accepts it, as should the audience. Last, the sidekick provides comic relief, a departure from the more serious matters of adventure and romance. Autry's films provided considerably more forms of entertainment than earlier Westerns: action, stunts, romance, and—new to the genre— music and systematic comedy and comic interplay and interaction. Departing from the previous lone wolf, able-to-handle-it-all-alone quality of the hero in Western films, Autry's movies often involved Frog, atop his horse Ring-Eyed Nellie, leading a company of riders to help Gene in the final confrontation with the villains. Something of a "big kid" himself, Smiley's character also worked well with child characters, and, as Autry himself related well to children on film as both a caring friend and a role model, child actors and actresses were often incorporated into the stories.

Besides the comic sidekick character crystalized by Smiley Burnette, along with the country and western music, and Autry's role as a new type of younger leading man infested with the Autry persona, there is one other key feature of the Gene Autry films that gave them a new kind of vitality. They were set in a world where frontier icons and milieu and modern civilization exist simultaneously. Unlike earlier Western films set in the 1880–1900 time period, Autry's films often were set in the 1930s, in the world of tractors, cars, radio technology, moving pictures, and the Depression. Yet Autry films also featured men carrying guns (Autry did not in some films, but he could always lay his hand on one if necessary), wearing standard western garb, and riding horses. Perhaps this strange blend first coincided with the mixture of science fiction and the Western in *The Phantom Empire*, but, whatever, it allowed for new dimensions in the B Western and helped engineer different kinds of plots and thematic concerns than had traditionally been conceived for the genre.

A number of Western purists and critics found the modern/historic Western coupling in Autry movies laughable. For them, Westerns must be set in a time when wilderness/savagery and civilization are in conflict, with the protagonist tipping the scales in favor of civilization. And, like Natty Bumppo, Shane, or so many of John Ford's Western heroes, the protagonist can never stay to enjoy the peace, safety, and security made possible by the trappings of civilization he has helped to institutionalize. There is a great sense of loss and pain and nostalgia in the traditional Western as the hero is usually a doomed, even a tragic individual. The talents and mind-set which bring about his triumph also alienate him from the civilized society he has allowed to supplant the wilderness and the ruffians previously in control.

In Autry films there is no real tension between the frontier and the new mechanized society. The villains are not emblems of freedom or open lawlessness but petty, materialistic schemers dressed in eastern banker-like suits employing western-garbed henchmen of low-grade intelligence. Whatever is necessary, be it horseflesh or technology, to thwart their plot is what Autry uses. One standard happening in Autry films involves, during the final chase scene, the automobile carrying the sheriff having a flat tire or being halted by a stream; on his horse Champion Gene simply storms past and succeeds in catching and apprehending the criminals. Another standard plot device involves Autry using a record player to deceive the villains into thinking he is one place when he is actually somewhere else or his using a recording device to gain evidence against the scoundrels while they are hatching a sinister plan.

The new twists in locale, plot, and persona distinguished Autry's films from those of the older stars who invariably were lawmen working undercover to infiltrate the outlaw gang and discern "the brains" behind the thievery and plundering. Much less a loner figure—indeed, not a loner figure at all—Autry is always associated with a group, the group being Depression rural farmers or ranchers coping with national or regional financial problems darkened by self-serving business schemers.

The way Autry's films reflect sociological, cultural, and even political concerns of the 1930s, 1940s, and 1950s is another aspect of his motion picture legacy that is generally overlooked. Even Autry in his autobiography, *Back in the Saddle Again*, emphasizes his musical contributions rather than his films. He asserts:

> Music has always been the better part of my career. Movies are wonderful fun, and they give you a famous face. But how the words and melody are joined, how they come together out of air and enter the mind, this is art. Songs are forever. We carry them with us, at work or play.[12]

Similar comments participate in the same mind-set. "Westerns were to movies what the sports page is to the daily newspaper: the best part of it. The toy department."[13] and "Trying to single out one of my pictures is like trying to recall a particular noodle you enjoyed during a spaghetti dinner."[14]

Autry, in his autobiography, testifies to some knowledge, however dismissive, of the trends set by his films: "(1) There wasn't a Repo truck or a wood-paneled station wagon on the road that my horse Champion couldn't outrun, and (2) Big Business and Special Interests and High-Handed Villains always lost to the pure of heart."[15] As for the basic formulas, Autry lists merely "(1) a decent story; (2) good music; (3) comedy relief; (4) enough action, with chases and fights; and (5) a little romance. And always we played it against the sweep of desert scenery, mountains, and untamed land and an ocean of sky."[16]

Certainly Autry has just cause to be proud of his contributions to twentieth-century popular music. Autry discovery and protegé Jimmy Wakely, who became a B-Western singing cowboy in his own right, once named Autry along with Bing Crosby, Frank Sinatra, and Elvis Presley as the four most prominent and influential singing talents of the period. Of the five best-selling Christmas songs of our time, Autry has three: "Rudolph the Red-Nosed Reindeer," "Frosty the Snowman," and "Here Comes Santa Claus," and his country and western songs, albums, and compositions have impacted both on the industry and on later performers. For example, Willie Nelson included a version of "Ridin' Down the Canyon" on an album with Leon Russell. But, notwithstanding the music included in them, Autry's individual films deserve more analysis than the "aw, shucks, they're all the same" stance that so many critics, fans, and even Autry himself have taken.

Of Autry's ninety-three B Westerns, fifty-six were completed by 1942 when Autry joined the Army Air Corps during World War II. Generally, these films concerned 1930s themes "such as political corruption, big business expansion, soil erosion, crop destruction, and various social problems."[17] Autry's fourth film *Red River Valley* (1936), for example, dealt with a scheme to foil the completion of an irrigation project that would provide water to a drought-parched valley. In a key, rather typical Autry scene, Gene, using his .45 as a baton, forces a group of angry dam workers who have been demanding their overdue pay to join together in a chorus led by agitator/villain George Chesebro. Autry's pronouncement, once they have finished, is, "Now, don't you feel better? There's nothing like a song." In *The Filming of the*

*West,* critic and motion picture historian Jon Tuska comments on what he calls the Autry fantasy, the use of music and "muscle" to initiate social change:

> I sincerely believe that Autry's massive appeal as a modest cowboy trou-badour leading a uniquely charmed life, a musical magician who could turn darkness into light, sorrow into happiness, tarnish into splendor, a Pied Piper able to control men and alter the course of world events by means of a song, is the most tremendous single occurrence in the history of the American Western cinema. Gene Autry in his magnificent outfits, yodeling a pop tune, is a vision so remote from the actual man of the frontier to rival any fairy tale. If you compare Autry to Tom Mix, or even William S. Hart, of the previous generation, he appears hopelessly inept. But once you accept him on his own terms and find yourself enthralled by the Autry Fantasy, the others begin to look clumsy, plebeian, vulgar. Whereas screen cowboys once flaunted their fast draw, Autry customarily carried his gloves between his gun butt and his holster. . . . Gene boasted that in his films he seldom threw the first punch, and he certainly never fought vigorously from 1936 to 1948. He insisted on never killing anyone, and I cannot remember that he did, save indirectly.[18]

Several other films of this early Autry, progressive era are worth noting. In *The Big Show* (1936), Autry plays a double role: a disagree-able, gambling-debt-ridden Western film star who can't sing and his stuntman/double named Gene Autry who replaces the star and finally wins audience support in his own right. During a rodeo performance, Autry apologizes for the masquerade, reveals his true identity, and hears a man in the crowd shout, "We don't care who you are. We're for you!" The Sons of the Pioneers, including Roy Rogers—then called Dick Weston—appear in the film as they do in a later Autry film that same year *The Old Corral*. The latter features a fight between Sheriff Autry and an impetuous Rogers that is won by Gene, who rehabilitates the younger songster and his pards who are only hoping for a show busi-ness break and who are enlisted in Autry's cause against a group of big-city gangsters.

*Round-up Time in Texas* (1937), perhaps Autry's weirdest feature, is set in Africa where Gene and Frog transport a herd of horses for use in Gene's brother's diamond mine. The depiction of the natives consti-tutes the worst racial stereotypes, and stock footage from old Tarzan films is in abundance. Still this is another effort to transplant the West-ern into yet another new locale.

*Yodelin' Kid from Pine Ridge* (1937) also has a new locale—cattle ranches in Florida—where Gene finds himself temporarily alienated

Gene Autry and Champion in *The Big Show* (1936). *Ray Merlock*

from his rancher-father in a fight between poor moonshiners and the cattlemen whose stock is being rustled. Rustling is also used in *Public Cowboy No. 1* (1937), in Autry's surrogate father figure, a sheriff played by William Farnum, is having trouble coping with thieves who are using refrigerated trucks, airplanes, and two-way radios in their enterprise. The townspeople are demanding the sheriff's resignation, feeling his Old West sensibility is a liability in dealing with modernized criminal tactics, until Gene uses some of the same devices (a radio broadcasting a "Calling All Cowboys" message) to apprehend the rustlers.

*The Old Barn Dance* (1938) also pits Old West versus New West conventions. Autry is a horse trader who, persuaded by a girl in trouble—her father's radio station is in financial jeopardy—becomes a radio star huckstering tractors. The company actually is composed of swindlers, but Autry is able to demonstrate the problem is with the unscrupulous businessmen and not with the premise that tractors are more practical and usable than horses for plowing purposes. *Git Along,*

Gene Autry in *Public Cowboy No. 1* (1937). *Ray Merlock*

*Little Dogies* (1937) has a similar twist. Originally against oil drilling, feeling it will pollute the streams, Autry changes his mind when he learns that if the well strikes oil the railroad will follow, so he encourages the good townspeople to invest in the capitalistic venture. *Stardust on the Sagebrush* (1942) uses the same plot and sequences with mining stock substituted for oil interests.

   *Melody Ranch* (1940) was an effort to reach a broader, more musically oriented audience. It also included non-western performers Jimmy Durante, Vera Vague, and dancer Ann Miller in the cast. Radio star Autry is first given the title of honorary sheriff. Then, as the need arises and the public demands, he runs for the office in earnest and wins an election the villains unsuccessfully try to fix. The climax involves Autry's driving a bus through the criminals' blockade.

   *Ride, Ranger, Ride* (1936) is one early Autry entry with a setting in the Old West instead of the modern period. Formerly a Texas Ranger, when the organization is disbanded Autry joins the cavalry (Frog and the boys faithfully follow his example) and discovers— initially to the Army's disbelief—that a corrupt Indian agent is inciting the Comanches to looting and plundering. As with blacks in *Round-up Time in Texas*, the portrayal of Indians in *Ride, Ranger, Ride* constitutes a distressing racial stereotype, as does the depiction of Mexicans in *Mexicali Rose* (1939), *South of the Border* (1939), and *Down Mexico Way* (1941). In *South of the Border*, for example, a group of Mexicans now engaged in subversive activities endangering American oil interests used to be happy and prosperous until, after listening to propaganda supplied by another country desiring their oil, they became "lazy, dissatisfied, and discontent." Duncan Renaldo, better known later for his role as the Cisco Kid, played the Mexican so easily duped by foreign powers. When he perishes, his sister, Autry's love interest, redeems the family honor by joining a convent, painfully separating herself from her country's singing Yankee savior. A later Columbia Autry film with the same pro-WASP, pro-grass roots Americana sentiment of *South of the Border* is *Gene Autry and the Mounties* (1951), in which a group of Canadian revolutionaries are fighting to set up a Marxist republic in Northwest Canada. To a Mountie's explanation, "They want to set up a welfare state—if you don't work, someone else will," Autry replies, "A good trick if it works—sort of like sending water uphill."

Another trace of this American jingoism strain in Autry films involves the fact that the scheming big business villains are generally mid-level officials, cheating both the working people and the big boss who has become separated from the true worth of the land and the value of hard, sweat-producing work by secluding himself or herself in an office or abroad. *Call of the Canyon* (1942) is one example of this plotline. A corrupt mid-level official offers the cattlemen $65 a head instead of the standard $80, pocketing the difference himself. Autry attempts to get word to the isolated corporate head who does, indeed, come in disguise to investigate the situation and help the abused rural folk. The "bigger-they-are-the-more-sympathetic-with-the-common-people" screenplay of *Call of the Canyon* was penned, interestingly enough, by silent film producer Harry Rapf's son, Maurice Rapf, later blacklisted in the 1950s and forced into academia (Dartmouth College Film Studies) rather than be permitted to pursue his career as a screenwriter and director.

Surprisingly and foolishly enough, standard B-Western plotlines such as *Call of the Canyon*'s sparked concern from the United States Office of War Information. Commenting on the usual procedure of casting the B-Western villain as a supposedly responsible head of the community, a memo stated, "This plot is becoming a Hollywood habit; the men who should be the town leaders are bandit leaders instead, and some itinerant cowboy has to administer justice for the people."[19] Autry, of course, generally was employed in his roles, so the term "itinerant" does not apply. Moreover, the association rural audiences (the largest segment of the B-Western's following) had with banker types in the 1930s simplified identifying villains. Any effort at insidious demoralization seems completely unintended.

Indeed, as world affairs grew increasingly bleaker, Autry's films changed their focus somewhat, turning to more updated national concerns. In *In Old Monterey* (1939), for example, Army Sergeant Gene Autry is dispatched to persuade a group of irate ranchers led by Gabby Hayes to permit the military to use out-of-the-way land for bombing practice exercises. In a town meeting to convince the ranchers they need to support the military operations, he uses film footage showing European refugees as a warning to the danger to this country if it is not prepared. He ends his speech by leading all in attendance in a rousing version of "Columbia, The Gem of the Ocean." Again unpatriotic, self-serving, mid-level villains sabotage the maneuvers for personal gain, and a young boy is killed during a bombing practice in one of the more somber deaths in a B Western. Accused and ostracized by the community, Autry does appear to sing at the boy's funeral, and later, with Frog's help, makes use of a miniature tank to capture the culprits and prevent an unnecessary skirmish between the homesteaders and regular Army cavalry troops.

The patriotism of both Autry the individual and Autry the film persona was further enhanced when he joined the Air Corps in 1942. According to his autobiography, "I was thirty-five. Married. Childless. But supporting two sisters and a brother. And for the first time in my career, in my life, the money had been pouring in: from movies, records, radio, rodeo appearances, and merchandising deals. In 1941, I had earned over $600,000."[20] In a widely circulated newspaper interview, Autry espoused his reasons for enlisting and his personal beliefs:

> Everybody ought to think of winning the war ahead of anything else. This is the most serious time in our history and our country is in more peril than any other time. . . . I think the He-Men in the movies belong in the

Army, Marine, Navy or Air Corps. All of these He-Men in the movies realize that right now is the time to get into the service. Every movie cowboy
ought to devote time to the Army winning or to helping win until the war
is won—the same as any other American citizen. The Army needs every
young man it can get, and if I can set a good example for the young men I'll
be mighty proud. Seventeen and eighteen year olds are needed, and some
of the boys are my fans. I say to them and to all you young men, every
young man should give everything he can for the war effort. If we train
young pilots and the war continues for a long stretch, those boys of seventeen or eighteen will be a protectorate over the whole country.[21]

The sentiments in the interview correlate with Autry's well-
known and, to his youthful fans, much revered Ten Commandments of
the Cowboy (a code Natty Bumppo would be proud to honor):

(1) A cowboy never takes unfair advantage—even of an enemy.
(2) A cowboy never betrays a trust.
(3) A cowboy always tells the truth.
(4) A cowboy is kind to small children, to old folks, and to animals.
(5) A cowboy is free from racial and religious prejudices.
(6) A cowboy is helpful and when anyone is in trouble he lends a hand.
(7) A cowboy is a good worker.
(8) A cowboy is clean about his person and in thought, word, and deed.
(9) A cowboy respects womanhood, his parents, and the laws of his
country.
(10) A cowboy is a patriot.

The years in the service and Roy Rogers's status as Republic's new
singing cowboy draw did not hamper Autry upon his discharge. Now
completely associated in the public's mind with the Ten Commandments of the Cowboy and still capable of pleasing his fans, he was an
institution. Despite putting on weight rather like an aging Elvis
Presley years later, he continued to hold the support and affection of
loyal fans who had grown up with him. After a series of five more films
(1946–47) for Republic, Autry made thirty-one additional films through
Gene Autry Productions with Columbia Pictures handling the releases.

Autry's first film for Republic upon his discharge, *Sioux City Sue*
(1947), has some comic touches and a flair similar to his prewar
Republic releases. Cattleman Autry is tricked into supplying the singing voice for an animated film donkey. In a rather warm scene, Gene,
not knowing how he has been used, attends the hometown premiere
and, with tears of embarrassment in his eyes, sits humiliated at the
screening. Of course, his "real-life" heroics catch the filmmakers' at-

tention finally, and he is given a legitimate movie contract and renewed respectability. The Autry-as-show-business-character plot once again proved durable.

As might be expected, there are some notable differences in Autry's prewar and postwar films, particularly after the move to Columbia. Although some of the Columbia films are set in the New West/Old West locale used so often at Republic, a sizable number are set in the standard post-Civil War West that is usually the domain of Western films. One picture, *Saginaw Trail* (1953), even involves a buckskin-clad Autry as a captain in Hamilton's Rangers in 1827 in northern Michigan coping with a French fur trapper who is leading a party of renegades. The film includes such memorable lines as "Some settlers have been massacred." "Not again?" and "Don't ever try to stop progress."

There were other new slants in the Columbia films. Autry was depicted as having considerable prowess with his fists and fast draw, implying that, despite his age and paunch, Autry was rougher than ever. Autry's dress also involved Levis or, on occasion, vests rather than the more flamboyant outfits of the Republic days.[22]

An early aspect of the Republic films is that they often contained vestiges of other 1930s popular genres. The screwball comedy (*It Happened One Night, Bringing Up Baby*, etc.) featured madcap love affairs between members of different social classes, all resolved in the most democratic way. In the Autry versions of screwball comedy merging with the Western, Gene—the hard-working, poor cowboy—comes in contact, quarrels, bickers, and fights, and ultimately falls in love with a wealthy society belle, usually played by June Storey. Also popular in the 1930s was the Shirley Temple/Freddie Bartholomew child performer film, and Autry and Frog were often caring for the cutest of orphans, forsaken children, or youngsters in jeopardy. This also carried over into the on-the-road/*It Happened One Night* film in which the characters discover how much they like each other during a journey. One example of this is *Gaucho Serenade*, also shown under the title *Keep Rolling* (1940), in which Gene and Frog accompany a British-educated boy to his western home, "Rancho San Quentin" (the boy's father has been wrongly convicted of a crime), picking up two sisters (June Storey and Mary Lee) on the way. The *Variety* critic complained of *Gaucho Serenade*, "First horse is not mounted until forty-four minutes have passed; first fist is not flung until fifty minutes have passed; first gun is not fired until fifty-six minutes have passed. What matter of western is this?"[23] The answer is the film is only part Western and part screwball comedy/child performer/on-the-road movie, several 1930s genres rolled into one film. Likewise, *Rovin' Tumbleweeds* (1939) takes its lead from another 1939 film, Frank Capra's *Mr. Smith Goes to Washington*, with an ending probably influenced by King Vidor's *Our Daily Bread* (1934). The Autry "Western" version has the poor, common people, who are suffering from a flood control bill/land scheme, electing radio singer Autry to represent them in Congress.

In the postwar Autry films, as in postwar films in general, producers and directors realized that the old genre stances were no longer workable and that changes were needed. This is not to suggest, however, that the durable, now almost sacred convention of Autry as the initiator of social progress was lost. In the 1947 Columbia release *The Last Round-up*, for example, Gene uses a closed circuit television broadcast to convince an Indian tribe to relocate to a more plush site so a much needed aqueduct can be built. The film is cited by Autry as his personal favorite, one might suspect, because of the prophetic and positive use of television, certainly a medium Autry was to explore to greater lengths beginning in 1950 with his *Gene Autry* series and then, under his Flying A Productions banner, with *Annie Oakley, The Range Rider, Buffalo Bill, Jr.*, and *The Adventures of Champion*.

Another element in the Columbia releases is the pairing of Autry and his frequent sidekick Pat Buttram[24] not with child performers but with troubled, on-the-verge-of-going-wrong adolescents, boys who initially fall in with bad company before they realize, under Autry's influence, the worth of the values implicit in The Ten Commandments of the Cowboy totally embodied in the Autry persona. In *Sons of New Mexico* (1950), Dick Jones, later known as The Range Rider's young sidekick Dick West and then as the lead in *Buffalo Bill, Jr.*, plays a headstrong youth for whom Gene is appointed guardian. A military camp, a love of horses, and Gene's example set the boy on the right path. In *Gene Autry and the Mounties* (1951), another potential juvenile deliquent, a teen-age boy who idolizes a French-Canadian revolutionary/outlaw leader, comes finally to realize that Gene represents the better, more adept man and way of life. Despite his weight problems—B-Western actor Don "Red" Barry enjoyed describing Autry's preparing for a scene by donning corset, hairpiece, and elevator boots—Gene Autry consistently evoked a stellar image for adolescents. To use another example from *Gene Autry and the Mounties*, Autry's response to sidekick Pat Buttram's question "You want a beer?" is "I'm particular about what I put in my stomach."

In real life, Autry was not that opposed to alcohol. In his autobiography, he admits to a drinking problem that developed in the Air Corps and was later intensified by business pressures. Presently he proposes to avoid situations and gatherings where heavy drinking occurs. Another less than relevant rumor about Autry concerned a onetime liaison with *Annie Oakley* star Gail Davis during his marriage of forty years to the former Ina Mae Spivey. Whatever the truth about Autry's drinking or womanizing, his success in business speaks for itself. His holdings include Golden West Broadcasters (four radio stations, KTLA television in Los Angeles, a ten-acre movie and TV production center, a national agency for selling radio time, the California Angels baseball organization) and privately owned enterprises such as a Palm Springs resort hotel, a television and two radio stations in Arizona, a twenty-thousand-acre Winslow, Arizona, ranch, a collection of vintage automobiles and locomotives, recording and music publishing companies, and the one-hundred-acre Melody Ranch.

As a performer, Autry remained in the public's eye on television until 1956 when his *Gene Autry* series ended reruns. The series, also involving Pat Buttram and Champion, included the same type of Autry/Americana/moralistic platitudes dispensed to young characters that figured so prominently in the Columbia film releases. The Wrigley's Chewing Gum-sponsored *Melody Show* radio program also ended in 1956 after a sixteen-year run. Autry was forty-nine years old and perhaps ready to shift his energies elsewhere. A longtime baseball fan—Gene presumably gave up a semipro career in Oklahoma because the $50-a-month pay could not match the $150 monthly wages offered by the railroad telegraph company—Autry purchased the Los Angeles/ now California Angels baseball franchise in 1961. Buttram, a longtime Autry friend and colleague, candidly suggests that when his show business career ended, Autry turned to the ownership of a baseball team not just for profit and enjoyment but as a way of keeping his name in the newspapers.

Re-release albums of Autry material have been prominent in the last decade in keeping with new interest in the country and western music heritage and the nostalgia craze. Although, as of 1986, the California Angels have yet to win a league championship and participate in a World Series, perhaps one of the few disappointments in Autry's life, they consistently have been a competitive and interesting team. And, although in the 1960s and 1970s, Autry films generally were available for viewing only at Western film festivals, in the 1980s a large number of Republic and Columbia Autry pictures frequently have been scheduled on television with the advent of national cable stations.

This seems fitting, for a consistent appeal of the Autry film character is his use of modern technology to convince and persuade settlers and townspeople of a better way of life. Even before Autry became a successful businessman/millionaire, the films, the *Melody Ranch* radio program, and the television episodes implied qualities that sanctified business success both as a possibility and as a desirable end, though never in a way that ran contrary to rural roots. In both his show business career, particularly in his films, and in his personal life, Autry represents commercial progress and the worth of American broadcasting and business enterprise in a way that no other Western star does. However dismissive many might be about his legacy, Autry has been a part of and a reflection of the twentieth century as well as a force that has helped utilize and shape modern entertainment and enterprise vehicles. Few have been involved, in the forefront, in as many areas of popular culture, including radio, records, films, television, and sports, for so long. The Gene Autry phenomenon has involved good luck, being in the right place at the right time, and is, indeed, more than the accomplishment of one individual. It is, however, an element that for over half a century has been instrumental in delineating, generally for better than for worse, how Americans have imagined and envisioned their potential and enjoyed themselves.

NOTES

1. Ron Base, "Gene Autry," *Persimmon Hill, A Publication of the National Cowboy Hall of Fame and Western Heritage Center*, 13, no. 3 (Fall 1983), p. 55.

2. Robert Warshow, "The Westerner." *The Immediate Experience* (Garden City, N.Y.: Doubleday and Co., Inc., 1962), pp. 135–54; rpt. in *Focus on the Western*, ed. Jack Nachbar (Englewood Cliffs, N.J.: Prentice-Hall, Inc., 1974), p. 49.

3. Professor Nachbar made this comment during a "Choosing the Best and Worst Western Films and Novels" panel with Dr. Ray White of Ball State's History Department and myself during the 1981 Cincinnati National Popular Culture Association National Convention. I admit Jack had an impish gleam in his eye when he said it.

4. Base, "Autry," p. 62.

5. Gene Autry with Mickey Herskowitz, *Back in the Saddle Again* (Garden City, N.Y.: Doubleday and Co., Inc., 1978), p. 3.

6. Autry, *Back in the Saddle Again*, p. 3.

7. David Rothel, *The Singing Cowboys* (South Brunswick and New York: A.S. Barnes and Co., 1978), p. 20.

8. Douglas B. Green, *Country Roots: The Origins of Country Music* (New York: Hawthorn Books, Inc., 1976), p. 23. Author Douglas Green is better known in some circles as "Ranger Doug" of Riders in the Sky, a country and western trio which hosts a series on singing cowboy Westerns on the Nashville Network.

9. Rothel, *The Singing Cowboys*, p. 22.

10. Autry, *Back in the Saddle Again*, p. 8.

11. Ibid., p. 39.

12. Ibid., p. 19.

13. Ibid., p. 41.

14. Ibid., p. 51.

15. Ibid., p. 52.

16. Ibid., pp. 39–40.

17. Richard Maurice Hurst, *Republic Studios: Between Poverty Row and the Majors* (Metuchen, N.J. & London: The Scarecrow Press, Inc., 1979), p. 142.

18. Jon Tuska, *The Filming of the West* (Garden City, N.Y.: Doubleday & Co., Inc., 1976), p. 305.

19. Hurst, *Republic Studios*, p. 128. From Gregory D. Black and Clayton R. Koppes, "OWI Goes to the Movies: The Bureau of Intelligence's Criticism of Hollywood, 1942–1943," *Prologue: The Journal of the National Archives*, VI (Spring, 1974), p. 50.

20. Autry, *Back in the Saddle Again*, p. 80.

21. Hurst, *Republic Studios*, p. 140. From "Gene Autry's Advice to Youth in Wartime," 1942 article from the Chamberlain and Lyman Brown Theatrical Agency Collection in the Theatrical Section of the New York Public Library.

22. Tuska, *Filming of the West*, p. 468.

23. Rothel, *The Singing Cowboys*, p. 55.

24. Smiley Burnette was involved with Columbia Pictures' Durango Kid/Charles Starrett series. Burnette did replace Pat Buttram in *Whirlwind* (1951) when Buttram was injured in an on-location accident, and Smiley did serve as Autry's sidekick in the final six films Gene made for Columbia. Autry's comment was: "We had gone in together and we would go out together. Fair is fair."

ARCHIE P. McDONALD

# John Wayne:
# Hero of the Western

JOHN WAYNE. The name calls the mind to focus on an image of a tall man embodying personal power, flint-like resolution, resourcefulness, uncanny endurance, and above all, heroism. And because he appears in boots, kerchief, and broad-brimmed hat, he especially personifies Western heroism. Wayne is America; not ordinary America, but super-America, an embodiment of our nationalism, our jingoistic, self-image of success, triumph, and prevalence. Wayne made that image vivid from a film career that spanned parts of five decades and numbered nearly 200 separate roles. He did not always play a Westerner; indeed, he portrayed diplomats, detectives, war correspondents, soldiers, businessmen, football players, and even prizefighters, but more than anything, he seemed suited to the Western image that he etched in the memory of moviegoers from the 1930s through the 1970s.

During those years, Wayne made film classics under the direction of John Ford and Howard Hawks, and developed a characterization that seemed to move from role to role and become familiar and mellow. When a person bought his ticket at the box office, he knew what he was buying—a John Wayne movie. Not that Wayne's movies were all alike, as some suggest, for they each offered something unique even if based on the same plot lines as, for example, *Rio Bravo, El Dorado*, and *Rio Lobo*. But each did offer a sameness that was satisfying and unsurprising and comfortable.

By the end of his career, Wayne made his work look deceptively easy. The drawl, the look, the gesture, practiced crafts that he learned by hard work and careful study, became as familiar to his audiences as were the speech patterns and gestures of their families. These traditions became so familiar to Wayne's life that his friends called them genuine, and used words to describe him like "sincere," or called him a "real man," and, in general, said that the screen image and the real person were the same. Some critics summarize this blend of personality by saying that Wayne played himself in every role and quoted his statement that he did not act—he re-acted. To accept this view on its face is to deny that Wayne really was an actor and to assign him to the status of a man with a gimmick—an image that happened to appeal to a couple of generations of moviegoers. Gimmicks and fads do not last as long as did his career. He *was* an actor, or at least he became one; more than that, he became an entertainer, an artist, an inspiration, a dependable guide for millions of people who never met him but who came to know him in the spirit of his performances. This status resulted from hard work, from exposure in two to four pictures a year over several decades (nearly twice the number of most actors), and from an inexplicable photogenesis that projected sincerity to large and varied audiences, and partially explains why his films grossed nearly $800 million and why, during the 1970s, he became the best-known movie actor in the world. People respected him even when they disagreed with his well-known political views.

These political views, or at least the popular notions they reflected, suited ideally the John Wayne cowboy figure. Actually, his interviews and public statements do not reveal the strident qualities his critics assume. Wayne's ideas are, as was he, grounded in nineteenth-century American values and mores. And because viewers see Wayne's Western hero in a nineteenth-century setting, the image and the views appear to merge. He was, in fact, tied to that century's value structure by the place and time of his birth and, later, by choice.

He did not live *in* the past so much as he lived *on* it, but its established truths came to him naturally from a midwestern orientation and later from life in near-frontier conditions in the desert of California. Wayne was born in Winterset, Iowa, on May 26, 1907, to Clyde and Mary (Brown) Morrison, and named Marion Robert Morrison. Wayne substituted "Michael" for "Robert" in later years. Despite the use of John Wayne for professional purposes, he continued to think of himself as Marion Morrison throughout his life, sometimes observ-

lost his white hat in a brawl, and who always fought with *fairness* regardless of what unfair tactics were used against him. Wayne believed that such actions were unrealistic. If he were hit with a chair in a saloon fight, he threw a table at his opponent, since real fighting is always done in anger and its goal is survival.

As Wayne's postwar career developed, such actions continued. In *The Man Who Shot Liberty Valance*, he shot a man from ambush. And, except for *Stagecoach*, there were few main street showdowns. When possible, he used a rifle or shotgun, which were more effective and devastating than pistols. He rarely attempted to give the appearance that he had a lightning-quick draw with a handgun, even when he used one, but rather worked to show that cunning or grit could help avoid shootouts. In *Tall in the Saddle* (1944), he cools an adversary by simply stating "Touch that gun and I'll kill you." The villain's hesitation earns him a blow on the head from Wayne's weapon rather than a bullet. And when a female bystander exclaims "Why, you hit him!" he grimly replies, "Yes ma'm, just as hard as I could."

In the later part of his career, Wayne's costuming became more a personal expression and less a badge of authenticity. Trademarks appeared: the battered campaign hat, the Winchester from *Stagecoach* with the large ring level, the buttoned-panel shirt, the belt buckle with the Red River D Brand, and the Viet-

(1971), *Cowboys* (1972), *Cahill* (1973), and, above all, *The Shootist* (1976), show him in the company of younger people who learn from his experiences.

*The Shootist*, Wayne's last picture, demonstrates this learning theme. Wayne portrays J.B. Book, an aged western gunfighter dying of cancer. In the opening sequences, by the use of clips in black and white from several previous western films, Book is clearly established as John Wayne. Then the film shifts to a panoramic scene in which a distant rider slowly approaches the camera's foreground, and an older Wayne/Book appears. A visit to a doctor confirms that he is dying of cancer. He is out of place at his dying, and although he prepares for an orderly and dignified death, his last days are spent in the presence of old enemies and new challengers. He determines to let his opponents kill him, to cheat the slower death, and to settle old scores. Preparing for the final shootout, he takes on the task of straightening out a youth and passes on the wisdom of his years. He teaches the boy (Ronnie Howard) to shoot a gun, chides him for drinking whiskey, and gives him a personal philosophy: "I won't be lied to and I won't be laid a hand on; I don't do these things to other people, and I won't have them do them to me." Book and Wayne are mutually conscious of the role of "passing it on," of striking a blow against what is wrong in the world. So in the end, Book/Wayne reacts characteristically: he kills the three who tried to kill him and then is shot in the back by a sneak he can not fight.

Archie P. McDonald.

*John Wayne as John T. Chance in Rio Bravo. (Photo courtesy of Wayne Enterprises.)*

for such Westerns as *Cahill*. His boots were rarely shined, his shirts fit loosely, his belt strained a bit with increasing weight; but the image congealed, solidified, and the quality of sincerity that Ford had recognized during the 1930s intensified. In the end, no matter that his continuing survivals or countless scrapes defied credibility; everyone knew that John Wayne survived.

Because the Wayne image included surviving and winning, most commentators on his movie *The Cowboys* (1972) express wonder that as Will Anderson he dies with thirty minutes remaining in the picture. Many critics argued that he had never before died on film. They had forgotten Sergeant Stryker in *Sands of Iwo Jima* (1949) and *Wake of the Red Witch* (1948). Perhaps they were talking only of Westerns, where he seemed always to prevail. But even in *Red River*, he loses his herd. The difference is, possibly, that in that role his stern character softens at the end of the film. Even in Wayne's meanness in the middle portions of *Red River*, one can identify with his motives if not his methods, could see humanity. Wayne might have changed the story and survived Bruce Dern's beating in *The Cowboys*, as he had changed other stories, to stress survival and winning; but he would have changed the story, and the story emphasized passing on wisdom to a younger generation. That is a key to appreciating Wayne's later Westerns. *The Alamo* (1960), *Comancheros* (1961), *Sons of Katie Elder* (1965), *True Grit* 1969), *Big Jake*

last movie, but that film became an icon ...
his life in motion pictures, especially as a western star. His death on June 13, 1979, from physical weakness that lingered following open-heart surgery the previous year and a reoccurrence of cancer, ended a career and an era. For many film goers, critics as well as hero-worshippers, he had come to personify the Western, its faults and its virtues. His films were violent, sometimes excessively so, but they did not dwell on violence for its own sake; his victims rarely spurted blood at the camera. Usually there was some point to the violence, some context that made it appropriate or even humorous. In *The Sons of Katie Elder* (1965), for example, he struck George Kennedy in the face with an axe handle to aid a friend, and the scene invariably moved audiences to laughter and chuckles rather than horror.

Wayne disdained open and obvious sex in his films claiming in an interview in *Playboy Magazine* that films employing such explicit scenes denied the audience the greatest gift of movies — illusion. Yet his characters even in advancing age, projected sexuality and virility. He was always a man's man and a woman's man as well.

Wayne's well-known conservative political views caused many liberal critics to deny his acting ability and made critics of some who otherwise enjoyed his brand of film escapism. Presumably, knowledge of his atti

ing that occasionally it made him feel like an imposter to use the name Wayne.

Clyde Morrison worked as a pharmacist in several Iowa towns, but most of Marion's younger years were spent in Winterset. Winterset had a formidable impact on his development, for it resembled the kind of country Frederick Jackson Turner experienced fifty years earlier; its graybeards were veterans of the Civil War (Union side), Indian difficulties, and scraps with Jesse James. From his parents he learned that domestic life could be stormy—they divorced before he became an adult—but also something about values. Young Morrison loved both parents, their disagreements tormented him, and they perhaps contributed to his own marital difficulties later. Clyde Morrison gave his son a personal philosophy that is directly connected to the unique development of the American frontier: keep your word, never insult someone unintentionally, and do not look for trouble but if it comes do not quit. This philosophy is so frequently quoted that the meaning is lost and seems more a caricature of his film image than a characteristic of his personal life. Except for the enigma in the second part, in which Clyde meant to teach his son that real gentlemen *never* insult anyone except purposely, it is just good nineteenth-century values translated to a personal code, and is a convenient way to teach a truth about truth. Interestingly, this is the same philosophy that Wayne, as the aged gunman J. B. Book, passed on to young Ronnie Howard in Wayne's last movie *The Shootist*. In that role, Book became Clyde Morrison.

Clyde Morrison developed a pulmonary health problem, and on medical advice moved his family in 1917 to a desert farm near Palmdale, California. There Marion learned horsemanship and marksmanship by riding the crop middles as his father worked, ready to shoot snakes and rabbits. The killing was disagreeable, but Marion persevered. From these experiences, he learned that a person could get through a thing if he kept on trying, no matter how afraid he became. His long travail in B Westerns and serials would put such lessons to severe tests. He also learned, one biographer claimed, that a person could get the snakes but he could never get all the rabbits. To discern that some things are beyond oneself is ultimately to be satisfied with reality.

Clyde Morrison farmed only two years, moved his family to Glendale to return to work in a pharmacy, and so Marion transferred to the Glendale schools, where he was graduated in 1925. He gave a good account of himself as a student, dressed well, and developed further his liking for football, which his father encouraged. He made deliveries for the various pharmacies where his father worked and delivered newspapers and handbills for a local theatre. The latter enterprise helped lead to his interest in movies. The industry was by then well established in southern California, especially in the Los Angeles area, and he could visit the locations and witness the filming process as well as see the finished products. During this time he acquired his lifelong nickname—Duke—from local firemen. He frequently visited their station house with a dog named Duke, and he became Big Duke to the men.

Following graduation from Glendale High School, Marion enrolled at the University of Southern California on a football scholarship. His father, and perhaps Marion as well, thought of Annapolis and a naval career, but Marion failed to secure a full appointment, so the scholarship and USC became a way to go to college. Marion remained there only two years, played football, joined Sigma Chi (a lifelong affiliation), and worked summers in the prop department at Fox Studios. Marion's coach, Howard Jones, arranged the job through Tom Mix, Fox's leading Western star. Marion felt some early disappointment with the work because he thought he would be Mix's athletic trainer. But he worked anyway, and the experience proved fortunate when he met John Ford at Fox Studios in 1926. They eventually became close friends, although their movie collaboration did not begin until the late 1930s.

Morrison got into a few silent films in the late 1920s, although mostly by accident. Sometimes his duties as prop man brought him into camera range, and unskilled or uncaring editing left his image in the pictures. Sometimes Ford deliberately cast Morrison in crowd scenes or walk-on roles which required little acting skill. In *Hangman's House* (1928), for example, Morrison simply stood before a judge to receive a sentence. He did not seem to manifest much interest in an acting career then. He worked steadily at his prop job to earn money to get married, and gained a lifelong appreciation for the role these professionals played in the making of pictures. Later, when he doubled for the actors in scenes of danger, he broadened this appreciation to include stunt men and women. Even at the height of his acting career, Wayne shared off-camera time with technical personnel, as well as with his co-stars. This appreciation resulted partly from his interest in learning every aspect of the business which grew into a desire to produce pictures instead of just acting in them, and partly from his having done the work himself and understanding its contribution to the product.

Morrison's football career at USC ended in 1927 because of an injury to his shoulder in a surfing accident. His urge to work full-time gained momentum as his courtship of Josephine Saenz, daughter of a Los Angeles businessman, progressed to a desire for marriage.

The summer of 1929 director Raoul Walsh saw Morrison working shirtless on a movie lot and asked Edward Goulding who he was. Walsh was having difficulty casting the part of a scout, the lead in a film called *The Big Trail* (1930) about a wagon train and the problems immigrants experienced. The film was revolutionary in several respects: It was among the early "talkies," and it would be filmed in 70mm, which required new cameras and projection equipment.

Walsh had already lined up established stage actors for most of the parts, following the pattern of early sound movies in casting actors who could speak lines convincingly. He had wanted Gary Cooper or another well-known actor to portray the scout, but had been unable to obtain a star for various reasons. Because the picture was ready to start, Walsh needed someone quickly. He saw Morrison's lean physique and boyish features, and decided to give him a screen test. With little time to prepare, and feeling the disdain of the professionals who were to be in the test scene with him, Morrison appeared flustered at first. Then temper appeared. He started hammering the actors with questions in the way they had been interrogating him, with the same angered contempt, and this time they became frustrated because their prepared lines did not accommodate his questions. Walsh liked what he saw and signed Morrison to a Fox contract and assigned him the lead in *The Big Trail*.

When the film finally appeared with Morrison in his first starring role, he had a new name: John Wayne. Walsh refused to use Morrison's real name, and after a while he and Goulding came up with John Wayne, borrowing some of it from General Anthony Wayne and settling on "John" because it seemed "American."

Morrison accepted the change grudgingly, but he was now making $75 a week, so he continued to use the name. He did his own stunts in the film, and acquired a knife-throwing skill the part required. After filming ended he was dispatched on a promotional tour in the East and forced to wear an elaborate costume. Such phoniness disgusted him, and he broke off the tour before its scheduled end. Then the film was released. Wayne's performance was adequate if amateurish, but the film proved a financial failure and a liability to him for several years.

Over the next decade, producers never seemed to forget the losses *The Big Trail* suffered, and refused to hire Wayne. Fox did cast him in a quick money-maker *Girls Demand Excitement* (1931), a basketball film, then dropped him. He signed then with Harry Cohn at Columbia Studios, but that association also ended when Cohn became jealous of Wayne's supposed attentions to a girl in whom Cohn was interested. He locked Wayne out of the studio, and later dropped his contract in 1932.

Unable to find work and feeling desperate because he could not marry Josephine Saenz until he could support her, Wayne contacted agent Al Kingston. Kingston introduced Wayne to Nat Levine at Mascot Films, a Poverty Row film maker of serials and five-reel melodramas. Levine immediately cast Wayne in *Shadow of the Eagle* (1932), an aviation serial, cashing in on the popularity of the Lone Eagle, Charles A. Lindbergh. Indeed, in the early 1930s Wayne starred in several serial Westerns, which are essentially a long film divided into twelve parts, two reels each, plus a "trailer," or promotional reel. Each episode ends with the hero or heroine in peril, and the next begins with the explanation of their escape. This suspense continues until a conclusion is reached in the final reel. Shooting these films quickly and with few retakes, the crew and actors worked before cameras or waited for setups from dawn until dusk, using the predawn hours for makeup and preparation. Often the cast and crew remained on the set all night to await the next day's shooting. Although exhausting, this kind of work paid well for the Depression times, and from these experiences and other B Westerns that followed in the 1930s, Wayne learned much about his trade, and made many lifelong friendships. He moved from the Mascot serials to a contract to remake several Ken Maynard silent films for Sid Rogell at Monogram in 1933. While still living, Maynard was older and heavier than when he had made the originals. So, clad in costumes identical to Maynard's, Wayne remade sound portions to be interspliced with distant shots of Maynard in action. Although not the best work in films, this work finally brought him enough income to marry Josephine Saenz on June 24, 1933.

Wayne continued his work by making sixteen five-reel Westerns for Monogram from 1933 to 1935. Included among his roles was that of one of the earliest Singing Cowboys, "Singing Sandy" Saunders, a secret Treasury agent. The role called for guitar playing and singing, and as Wayne did neither to the director's satisfaction, these scenes were dubbed in. He quickly rejected such phoniness because he was expected to sing and play in personal appearances and could not do so.

In 1935 Wayne signed with Herbert B. Yates at Republic, beginning a long and sometimes rocky relationship. Still making B Westerns, he was at least working and supporting his growing family.

The Saturday matinee movies and serials Wayne filmed during the 1930s proved tiresome, grueling and unrewarding—except financially. While much of America hungered for a job, Wayne earned from $100 to $500 per week, and learned more about his trade. From Jack Padgin he learned western riding, movie style; he learned to throw a rope, handle a pistol, and how to look tough. From Enos Canutt he learned safer yet more daring ways to do his stunts. Wayne met Canutt on location in his first serial when they spent the night on the set in the open to avoid the long ride back to Los Angeles. That began a lifelong, mutual appreciation of each other's work; Canutt became the best-known stunt man in the business, often making more money than the stars he doubled for, and eventually achieved notice as a second-unit director, winning an Academy Award for the chariot race in *Ben Hur*. From Bob Bradbury, who directed many of Wayne's 1930s Westerns, he learned the pass system in movie fighting. Prior to the adoption of this technique, actors literally struck each other in fights, usually around the shoulders. The pass system, which incorporates camera angles, sound effects, and other gimmicks, enables actors to put full force into their punches, yet miss their colleague's chin by an inch.

But most of all these movies taught Wayne how to deliver expository speech. Even though they thrived on action, the films had to stop periodically to allow the actors to advance the story through dialogue exchanges that explained the action's purpose. Through these experiences, Wayne learned to give convincing statements of fact without self-conscious overtones. Later, in more ambitious films, he already knew what was taken for granted—how to speak easily before a camera. Throughout his life Wayne always experienced a bit of stage fright in front of a live audience, but long hours making B Westerns helped overcome camera shyness years before his next break in films came—The Stage to Lordsburg.

Before he caught that stagecoach, Wayne made a trail of Westerns, some shot in as few as four days, joining a long line of Western heroes that extended back to John Smith, continued in the careers of such folk heroes as Daniel Boone, Kit Carson, and David Crockett, and appeared on the screen as early as 1908 when Broncho Billy Anderson emerged from *The Great Train Robbery* to become the first movie cowboy. Later William Surrey Hart succeeded Anderson as the premier film Westerner and added realism to the role; real cowboys Tom Mix and Buck Jones joined Hart in the 1920s and became superstars of that era in cowboy movies, along with lesser actors such as Johnny Mack Brown, Bob Steele, Rocky Lane, and William Boyd, while Roy Rogers and Gene Autry finally developed the singing cowboy. During the 1930s, Wayne was there among them in single starring roles or joining with others as one of the Three Musketeers in the Republic series.

Then came the Stage to Lordsburg, John Ford, Monument Valley, and forty years of stardom. From 1940 until his death in 1979, he made nearly 100 films, 20 of which figure among the top grossing films in Hollywood's history; he appeared in the top ten box-office poll more consistently than any other individual after World War II, and his films finally achieved artistic acclaim, including an Academy Award in 1969 for his portrayal of Rooster Cogburn in *True Grit*. Not all of these films were good, and not all were Westerns. But over the years, Wayne so molded scripts and the direction and image they projected that by the late 1950s a film in which he appeared in a major role had made a commitment to its audience simply by his being cast in it. Less than half of his last 50 films were "Westerns," a story set between 1865 and 1890. Yet his best work was in classic Westerns, mostly directed by either Ford or Howard Hawks, and in a majority of the others he played a kind of Western American heroic character.

The road to this success began with John Ford and *Stagecoach* (1939). Ford purchased Ernest Haycox's story about a stage ride to Lordsburg, New Mexico, which was endangered by an Apache raid and threatened within by the conflicting personalities of the passengers. Ford had a screenplay drafted, probably to fit Wayne, but he had teased Wayne for years about the quickie Westerns in which the latter worked, so when he asked Wayne's advice on who should play the Ringo Kid, the central character, Wayne did not believe that Ford would ask him to play the role. So he suggested Lloyd Nolan. Later Ford told Wayne that the part was his. *Stagecoach* was shot in Monument Valley, the first film done there, and remains a film classic. In addition to Wayne, the cast included Thomas Mitchell, who won a supporting Academy Award for his role as drunken Doc Boone, along with Claire Trevor, Andy Devine, John Carradine, Louise Platt, George Bancroft, Benton Churchill, and Donald Meek. The film employed unique camera work, a memorable *agitato* for the scene of the stagecoach fleeing from the Indians, and marked the beginning of a remarkable partnership between director and actor. Together, Wayne and Ford made some of

John Wayne. *Archie P. McDonald*

America's best Western movies. Wayne for some time labored under the judgment that he was only good in Ford Westerns; upon reflection, however, it is obvious that Ford's best Westerns, indeed his best films after 1939, starred John Wayne. Each complemented the other's best efforts, based largely on mutual trust and friendship.

Another major factor of this relationship was the large cast of characters appearing so frequently in Ford's films that they were sometimes called the John Ford Stock Company, and later they appeared in Wayne's own productions. The list included, among others, Ward Bond, Victor McLaglen, Jack Pennick, Hank Worden, Paul Fix, John Qualen, and Grant Withers. It would be difficult to distinguish between the Ford and Wayne groups because so many actors were in both, and one succeeded the other. These actors became, and for the most part remained, lifelong friends. They respected each other's professionalism, they liked each other's company, and they were able to merge social and working relationships. Wayne already understood the value of friendship and loyalty before he met Ford, but the latter reinforced those feelings because he too expressed them. Following Ford's traditions, Wayne continued to employ many of these cronies when he produced his films at Republic and later for his company, Batjac. And he became attached to some of his leading ladies. Maureen O'Hara, for example, made three films with him and became extremely close; in the early 1940s, he also enjoyed a celebrated friendship with Marlene Dietrich. But O'Hara remained his most consistent actress-friend.

Despite the success of *Stagecoach*, Wayne was still under contract to Yates at Republic, and Yates exploited Wayne's new popularity outside the matinee set with a burst of melodrama. Wayne made eleven pictures in three years, some working off the Republic contract, some with Ford, such as *The Long Voyage Home* (1940), and some with Randolph Scott and Marlene Dietrich. Only the Republic features were Westerns.

Then came World War II. Because of the shoulder he had injured in 1926, his age, and the fact that he was the father of four children, Wayne did not serve on active duty in the war. This circumstance was something of an embarrassment in later years, but immediately his career was helped by his continuing to make films. When stars left for the service, lesser-known actors were left to play major roles. And there was a big demand for heavy action war movies. Wayne was available, so he began to play a different kind of Western hero, one who fought America's current enemies instead of Indians, and from airplanes and landing craft instead of on horseback. Wayne became the consummate war movie actor, much associated with the Marines even as he was associated with the Cavalry in period Westerns. His role as Sergeant Stryker in *Sands of Iwo Jima* earned him an Academy Award nomination in 1949. And he also became a producer. Yates permitted him to produce films at Republic to hold him, but afterwards Wayne and Robert Fellows founded an independent production company. He was one of the first actors to do so. Later, Wayne ran Batjac with the aid of his family. Although most of the company's productions starred Wayne, Batjac also produced films in which he did not appear.

In the late 1940s, the modern image of Wayne as a Westerner surfaced again when he returned to making films such as *Red River* (1948), *Fort Apache* (1948), *Three Godfathers* (1948), and *She Wore a Yellow Ribbon* (1949). Unlike his Westerns of the early 1930s, these films enjoyed top-level direction and technical support. It is this image that has inspired hundreds of magazine pieces, cartoons, impersonations by Rich Little and others, and in his last year a commemorative gold medal authorized by the United States Congress. This image is the John Wayne who won, that endeared him to people from all walks of life, in short, that made him an authentic folk hero. It is the image of Kirby York in *Fort Apache*, Tom Dunson in *Red River*, Nathan Brittles in *She Wore a Yellow Ribbon*, Ethan Edwards in *The Searchers* (1956), Rooster Cogburn in *True Grit* (1969), and finally J. B. Book in *The Shootist* (1976). It is the driven fanatic, unyielding but with a soft heart; the hardhanded man who quests for a grail of truth, the real man with human appetites and even weaknesses. Wayne's roles are of individuals who are resourceful, who believe in work, in right, and in winning.

In *Three Godfathers*, Wayne, Pedro Armendariz, and Harry Carey, Jr., rob a New Mexico community and flee into the desert. As they are pursued by the sheriff (Ward Bond), they come upon a wagon. The owner had left for help and was killed by Indians, and his wife was in the process of giving birth to their son. She died shortly after delivery, but her deathbed wish was for the three outlaws to assume responsibility for the child. These "Three Wise Men" are thus a part of a Ford version of the Nativity. Carey and Armendariz died in the process of taking the child to civilization, and Wayne's character, Bob Slaughter, barely survived the ordeal of bringing the child to "Jerusalem," New

Mexico, where he is captured and sentenced to prison. The act of saving the baby gained him sympathy, friendship with the sheriff, and the promise of a better life.

*Fort Apache* and *She Wore a Yellow Ribbon* are the major works of Ford and Wayne's trilogy on the U.S. Cavalry. *Rio Grande* (1950) completed the set, but is less important than the other two films. *Fort Apache* is a kind of George A. Custer story, with Henry Fonda playing Colonel Owen Thursday, commander of a regiment at a duty station in Apache country he considered beneath him. Wayne's character, Capt. Kirby York, is considerably wiser in the ways of the West, particularly in dealing with the Indian chief Cochise, but his advice is disregarded in Thursday's quest for a victory that will rescue him from the frontier and gain reassignment in the East. Thursday dreams of being known as the man who captured Cochise. In a clash of wills, Thursday ordered York's arrest for failing to cooperate in a scheme to trick Cochise, to whom the latter had given his word. "Your word, Mister, means nothing to a savage," Thursday ordered. "It does to me," was York's response. In the battle which followed, Thursday was slain while York survived in arrest at the rear of the action, and later he commanded the regiment. In a concluding scene, York held a conference with eastern reporters—similar to the conclusion of *Liberty Valance*—in which for the good of the regiment he paints Thursday's action as heroic.

In *She Wore a Yellow Ribbon*, the second of the Ford trilogy films, Wayne portrayed Captain Nathan Brittles. Principal characters are the colonel played by George O'Brien, Sergeant Quincannon played by Victor McLaglen, and Corporal Tyree played by Ben Johnson. Brittles had come to the end of a military career which had already won for him a Congressional Medal of Honor, but was faced with failure on his last patrol because of Indian difficulties. In the climax of the film, he disobeyed orders to engineer a successful end to the trouble, then is rewarded by a permanent appointment as Chief of Scouts.

*Red River* was director Howard Hawks's first Western, and was one of Wayne's best films. With the possible exception of his Ethan Edwards's character in *The Searchers*, it remains the best example of his driven hero role. The film begins with Tom Dunson's departure from a wagon train headed for California in the 1850s. Instead he turned south for Texas, accompanied by Groot (Walter Brennan) and he later picked up Matthew Garth (Montgomery Clift) after the wagon train was attacked by Indians. Together the three established the Red River Ranch in the south Texas bush country after taking the land from its Mexican owner. They prospered until the Civil War when Matthew left

John Wayne. *Archie P. McDonald*

for military service. During the Reconstruction period, there were plenty of cows but no money, so Dunson started to trail the herd to Sedalia, Missouri. Indian problems, desertions, and endless trailing turned Dunson into a hard man. He had pledged all the men to complete the drive, and killed several who tried to desert. He refused to accept evidence that a railroad terminal could be reached at Abilene, Kansas, so Garth seized control of the drive to prevent the deaths of additional cowboys, and gambled that the railroad would really be available at Abilene. Dunson pursued them, and in a final scene the two fight in the street until Tess Millay (Joanne Dru) forces them to stop. The two are reconciled, and sitting in the dusty street, a softened Dunson made Garth a full partner in the ranch.

In these strong characterizations, whether as Bob Slaughter, Kirby York, Nathan Brittles, or Tom Dunson, Wayne permanently established himself as the iron-willed, successful survivor. This obsessed hero role continued through his performance as Rooster Cogburn in *True Grit.*

This John Wayne image grew larger than life in the last three decades of his career, but its original first vestiges appeared in the B Westerns of the 1930s. Even then, Wayne attempted to give the ticket buyer his money's worth by presenting the cowboy, or Westerner, with realism and virility. As soon as possible, he spurned gaudy costumes and wore dusty, even frayed, jeans and shirts, and kerchiefs, as in the role of Ringo in *Stagecoach*. He traded the white-hat trademark of the "Good Guy" for the more practical, darker hat that real men wore. His screen fights included tactics avoided by fancier cowboys such as Roy Rogers, who rarely if ever lost his white hat in a brawl, and who always fought with *fairness* regardless of what unfair tactics were used against him. Wayne believed that such manners were unrealistic. If he were hit with a chair in a saloon fight, he threw a table at his opponent, since real fighting is always done in anger and its goal is survival.

As Wayne's postwar career developed, such activities continued. In *The Man Who Shot Liberty Valance* (1962), he shot a man from ambush. And except for *Stagecoach*, there were few main-street showdowns. When possible, he used a rifle or shotgun, which were more effective and devastating weapons. He rarely attempted to give the appearance that he had a lightning-like draw with a pistol, even when he used one, but rather worked to show that cunning or grit could avoid shooting by guile or intimidation. In *Tall in the Saddle* (1944), he cooled an adversary by simply stating "Touch that gun and I'll kill you." The villain's hesitation earned him a blow on the head from Wayne's weapon rather than a bullet. And when a female bystander exclaimed "Why, you hit him!" he grimly replied, "Yes, ma'am, just as hard as I could."

In the latter part of his career, Wayne's costuming became more a personal expression and less concerned with authenticity. Trademarks appeared: the battered campaign hat, the Winchester from *Stagecoach* with the large ring level, the buttoned panel shirt, the belt buckle with the Red River D Brand, and the Vietnamese bracelet that appeared during the southeastern Asian war, even for such Westerns as *Cahill*. His boots were rarely shined, his shirts fit loosely, his belt strained a bit with increasing weight. But the image strengthened, and the quality of sincerity intensified that Ford had recognized during the 1930s. At the end it did not matter that his continuing survivals or countless scrapes defied credibility. Everyone knew that John Wayne survived.

Because the Wayne image included survival and winning, most commentators on his movie *The Cowboys* (1972) express wonder that he permitted his character, Wil Andersen, to die with thirty minutes remaining in the picture. Many critics argued that he had never before

John Wayne. *Archie P. McDonald*

died on film. They had forgotten Sergeant Stryker in *Sands of Iwo Jima* (1949) and his role in *Wake of the Red Witch* (1948). Perhaps they were talking only of Westerns, where he seemed always to prevail. But even in *Red River*, he lost the herd. The difference is, possibly, that in that role his stern character softened at the end of the film. Even in his meanness in the middle part of the picture, the viewer could identify with his motives if not his methods, could see humanity in his characterizations. Wayne might have changed the story and survived Bruce Dern's beating in *The Cowboys*, as he had changed other stories to stress survival and winning, but he would have changed the story, and the story emphasized passing on wisdom to a younger generation. That is a key to appreciating Wayne's later Westerns. *The Alamo* (1960), *The Cowboys* (1972), *Cahill* (1973), *Comancheros* (1961), *True Grit* (1969), *Sons of Katie Elder* (1965), *Big Jake* (1971), and, above all, *The Shootist*, show him in the company of younger people who learn from his experiences.

*The Shootist* demonstrates this well and it was his last picture. In this film, Wayne portrayed J. B. Book, an aged Western gunfighter dying of cancer. In the opening sequences, by the use of clips in black and white from several previous Western films, Book is clearly John Wayne. Then the film shifts to a panoramic scene in which a distant rider slowly approaches the camera's foreground, and an older Wayne/ Book appears. A visit to a doctor confirms that he is dying of cancer. He is out of place at his dying, and although he prepares for an orderly and dignified death, his last days are spent where old enemies and new challengers abound. He determines to let them kill him, to cheat the slower death, and to settle old scores. Preparing for the final shoot-out, he takes on the task of straightening out a youth and passes on the wisdom of his years. He teaches the boy, played by Ronnie Howard, to shoot a gun, chides him for drinking whiskey, and gives him a personal philosophy: "I won't be lied to and I won't be laid a hand on; I don't do these things to other people, and I won't have them do them to me." Book and Wayne are mutually conscious of the role of "passing it on," of striking a blow against what is wrong in the world. So in the end, he reacts characteristically: Book/Wayne kills the three who tried to kill him and then is shot in the back by a sneak he could not fight.

No one realized that *The Shootist* was to be Wayne's last movie, but that film did become an ironic conclusion to his life in motion pictures, especially as a Western star. His death on June 13, 1979, from physical weakness which lingered following open heart surgery the previous year and a reoccurrence of cancer, ended a career and an era. For many filmgoers, critics as well as hero-worshipers, he had come to personify the Western film in both fault and virtue. His films were violent, sometimes excessively so, but they did not dwell on violence for its own sake; his victims rarely spurted blood at the camera. And usually there was some point to the violence, some context which made it appropriate or even humorous. In *The Sons of Katie Elder* (1965), he struck George Kennedy in the face with an axe handle, and the scene invariably moved audiences to groans and chuckles rather than horror.

Wayne disdained open and obvious sex in his films, claiming in an interview in *Playboy* magazine that films employing such explicit scenes denied the audience the greatest gift of movies—illusion. Yet his characters, even in advancing age, projected sexuality and virility. He was always a man's man and a woman's man as well.

Wayne's well-known conservative political views caused many liberal critics to deny his acting ability, and made critics of some who otherwise enjoyed his brand of film escapism. Presumably, knowledge of his attitudes made some conservatives respect him all the more. By whatever means he came to his image, Wayne personified for both sides the spirit of the closing frontier. Born in the American West just as the nation's frontier experience ended, he seemed to carry the frontier spirit on in an alien world of metropolis. So, at the end, millions worried about him and prayed for him during the final illness. His attitudes and statements were reviewed on national news programs. His passing was noted by world political leaders, as well as by fellow actors. Some remembered him as uncompromising, prejudiced, fearless, opinionated, and suspicious of liberals and modern ideas; others saw his life and career in more attractive ways, calling him gentle, compassionate, a good friend, tolerant, intelligent, and patriotic. By 1979, he had become a blend of so many qualities as to deny accurate labeling; his life and career were so intertwined as to become inseparable.

In *Liberty Valance*, John Ford had a character say that when the legend became fact, print the legend. At that time, Wayne had already become a legend.

BIBLIOGRAPHIC ESSAY

No first-rate biography of Wayne exists, but the following studies offer some insight into his career: Maurice Zolotow, *Shooting Star* (New York: Simon and Schuster, 1974); George Carpozi, *The John Wayne Story* (New Rochelle, N.Y.: Arlington House, 1972); Jean Ramer, *Duke: The Real Story of John Wayne* (New York: Award Books, 1973); and Mike Tomkies, *Duke: The Story of John Wayne* (New York: Avon, 1971).

Filmographies featuring photos and plot lines of Wayne's films include Alan G. Barbour, *John Wayne* (New York: Pyramid, 1974); Mark Ricci, Boris Zmijewsky, and Steve Zmijewsky, *The Films of John Wayne* (Secaucus, N.J.: Citadel, 1970); and Allen Eyles, *John Wayne and The Movies* (New York: Grosset & Dunlap, 1976).

Film histories and analyses of Westerns that feature Wayne include Jon Tuska, *The Filming of the West* (Garden City, N.Y.: Doubleday, 1976); George N. Fenin and William K. Everson, *The Western: From Silents to the Seventies* (New York: Penguin, 1973); and John Lenihan, *Showdown: Confronting Modern America In the Western Film* (Urbana: University of Illinois Press, 1980).

This essay originally appeared in *The Journal of the West*, XXII, 4 (October 1983), 53–63. Copyright 1983 by The Journal of the West, Inc., 1531 Yuma, Manhattan, Kansas 66502; reprinted with permission.

DON B. GRAHAM

# Audie Murphy:
# Kid With a Gun

Out of the greatest mass warfare in history, one American emerged as the archetype of the common soldier. Audie Murphy was the Sergeant York of World War II. Like York, Murphy expressed something essential about American mythology. The anonymous dogface soldier had to be personalized, turned into the cult of the individual, and Murphy, through no action other than incredible heroism and luck, was the chosen vessel. The buildup climaxed with the famous *Life* cover of July 16, 1945. There, on the front of America's most popular magazine, was the American soldier as barefoot-boy-with-cheeks-of-tan, smiling, his chest laden with medals.

Murphy was an adman's dream. The son of a destitute share-cropper family, he personified the Horatio Alger story of rise from obscurity to fame and fortune. He was wholesome, handsome, and modest. He looked like the boy who delivered the newspaper in a Norman Rockwell drawing. He was also a Texan, a fact of some importance. A poll taken in 1940 showed that the three words with the most box-office appeal were Texas, Brooklyn, and Heaven.[1] The American hero could not be from Brooklyn because that would give him too much of an ethnic flavor; he obviously could not be from heaven; that left Texas, which suggested frontier values, the Alamo, and a bigger-than-life aura. Murphy had two other appealing qualities: he was not a 6-foot 2-inch Texan in the stereotypical mode—he was a pint-sized 5-foot 8-inches or thereabouts and he was Irish, which meant he was a scrapper. It was a potent combination, and yet there was nothing inevitable about Murphy's success after the war. He could have chosen Sergeant York's way and retired to quiet obscurity. Instead he chose to become a highly visible figure. He did not capitalize directly on his military career and refused to allow his studio, Universal-International, to exploit his war record in promoting his films. Yet as long as he remained before the public, that record was an inescapable dimension of his appeal.

Murphy spoke softly, he was mild-mannered and polite, but there was something menacing about him, too. He was no one to trifle with. He had a pouty look and the fastest hands in Hollywood. Mothers wanted to mother him, girls said he was the kid brother they never had, and men respected his calm, cool professionalism. He rode the lonely cinematic terrain of the West from 1950 to 1969 when most of the others had died or retired or gone on to megastardom. Gary Cooper died in 1961, Randolph Scott retired in 1962, television was in the saddle, the only new star on the horizon was Clint Eastwood, and among the old giants only John Wayne kept making Westerns on a regular basis. But Wayne made A Westerns; he had not made a true B Western since 1939. That left only Audie Murphy to carry on the tradition, and he did so right up until his death in an airplane crash in 1971. The last of the B stars held a realistic view of his position: "I guess all those Westerns on television killed the market. I seem to be the only one left. I'll keep on making them until they get wise to me."² Murphy *was* the postwar Western star as much as Cooper, Scott, Wayne, or anyone else.

The beginning of Murphy's film career was itself the stuff of movie legend. When James Cagney saw the Irish kid's face on the cover of *Life*, he invited him to Hollywood. He went, and despite diffidence about pursuing an acting career, he stuck around long enough to get a small part in *Beyond Glory* (1948), a West Point story starring Alan Ladd. This was the first of many ironies in Murphy's career. During the war his combat exploits earned him a chance undreamed of for a sharecropper's son, to enter West Point, but when he received a third wound that resulted in a 50 percent disability, he became ineligible. Thus he became a cadet only in the fantasy life of films.

James Cagney thought he saw something special in the young war hero: "I saw in Audie poise and assurance without aggressiveness. You might call it a spiritual overtone, a quality that we could certainly use in Hollywood."³ Hollywood must have seen something different. When Murphy got his first starring role, as a juvenile delinquent in *Bad Boy*

(1949), the part called for the exact opposite of that spiritual quality that Cagney glimpsed in him. Murphy played a "teen-age, trigger-happy, baby-faced thug."[4] Said one reviewer: "Only the boyish appeal of Audie Murphy keeps the character of the boy from becoming completely unsympathetic, for a more oily and unregenerate young felon never existed."[5] He received a prophetic notice in *Variety*: "He has an ingratiating personality and some latent thespic ability that should register with the younger set of filmgoers. With continued experience and good roles, he has possibilities."[6]

The chance to develop into a star with a solid career came in 1950 with a long-term contract at Universal-International. Studio executives pegged Murphy as a natural action player, and the principal action genre was the Western. Murphy's lifelong involvement with the shoot-'em-ups began with *The Kid from Texas* (1950). Murphy played in forty-four movies in all. Three were bit parts; four were war movies, including Universal-International's top grossing film of all time, *To Hell and Back* (1955), which Murphy called "a Western with uniforms";[7] one was a lame thriller (*Trunk to Cairo*, 1965); one was a boxing story (*The World in My Corner*, 1956); and two were set in the Orient (*The Quiet American*, 1958, and *Joe Butterfly*, 1957). The rest were Westerns. He played in thirty-three Westerns and starred in thirty of them. For nearly twenty years, as the trade reviews steadily reported, Audie Murphy was a guaranteed drawing card in the "outdoor pic" category. At the height of his success in 1956 he was an "equally fast draw with the guns and at the box office."[8] Murphy's climb to the top was confirmed by two prizes. In 1955 U.S. exhibitors named him the year's most popular Western Star, and in 1957 he was voted the top Western Star in England.[9]

There are misconceptions about Murphy's Western career. One is that he could not act. Murphy himself contributed to this impression more than once. He had a natural sense of humor and a gift for one-liners, and many of his most quoted remarks denigrated his Western roles. Newspapers liked to quote his quip about low-budget Westerns: "The plot in them is always the same, only the horse and the girl change."[10] He made similar remarks on other occasions: "The studio gave me a change of horses but not a change in stories" and "All I am required to do is ride a horse, shoot straight, and look somber."[11] In putting down both his own acting and the genre with which he was identified, Murphy was behaving no differently from the mass of reviewers, moviemakers, and audiences of the day. Westerns were regarded as an embarrassment to the American movie industry. They were steady earners but held no prestige value.

In the early fifties, before the widespread dissemination of film criticism, especially European appreciations of the Western, the condescension was apparent everywhere. John Ford was revered for his literary films such as *The Informer* and *The Grapes of Wrath*, not for his Westerns. Years later when Ford announced to Peter Bogdanovich, "My name's John Ford. I make Westerns," the statement was startling.[12] It is no wonder, then, that Audie Murphy said discouraging words about Westerns. News from France that the Western was America's epic had not reached Hunt County, Texas, in the late 1940s. Coming from where he did, a rural background in which the movies were a popular form of escapism, Murphy felt that the Western was simply an entertainment, a shoot-'em-up pure and simple. Westerns, he said, were "something the kids go for."[13]

Murphy undervalued film acting. Certainly he undervalued his own work. He told a reporter in 1956, "Somehow I don't think I'd ever find complete satisfaction in life being just an actor."[14] Yet he also respected good film acting and wished to be regarded as a professional. On the set of *The Red Badge of Courage* (1951) he talked about his chosen career: "Certain people said I cashed in on my record when I went to Hollywood. I just would like to continue in the movies long enough to make those people think I wasn't just using pictures as a soft touch."[15]

Murphy's ambivalence about film acting has its corollary in audience attitudes about motion pictures today. According to a widespread view, a star such as Robert DeNiro, for example, is an *actor*, while Clint Eastwood is a personality, an icon, but not somehow an actor. DeNiro vanishes into whatever role he plays, while Eastwood is always Eastwood, just as Wayne was Wayne, Cooper was Cooper, and Audie Murphy was Audie Murphy. A reviewer said as much in 1964 while writing of Murphy's performance in *The Quick Gun*: "With every film he makes Audie Murphy wraps closer and closer around himself the mantle he has inherited from Gary Cooper and Randolph Scott, that of the supreme non-actor which symbolizes, as far as Hollywood is concerned, the strong silent type who inhabited the Old West."[16]

"Supreme non-actors" are made, not born. Murphy had to learn technique. *Restraint* and *underplaying* are recurrent terms in reviews of Murphy's film roles. Like Cooper, Wayne, Scott, and Eastwood, Murphy tended to "re-act instead of act," as Wayne once put it.[17] Eastwood admitted that he deliberately underplayed his character of the Man-With-No-Name in the Sergio Leone trilogy of spaghetti Westerns that made him into an international star. He had to underplay in order to make any impression upon what he termed the "hellzapoppin" school of Italian film acting.[18]

What Murphy had to do as an actor was to become comfortable in the parts for which he seemed naturally cast—an action star who said little and said that laconically—but such roles require intelligence, skill, and dedication. Had Murphy not worked hard and studied his craft he would not have lasted and would not have become the sturdy, reliable star and box-office draw that he did become.[19]

Murphy probably suffered from the Steve McQueen syndrome in that he underrated the value of the action-performer. McQueen, a great action-star, fell under the spell of high culture and wanted to make himself into an "actor" late in his life. Thus he spent several years trying to promote a film that he insisted on making and starring in, Ibsen's talky, third-rate play, *An Enemy of the People*. Murphy did not go so far astray from his natural talents, but he also failed to appreciate his own best work in Westerns. His favorite movie and favorite role, one for which he received excellent reviews, was the Civil War film *The Red Badge of Courage* (1951). This was a typical John Huston "literary" film that followed the novel reverentially. A commercial disaster, it still has a following among Audie Murphy fans and cinema devotees, the only one of his works that appeals to both these groups. With a few exceptions, Murphy's ventures outside the Western did not yield glowing reviews. In such departures as *The Quiet American* (1958) he was thought by some to be out of his league in playing opposite such polished actors as Michael Redgrave.[20] In any event Murphy always came back to the Western. After he began making Westerns in 1950, only once in his career did he make two non-Westerns in a row (*The Quiet American*, 1958, and *The Gun Runners*, 1959).

Murphy earned an enviable record of favorable reviews. His standing in the trade magazines that monitored films and actors closely showed a steady growth and uniformity of opinion regarding his developing acting skills. In his first Western he received mixed reviews. Four rated his performance in *The Kid from Texas* solid, but two said he had still to learn the craft of acting.[21] According to one reviewer, "Rome wasn't built in a day, and merely saying Audie is an actor doesn't make him one."[22] After his next Western, *Kansas Raiders* (1950), reviews were again mixed. One felt that he "seems to have still a way to go before reaching starring caliber,"[23] but another praised his "brilliant and convincing performance as the young Jesse James."[24]

National publications began to recognize Murphy's abilities as early as 1952. *Newsweek* said of *The Duel at Silver Creek*: "It also has Audie Murphy, who has long since demonstrated that he can act as well as go to war."[25] According to numerous reviewers, Murphy kept getting better. *Tumbleweed* (1953) was "for the ever-improving Audie Murphy . . . his best performance yet."[26] Murphy was thus receiving the kind of acceptance the "supreme non-actor" must, that of appearing natural and tailored to a particular role or genre. In *Ride Clear of Diablo* (1954) Murphy's performance convinced one reviewer to conclude that "it is very difficult for Murphy to appear unnatural in anything he does, whether it be first-class motion pictures like 'Red Badge of Courage' or the present routine job."[27] By now, phrases such as "another solid performance" had become familiar judgments in the trade magazines.[28]

Perhaps the best proof of Murphy's acceptance as a star is that he won excellent reviews for his role in *Destry* (1955), a remake of a Jimmy Stewart classic, *Destry Rides Again* (1939). One reviewer pronounced Murphy's work "a most capable job" and said that he "has been improving steadily."[29] Other reviews compared him with Stewart. One thought that Murphy "probably better fits the original Brand conception than his predecessors" and that he performed "exceptionally well."[30] Another praised the suitability of Murphy for the character of Destry: "In picking Audie Murphy for the Jimmy Stewart role, Rubin made an amazingly apt bit of casting." The review concluded, "As an actor, the young fellow seems to have come into his own."[31]

In the 1960s, when the quality of his Westerns is thought to have declined, Murphy still drew admiration for his performances. A poor vehicle such as *Gunfight at Comanche Creek* (1963) was "tailor-made," said one review, "to satisfy the tastes of the Audy Murphy branch of the International Society of Western Film Addicts."[32] In *Arizona Raiders* (1965), one of the superior Murphy Westerns of this era, he earned high marks also: "Audie Murphy is the star not only in billing but by right of his sincerely studied performance. He cuts a heroic figure."[33] Near the end of his career he had become something of an institution. In a retrospective look across the years, a reviewer said of *Gunpoint* (1966): "Despite the dozens of Westerns he has starred in, and the thousands of dusty miles he has traveled on horseback, Audie Murphy still looks good in the saddle."[34]

Murphy's last Western was a final, if rarely seen, testimony to his

A dramatic moment in *The Guns of Fort Petticoat* (1957).
Murphy co-produced this film about a cavalry officer who
helps women learn to defend themselves from Indian attacks
while their husbands and kin are fighting in the Civil War.
*Don B. Graham*

professional abilities as an actor. In *A Time for Dying* (1969) Murphy
made a brief cameo appearance as Jesse James. When the film was
released after Murphy's death in 1971, Budd Boetticher, director and
co-producer with Murphy, spoke of the actor's last appearance and his
consistent underrating of a long career: "He was excellent even if he
didn't think of himself as much of an actor."[35]

Although Murphy belittled his roles in Westerns, his remarks are
far from a complete picture of his career. The facts suggest seriousness
of purpose and thoroughgoing professionalism. When Murphy tried to
produce films, as he did on at least two occasions, his choice each time
was a Western. In 1956 he joined producer Harry Joe Brown to make
*The Guns of Fort Petticoat*, a Western with an original twist to the plot.
Murphy played a Union officer who trains a group of pioneer women to

defend themselves against Indian attacks while their husbands and relatives are away fighting Yankees. Years later, in 1968, Murphy teamed up with Budd Boetticher in a multipicture deal reminiscent of the Boetticher-Brown series of seven films starring Randolph Scott from 1955 to 1960. Only one film was completed, *A Time for Dying* (1969), before Murphy's death ended what might have been a creative union of talents.[36] Both *A Time for Dying* and *The Guns of Fort Petticoat* convey a seriousness of purpose and intelligence of conception that suggest a sophisticated understanding of the Western genre. In Boetticher's view, Murphy was a "professional," who was intelligent and sophisticated.[37]

There were also occasions when Murphy talked seriously about the Western. In publicity material generated for *Arizona Raiders* (1965) Murphy tried to explain the Western's appeal. "Westerns," he said, "are nothing but American swashbucklers. They concern knights and crusaders, pirates and racketeers, except they are in a more familiar setting." He drew the familiar comparison between the Western outlaw hero and Robin Hood, and commented on the basic appeal of the outdoor setting: "The pressure of modern life in hustling, crowded communities is not a natural state for man. It's no wonder that he unconsciously harks back to his beginnings, when there were truly such places as open spaces." He concluded by speculating that "movie Westerns are doing an international job of getting families out into the fresh air and the sunlight."[38]

Murphy also gave considerable thought to the kind of hero he was asked to play in Westerns. He was of course preeminently qualified to talk about heroism, and his statements on the subject are worthy of attention. The nature of the Western hero bothered Murphy because, he wrote, "If a Western hero ever showed signs of fright he would be laughed off the screen, even though he comes up against a life and death matter. He can be tense—but not scared." The ironclad convention that kept the Western hero from showing fear made war movies more "honest" than Westerns, Murphy felt. He hoped in the future, he said, that the "adult" Western would mature enough to allow the Western hero to show fear, an emotion that was fundamental to the encounter with death.[39]

In none of Murphy's Westerns, though, was the hero ever allowed to do so. He tried to bring realism to his roles and succeeded in such areas as naturalness of movement, style of dress,[40] horsemanship—he was a skilled rider—and laconic humor. But the genre would not permit that emotional dimension that Murphy knew to be true in combat. In his own vivid account of his wartime experiences, recorded in *To Hell and Back* (1949), Murphy characterized bravery as compounded of two elements: fear and something like insanity. Neither was permissible in the Western hero; in fact both were attributes of lesser characters such as villains and cowards. Perhaps Murphy's disparaging remarks about his roles in Western movies grew out of his hard-earned knowledge of the true nature of combat and his awareness of the artificial and unrealistic requirements of the genre with the hero-who-never-shows-fear.

Murphy's entrance into films coincided with a number of postwar trends. One was a new generation of youthful-looking and diminutive stars. An acute reviewer spotted the similarity between Murphy and two other newcomers, Montgomery Clift and John Derek. Ruth Waterbury wrote, "They are all so different—Clift, the best actor, Derek the most devastating in appearance and now, Audie, the most warmly appealing."[41] Murphy's roles quickly placed him in the center of another trend, movies about young, misunderstood, often tragically doomed heroes. In *They Live By Night* (1948), Nicholas Ray's first film, Farley Granger depicted a young innocent trapped in a life of crime. John Derek played a similar character in another Ray film, *Knock on Any Door* (1949). Derek was a juvenile delinquent with a defiant motto: "Live fast, die young, and leave a good-looking corpse."[42] *Bad Boy* was Murphy's version of the role. Then came a string of Westerns with Murphy playing one kid after another. These kids were bad to a degree, and they were good as well. *Society* was the problem; each of these films was a popular study in environmentalism. The incongruity of the young war hero being cast as a social misfit, an outlaw, was not lost on the studio that did the casting. The publicity campaign that Universal-International used to promote Murphy for *Kansas Raiders* pointed this out in a list of suggestions on how to sell the film: "A story on the irony of the fact that Audie Murphy, an American war hero, has achieved film fame by playing dirty rascals like 'Bad Boy,' Billy the Kid in *The Kid from Texas*, and now Jesse James in *Kansas Raiders*."[43]

There were more dirty rascals to come. Murphy played the angry, antisocial son of an outlaw in *Sierra* (1950); an outlaw in *The Cimarron Kid* (1952); "a sort of Dead End kid on horseback" in *Gunsmoke* (1953);[44] and the cynical, humorous, and menacing brother of Jimmy Stewart in *Night Passage* (1957). His studio became sensitive about casting Murphy in such unsavory roles. When producer Paul Short received letters complaining about Murphy's playing a "meanie" role in *The Kid from Texas*, he responded with a roll call of stars such as Alan Ladd, James Cagney, and Edward G. Robinson who had launched their careers as bad guys and had gone on to play positive heroes.[45] The "bad boy" connection was also difficult for the studio to handle. A studio memo concerning promotional ploys for *The Kid from Texas* said that ads should be careful to indicate that "'Bad Boy' was a title of a motion picture and . . . not a descriptive phrase for Audie Murphy."[46]

The studio wanted to promote Murphy as an action star, not a romantic one. A Universal-International publicity man warned that the advance promotion for *The Kid from Texas* was poor because "a still of Audie Murphy looking at a girl certainly won't sell any tickets."[47] Such concerns, expressed repeatedly in studio correspondence, suggests the meticulous care with which Murphy's screen persona was monitored and nourished in the direction the studio wanted. His war record was a great temptation, and without Murphy's dogged resistance, it is easy to imagine that Universal-International would have exploited the military angle relentlessly. The publicity staff proved to be inventive in conjuring up military tie-ins, including, for *The Kid from Texas*, an Armistice Day photo-layout showing Murphy "in civilian clothes with American Flag and racked guns in background," "Audie hunting ducks—pointing up this is way he prefers to use guns," and "Audie at home in den with guns and keepsakes from Europe in background."[48]

They were dealing with a young man who had given away most of his medals and refused to let his war record be exploited. During the publicity campaign for *The Cimarron Kid* one executive wrote to another: "He is very touchy about being identified with veterans' organizations. We should stay completely away from any affair of this type, including making him an honorary member of any post or unit. The explanation is that he does not want in any way to trade on his war record."[49] Murphy's stand sometimes created tactical problems for Universal-International's publicity department. Scripting a radio interview plugging *The Kid from Texas*, a member of the studio's staff found himself stymied because "Murphy will not talk on either his war record or his personal life. And, without either one of these two ingredients the script would be very dull."[50] In this case there was a way round the difficulty. The writer was advised to bypass Murphy's objections and make his war record part of the announcer's commentary: "I am sure Mr. Murphy will never see nor know the prepared scripts as they finally go out to the radio stations."[51]

Murphy's youthfulness and his fame as a war hero were the chief ingredients of his early appeal in the movies. Moviegoers responded warmly to the young Murphy's persona at a preview screening of *The Kid from Texas*. Said one viewer: "Audie is good as the 'Kid'—but no one can surpass John Wayne as 'the man.' Audie is here to stay but he should have snatched a kiss somewhere." Another commented on his acting ability: "Audie Murphy is a great potential actor. At first I thought the movies were only cashing in on his fame as a war hero but he's OK for my dough." A third drew special attention to the combat skills that had made Murphy famous: "I thought Audie Murphy's ability to handle guns was extremely fascinating and thus I liked those scenes."[52]

Thematically the bad boy-kid roles displayed a fundamental ambivalence about the function and morality of violence in American society. Audie Murphy had done exactly what the Army demanded: He had become an expert killer. John Huston, Murphy's favorite director, called him a "gentle little killer."[53] In casting Murphy as an outlaw or misunderstood young killer, Universal-International played to postwar anxieties about returning veterans. While Westerns such as *She Wore a Yellow Ribbon* (1949) and *Red River* (1948), both with John Wayne, addressed the question of old leadership and the transition to a responsible new generation, Murphy's Westerns addressed such issues as the question of a socially trained killer trying to find a way to live without violence.[54] In *The Kid from Texas*, Billy the Kid never discovers a way out of the cycle of violence. When Billy's father figure, the kindly English rancher Jameson (based on the historical figure John Henry Tunstall), is slain, Billy straps on his guns, never to take them off again. Billy's death at the hands of Pat Garrett bothered both Murphy's fans and the Hays office, the board of censorship that reviewed movies for immoral content. In his review of the script, Joseph I. Breen cautioned the studio: "Please handle this death of Billy without any suggestion of a glorified suicide."[55] The studio claimed that it changed the original ending of *The Cimarron Kid*, which called for Murphy's death, in order to assuage the outrage of his many fans.[56]

Though fans may not have liked Murphy's dying in *The Kid from Texas*, such an ending was faithful to history and satisfied the demands of conventional morality. Such was decidedly not the case with *Kansas*

*Raiders* (1950), the most disturbing of the Kid Westerns that Murphy made early in his career. The sense of war is so strong in this Western that one reviewer called it a "war film."[57] It focuses on that segment of Jesse James's life during the American Civil War when he rode with William Quantrill's raiders. Jesse James, played by Murphy, brings a band of young men into Quantrill's camp and pledges their services to fight Yankees. The issue is clear to Jesse: "Some men need killing," especially the kind who maimed his mother, destroyed the family home, and killed his father. Quantrill offers revenge and glorious victories, but what Jesse learns is that Quantrill makes war against outnumbered and outgunned civilians, not Yankee soldiers. His "battles" are really massacres. Sickened by the slaying of innocent people, Jesse refuses to ride with Quantrill. Still, Jesse cannot leave Quantrill because he seems to be under the older man's spell. Played ably by Brian Donlevy, Quantrill is a charming, seductive father-figure. As a woman in the film points out, Quantrill has a "winning way with children." This emphasis on the youthfulness of Jesse and his gang is a constant refrain in the film, as it is in most of Murphy's early Westerns. References to kids, baby faces, and the like suggest that scripts were written to fit Murphy's astonishing youthfulness. Even in his early forties, he still drew comment about his youthful appearance.

This focuses on one of Murphy's central contributions to the Western: He was the principal star to play the kid role. The Western youth movement, as it might be called, affected the genre all during the 1950s. Nicholas Ray's *The True Story of Jesse James* (1957), starring Robert Wagner and Jeffrey Hunter, seems to have been influenced by the youthful Western outlaws played by Murphy and his supporting actors such as James Best and Tony Curtis. Murphy was in the vanguard of the troubled youth film that received its most popular treatment in contemporary sociological melodramas such as *Rebel Without a Cause, The Blackboard Jungle,* and *The Wild Ones.*

The young outlaw as a troubled adolescent invariably drew fire from the Hays office and raised questions in the minds of reviewers. Joseph I. Breen expressed concerns about *The Cimarron Kid* that were typical of letters from the Hays office during this period. Breen advised that the film should minimize "sympathizing with an outlaw," and worried about "featuring a religious medallion on a criminal such as Bitter Creek [James Best]."[58] To reviewers, the psychology of the young hero committed to lawlessness but somehow innocent, resulted in ambivalences of character motivation. This was especially true of

*Kansas Raiders.* One reviewer called Murphy's character "strangely indecisive for one who later became a notorious desperado."[59] Another pointed to the "difficult" job that the role required of Murphy "because the lad is torn between killing for revenge and horror of killing."[60] The juvenile delinquent hero reflected in the Western genre tried to address a modern concern in a frontier setting. The results were a series of disquieting outlaw Westerns, and America's greatest war hero played in the most unsettling of them.

As Murphy grew more comfortable in his Western roles, his films began to develop other kinds of heroes than the kid-outlaw types. Still, in Westerns such as *Tumbleweed* (1954), in which Murphy plays a wagon train scout, his youthfulness is an issue. He has to prove his abilities to skeptical older men, a situation rather like the one he faced with the reviewers. In his fifth Western, *The Duel at Silver Creek* (1952), for the first time Murphy played a character on the right side of the law. Cast as deputy to Stephen McNally's sheriff, Murphy still bore a sign of the socially unaligned type, because he played an orphan. Reviewers commented on another dimension in Murphy's persona in this film, a "laconic humor" that became of paramount importance in several future films.[61] In his next film, *Gunsmoke* (1953), he was praised for his "sardonic humor."[62] In this film Murphy was back on the wrong side of the law, playing an "assassin for hire," as one review put it.[63]

Murphy continued to work variations into the basic persona he was developing. He played good-guy parts in several Westerns in this period: dutiful son to a good father, *Drums Across the River* (1954); cavalry officer sympathetic to Indians, *Column South* (1953); saintly Indian agent John P. Clum, *Walk the Proud Land* (1956).[64] In each of these films Murphy the war hero found himself at odds with either his government, Army policy, or the official citizenry inhabiting Western towns. In his long career Murphy rarely played a completely "good" character. *The Gunfight at Comanche Creek* (1963) is a prime example. Here Murphy plays a heroic detective who takes on a dangerous undercover job. As usual his character is given a slightly seedy twist. An inveterate womanizer, he cavorts with a floozy in the opening scene. Such touches are both a part of the increasingly realistic coloration given to Western heroes in the 1960s and a recognition of the edgy, less than respectable, something that many directors saw in Murphy's style.

The Murphy persona developed shadings and precise articulations, but it always remained rooted in qualities that reviewers and the public recognized and valued. Always there was the intersection of on- and off-screen lives. Thus one reviewer said of *Posse From Hell* (1961): "Murphy, whose heroic exploits in real life made him ideally suitable for, and extra-believable in, super-heroic roles, does his usual commendably restrained job here."[65] Another noted the power of the biographical parallel in a review of *Hell Bent for Leather* (1959): "The entire film gains strength through the fact that audiences know Murphy really can perform the feats of marksmanship his role requires."[66] A Maryland theatre owner stated it best: "Everybody believes Audie. Another kid that young-looking, handling those guns and they wouldn't. But when Audie looks out of that smiling Irish face with those clear, calculating eyes, everybody believes him. I can see the show four times, and believe it every time, myself."[67] The overwhelming box-office success of *To Hell and Back* (1955) recalled for an older generation Murphy's war exploits and introduced him to a new generation of moviegoers. In 1955 Audie Murphy and Davy Crockett were the hottest cinematic heroes on American screens.

Over the years reviewers attempted to define the essence of the Murphy persona. His portrayal of the dedicated Indian agent in *Walk the Proud Land* seemed exactly right to one reviewer: "Murphy is probably one of the few actors who could successfully carry off this part. Although he is not a big man, he never implies weakness and the connotations of his name and career effectively underscore his determinedly mild behavior."[68] Another attempt to capture the Murphy persona appeared in a review of *Seven Ways From Sundown* (1960): "In this one Audie plays the type of character with which he is strongly identified—the shy and unassuming youth who displays unexpected resources when the showdown with the badmen comes."[69] At this time the "youth" was thirty-six years of age. The fullest definition of what Murphy brought to a film appeared in a review of *The Gun Runners* (1958), a remake of the Hemingway novel (and film), *To Have and Have Not*. The reviewer identified the Murphy "trademarks" as "a stubborn innocence, taciturn and firm character, an uncommunicative bravery, and suddenly a tight-lipped whirl of violence and vengeance."[70] To this list should be added humor. The composite is a sturdy, reliant, enduring Western persona worthy of the great tradition from William S. Hart through Gary Cooper. To most fans and reviewers, that is where Murphy belonged. A review of *Arizona Raiders* (1965) spoke to this question directly: "Audie Murphy has carved a niche for himself in the standard Western field comparable to that held by Randolph Scott a few years ago. While Murphy does not make such films as frequently as Scott did, the effect of their appearances is the same: the fans always know exactly what to expect and are thus seldom, if ever, disappointed."[71] Studio production notes repeatedly placed Murphy in that line of succession, but with a difference. In the promotional materials for *Tumbleweed*, for example, Universal-International stressed the tradition *and* the Murphy difference: "But just when the brawn seemed to have taken over entirely, along came a slight (150 pounds), not so tall (5'10"), freckled lad named Murphy to give the screen skyscrapers a run for their money."[72]

If Murphy summed up the past, he also pointed to the future. His 1959 film, *No Name on the Bullet*, was treated upon its release as just another Murphy Western. In retrospect it is one of the most interesting Westerns that he made. The philosophical cleverness of its script and the dark role played by Murphy resemble, with hindsight, a trial run for the spaghetti Westerns of the next decade. The original title, "Stranger from Nowhere," recalls both *Shane*, originally titled "Man from Nowhere," and Clint Eastwood's The Man With No Name.

*No Name on the Bullet* is one of those stunning B Westerns that the studios used to turn out now and then. The plot concerns the arrival of a hired assassin in a small town and the effect of his presence upon the community. Everyone who has anything to be guilty about believes that John Gant (Murphy) has come to kill him. The script describes Gant as a man almost preternatural in his icy detachment from ordinary life: "His eyes are cold, steady and piercing, his lips thin, his face white. . . . He is calm, serene, untouchable by externals."[73] Then there is this even more chilling note: "Perhaps his face might appear dead, but his eyes are always alive, always on the alert, searching, watching . . . careful eyes."[74] Besides his death-like appearance, Gant possesses a philosophical aloofness as well. He gets pleasure from watching people squirm: "Gant knows exactly what is going to happen, and he's already bored by it . . . men afraid, who come to him under the drivings of their secret guilt, to make a deal. He is contemptuous of them."[75] Gant's profound boredom is the most compelling dimension of this portrait of a killer.

Such boredom had its corollary in Murphy's off-screen life. His combat experiences haunted him. In *To Hell and Back* he wrote of how he felt after killing his first two men: "I feel no qualms; no pride; no remorse. There is only a weary indifference that will follow me throughout the war."[76] At the end of the book Murphy pledged that he

Audie Murphy in one of his most arresting films, *No Name on the Bullet* (1959). In this pre-spaghetti-style Western Murphy played a grim assassin with a cynical sense of humor. *Don B. Graham*

would "learn to look at life through uncynical eyes."[77] As late as 1967 he said, "With me, it's been a fight for a long, long time to keep from being bored to death."[78] He also spoke of the great difficulty of becoming an "executioner, somebody cold and analytical, to be trained to kill, and then to come back into civilian life and be alone in the crowd."[79]

To ward off such feelings of boredom and weariness, Murphy turned to gambling. It was one of the few activities that gave him a sense of stimulation. A friend said that Murphy would bet on anything, even on which of two birds on a telephone line would fly first.[80]

These biographical facts are especially pertinent to John Gant in *No Name on the Bullet*. Gant likes to play chess, and he likes to talk about the darker side of the human condition. He seems obsessed with death and his role as executioner. The only man Gant likes is Luke

(Charles Drake), the doctor, whom Gant always calls "physician." In one exchange the philosophical richness of this film and its relevance to Murphy's private as opposed to his public persona are striking:

> Luke: "Gant, I'm a healer. I've devoted my life to it and I intend to continue. Right now I've got one big public health problem, and I'm looking at it."
> Gant: "I like you, physician. You're like me. Why, you and I may well be the only two honest men in town."
> Luke: "Don't compare us, Gant. We've got nothing in common."
> Gant: "Everybody *dies*."[81]

The resolution of *No Name on the Bullet* is startling to anybody who believes that Murphy always played sterling types. Gant's target is an old man, a corrupt judge dying of consumption. His daughter discovers Gant's intentions and goes to tell him that her father will thwart his murderous plan by refusing to take arms against him. But Gant will not be stopped. He rips the daughter's bodice and takes a strip of her dress to taunt her father into trying to kill him. Although the father dies of natural causes just as Gant is about to shoot him, the point has been made. At this moment Gant wears on his face "a terrible smile, insinuating anything . . . everything."[82] Murphy's role as John Gant came as close to revealing the real Audie Murphy as did his self-portrayal in his best-known film, *To Hell and Back*, or the many Western heroes he played over the years.

In the late 1960s Murphy's career as a Western star took a downturn. Cheap Westerns, long a staple item for double bills, were no longer in demand, and Murphy found himself relegated to inferior vehicles such as *The Texican* (1967), which was filmed in Spain. There was of course Murphy's own bid, with Budd Boetticher, to make a series of quality B Westerns, but only *A Time for Dying* (1969) was completed. Tied for nearly twenty years to the popularity of the Western genre, Murphy's career suffered along with its decline.

His private life, always rocky, saw setbacks, too. First, there had been the much-celebrated, troubled, and short-lived marriage to starlet Wanda Hendrix, back in 1949, then remarriage to Pamela Archer in 1951, a union that produced some years of domestic tranquility, two children, and strains that led to publicized separations. Murphy also experienced several financial reversals, including bankruptcy in 1968. There were incidents of violent encounters that made the newspapers. Through all these adversities, many caused by his own actions,

Murphy kept fighting back, recovering his equilibrium, continuing to meet life as he always had, head on and with world-weary humor. Then, in May 1971, on a flight to North Carolina, the plane carrying Murphy and some business associates crashed into a mountain.[83] The forever-young war hero and Western star was dead at age forty-six. Dead but not forgotten. His military legend lives on, enhanced by his gravesite at Arlington National Cemetery and by statues commemorating his accomplishments. His movie legend lives on, too, perpetuated by televison. In his Westerns and in his war movies—they were the same, really—Murphy created a screen persona that will not fade away: legitimate hero, trained executioner, all-American boy, and dark, doomed victim of America's greatest war.

NOTES

I wish to thank the University Research Institute of the University of Texas for a Faculty Research Grant which provided support for this project. Special thanks are also due two librarians who gave invaluable assistance: Ned Comstock of the University of Southern California and Carol Epstein of the Academy of Motion Picture Arts and Sciences.

1. "Hollywood 'Rambling Reporter,'" *Hollywood Reporter*, September 15, 1983. Academy of Motion Picture Arts and Sciences. Subsequent references to this collection are listed as Academy.

2. Bob Thomas, "Texas Audie Making 29th Western," Dallas *Morning News*, November 27, 1963, section 1, p. 11.

3. "Profile of Audie Murphy, the Kid from Texas," Paul Short Productions. n.d. Academy.

4. "*Bad Boy*," *Cue*, March 26, 1949. Academy.

5. Ann Helming, "Audie Murphy Gives Good Performance," Hollywood *Citizen-News*, March 16, 1949. Academy.

6. Brog., "*Bad Boy*," *Variety*, January 26, 1949, p. 11.

7. Bob Thomas, "Audie Recalls Told to Kill," Greenville, Texas, *Banner*, December 2, 1960.

8. Lynn Bowers, "'Fort Petticoat' Unique Western," Los Angeles *Examiner*, April 4, 1957. Academy.

9. "Audie Murphy," Promotional materials for *Arizona Raiders*, Admiral Pictures. n.d. Special Collections, Doheny Library, University of Southern California. Subsequent references to this collection are listed as USC.

10. Harold B. Simpson, *Audie Murphy, American Soldier*, Veterans Edition (Dallas: Alcor Publishing, 1982), p. 266.

11. *Audie Murphy, American Soldier*, pp. 266 and 270.

12. Peter Bogdanovich, *John Ford* (Berkeley: University of California Press, 1968), p. 6.

13. A. H. Weiler, "By Way of Report," New York *Times*, October 14, 1951.

14. Simpson, p. 257.

15. Weiler, "By Way of Report."

16. Richard Davis, *"The Quiet Gun," Films and Filming*, June 1964. Academy.

17. Allen Eyles, *John Wayne* (South Brunswick, N.J.: A. S. Barnes, 1979), p. 12.

18. Christopher Frayling, *Spaghetti Westerns: Cowboys and Europeans from Karl May to Sergio Leone* (London: Routledge & Kegan Paul, 1981), p. 146.

19. By contrast, John Kimbrough, an All-American fullback from Texas A&M, made two Westerns in the early 1940s. *Variety* said after the second that he was a much better football player than actor. It was his last Western.

20. Typical of the negative judgments was the following: "As the hero, Mr. Murphy tries hard to keep up with such professionals as Mr. Redgrave and Claude Dauphin.... I'd give him an A for effort, but not for accomplishment, by a long shot." John McCarten, "Current Cinema," *New Yorker*, February 15, 1958. Academy. On the other hand, Bosley Crowther praised Murphy for a "very interesting and mettlesome performance." *"The Quiet American,"* New York *Times*, February 6, 1958, 24: 1.

21. The three positive reviews were: *"The Kid from Texas," Film Daily*, February 23, 1950. Academy; *"The Kid from Texas," Independent Film Journal*, February 25, 1950. Academy; *"The Kid from Texas," Variety*, March 1, 1950. Academy. On the negative side one reviewer wrote: "The part of Billy the Kid is a bit more than the limited talents of Audie Murphy can make convincing." "Complicated Story Slows Down Action," *Hollywood Reporter*, February 22, 1950. Academy.

22. *"The Kid from Texas," Fortnight*, March 31, 1950, p. 31.

23. Charles S. Aaronson, *"Kansas Raiders," Motion Picture Herald*, November 11, 1950. Academy.

24. "Cast, Production Excel in War Film," *Hollywood Reporter*, November 8, 1950. Academy.

25. *"Duel at Silver Creek," Newsweek*, August 4, 1952. Academy.

26. "Good Acting Keys Well-Handled Oater," *Hollywood Reporter*, November 17, 1953. Academy.

27. *"Ride Clear of Diablo," Newsweek*, March 15, 1954, p. 106.

28. Milton Luban, "Lively Action in Rogers-Hibbs Pic," *Hollywood Reporter*, February 3, 1954. Academy.

29. S. A. Desick, "'Destry' Again Rides Well," Los Angeles *Examiner*, January 20, 1955. Academy.

30. *"Destry," Variety (Weekly)*, December 2, 1954. Academy.

31. Jack Moffitt, "New 'Destry' Should Ride Into Easy Boxoffice Favor," *Hollywood Reporter*, December 2, 1954. Academy.

32. Tube., *"Gunfight at Comanche Creek," Variety*, February 26, 1964, p. 3.

33. Reed Porter, "Whytock-Whitney Film Well Done," *Hollywood Reporter*, July 21, 1965. Academy.

34. Sy Oshinsky, *"Gunpoint," Motion Picture Herald*, March 30, 1966. Academy.

35. Dorothy Manners, "Audie Murphy's Final Film To Be Released," Los Angeles *Examiner*, July 28, 1971. Academy.

36. FIPCO, the production company formed by Boetticher and Murphy, announced plans to make two more films: "When There's Sumpthin' To Do," scheduled for shooting in northern Mexico in October 1969, and "A Horse for Mr. Barnum," set for Spain in April 1970. None of these plans were realized. "Audie, Boetticher to Film 'Sumpthin' South of Border," *Variety (Daily)*, June 20, 1969. Academy.

37. Interview with Budd Boetticher, Ramona, California, March 4, 1985.

38. "Westerns Whet Appetites of Tourists Says Audie Murphy," publicity release for *Arizona Raiders*, Sherman Company, n.d. USC.

39. Audie Murphy, "Taps Never Blow for War Stories," *Hollywood Reporter*, November 16, 1959. Section 2. USC.

40. Murphy discussed his ideas about appropriate clothing in an interview when he was making *Ride Clear of Diablo*: "Kids nowadays are led to believe that the great western plainsmen all wore two-hundred dollar Stetson hats, expensively-tailored Technicolor shirts and solid gold buckles on their belts. Most of the famous western pioneers portrayed on the screen today rode around the plains in home made pants and the tops of their union suits. I don't insist on going that far, but I do try to look as near 'natural' as possible in the sartorial line." "*Ride Clear of Diablo*" (Production Notes), Universal-International. n.d. USC.

41. Ruth Waterbury, "'Bad Boy' Looks Like Hit," Los Angeles *Examiner*, March 16, 1949. Academy.

42. Quoted in Peter Biskind, *Seeing Is Believing: How Hollywood Taught Us to Stop Worrying and Love the Fifties* (New York: Pantheon Books, 1983), p. 198.

43. Promotional material for *Kansas Raiders*, Universal-International, n.d. USC.

44. "Rustlers and Redskins," *Time*, February 23, 1953. Academy.

45. "*The Cimarron Kid*," Production Notes, Universal-International, n.d. USC.

46. Memo from Clark Ramsey to Archie Herzoff, Mischa Kallis, Herman Levy, James Raker, August 1, 1949. USC. A follow-up letter from Herzoff to Hank Linet pointed out that ". . . the feeling up front is that the 'Bad Boy' reference adds nothing to Murphy's stature and also that as a personality he is well enough known to get along without the line." September 27, 1949. USC.

47. Herman Levy to Don Green, November 18, 1949. USC. It is instructive to see how another facet of Murphy's private life affected the publicity campaign for *The Kid from Texas*. His much celebrated marriage to actress Wanda Hendrix in late 1949 broke up suddenly early in 1950. Effects in the studio were felt immediately, as seen in one letter: "That's right—the Quaker Oats tie-up on 'The Kid from Texas' was killed because of the publicity on Audie Murphy's separation from Wanda Hendrix." Harry Ormiston to Charley Cohn, October 25, 1949. USC.

48. "Kid From Texas," promotional material, Universal-International, n.d. USC.

49. Frank McFadden to Bob Ungerfield, December 19, 1951. USC.

50. Bob Rains to Hank Linet, December 30, 1949. USC.

51. Hank Linet to Bob Rains, January 11, 1950. USC.

52. Summary of sneak preview cards, August 19, 1949. USC.

53. Lillian Ross, *Picture* (New York: Rinehart & Company, 1952), p. 9.

54. For a good discussion of postwar themes in fifties Westerns, see John

H. Lenihan, *Showdown: Confronting Modern America in the Western Film* (Urbana: University of Illinois Press, 1980), pp. 115–147.

55. Joseph I. Breen to William Gordon, May 25, 1949. USC.

56. *"The Cimarron Kid,"* production notes, Universal-International, n.d. USC.

57. "Cast, Production Excel in War Film," *Hollywood Reporter*, November 8, 1950. Academy.

58. Joseph I. Breen to William Gordon, May 3, 10, 1951. USC.

59. Ann Helming, "Quantrill's Raiders Ride Again," Hollywood *Citizen-News*, November 15, 1950. Academy.

60. John L. Scott, "Quantrill's Villains Take Over Screens," Los Angeles *Times*, November 15, 1950. Academy.

61. "Lively Sagebrusher Loaded with Action," *Hollywood Reporter*, February 6, 1953. Academy.

62. "Good Performances in Sardonic Oater," *Hollywood Reporter*, February 6, 1953. Academy.

63. Philip K. Scheuer, "Audie Murphy Assassin for Hire in 'Gunsmoke,'" Los Angeles *Times*, February 12, 1953. Academy. Scheuer also spotted something important about the development of the Murphy persona: "Audie displays an increasing confidence in the characterization *he has set for himself on the screen*" (emphasis mine).

64. John H. Lenihan discusses these and other Murphy Westerns in an excellent paper delivered at the Texas State Historical Association in Austin, Texas, in 1983, "The Kid From Texas: The Movie Heroism of Audie Murphy." This paper will be published in the *New Mexico Historical Quarterly*.

65. Tube., *"Posse From Hell,"* *Variety (Weekly)*, March 15, 1961. Academy.

66. Jack Moffitt, "Kay-Sherman Film Upgraded By Acting of Audie Murphy," *Hollywood Reporter*, January 12, 1960. Academy.

67. "Tumbleweed," Production Notes, Universal-International, n.d. USC.

68. *"Walk the Proud Land,"* *Hollywood Reporter*, July 10, 1956. Academy.

69. *"Seven Ways From Sundown,"* *Motion Picture Herald*, September 17, 1960. Academy.

70. *"The Gun Runners,"* *Motion Picture Herald*, September 20, 1958. Academy.

71. Richard Gertner, *"Arizona Raiders,"* *Motion Picture Herald*, August 4, 1965. Academy.

72. "Tumbleweed," Production Notes, Universal-International, n.d. USC.

73. Gene Coon, *No Name on the Bullet*, Revised Final Script, August 20, 1958, p. 2. USC.

74. Ibid., p. 4.

75. Ibid., p. 37.

76. Audie Murphy, *To Hell and Back* (New York: Henry Holt and Company, 1949), p. 11.

77. Ibid., p. 274.

78. Thomas B. Morgan, "The War Hero," *Esquire*, 100 (December 1983), p. 602.

79. Ibid., p. 603.

80. Interview with Budd Boetticher, Ramona, California, March 4, 1985.

81. *No Name on the Bullet*, p. 77.

82. Ibid., p. 104.

83. This brief overview is drawn from Simpson's *Audie Murphy, American Soldier*.

MICHAEL E. WELSH

# Western Film, Ronald Reagan, and the Western Metaphor

In the summer of 1985 President Ronald Wilson Reagan entered the United States Navy Hospital in Bethesda, Maryland. After conflicting reports filtered out on his physical condition, doctors announced that Reagan suffered from cancer of the colon, and that surgery had success-fully removed the tumor. In this moment of crisis the national news media characterized the President's recovery as they had done at other stages of the former actor's political career. Reporters and columnists made reference to Reagan's avowed connection to the virtues of the nineteenth-century American West as he overcame the trauma of the disease. His battle for survival reminded some of his image as a rugged individualist, while others speculated whether Reagan could soon enjoy the benefits of the outdoor life at his California ranch. The President himself added to this characterization by telling newspeople that he was "chomping at the bit" while hospitalized, and that he had begun reading the novel, *Jubal Sackett,* written by his favorite author, Louis L'Amour.

This latest phase of "Reagan-the-cowboy" journalism only accented one of the more intriguing questions of the 1980s: the ability of the President to rise above controversies that would harm other political officials. Speculation on this trait ranged from Reagan's boyish charm to his heartfelt conviction about the rightness of his personal beliefs. Inevitably the reference to Reagan and the West would surface, and public opinion either accepted this as proof of his goodness, or evidence of his shortcomings. Not since Theodore Roosevelt had a chief executive of the United States attached himself so closely to the myths of the American West, and in each case the public could not ignore the power of the symbolism.

Reagan's link to the simpler times of the past came at an opportune moment for himself and, said his supporters, for the nation as a whole. America had searched for two decades to find security and comfort amidst the shocks of Vietnam, civil rights, environmental despoliation, Watergate, and energy shortages. The challenge to understand these questions grew as traditional American optimism failed to assuage the doubts in many minds. President Jimmy Carter remarked on this loss of national spirit, and warned of darker days ahead. Scholars and journalists trumpeted the "Age of Limits," and books with titles like *Small is Beautiful* proliferated on best-seller lists.

This cycle of despondency and retrenchment seemed to many individuals as a cry for new vision from America's political leadership. The competitive economy of the United States requires constant expansion, and the bonds of inflation and high interest rates that prevailed in the 1970s threatened the American Dream. Then, in 1980, a voice echoing an earlier time promised to restore that lost American confidence, rebuild national prestige, and slay the villains unleashed by liberalism and bureaucracy since the days of Franklin D. Roosevelt.

That voice belonged to Ronald Reagan, born on February 6, 1911, to an Irish father and a Scots-Irish mother in the small town of Tampico, Illinois. The message delivered by presidential candidate Reagan had been refined through his personal experiences in the Midwest and in California, as well as from his observations of the changing American scene. Reagan spoke of a time when individualism dominated relationships, and when one's reputation and community standing counted heavily in one's favor. These values and perceptions had faded before the onslaught of organization in American life, whether from the corporate world or the expanding federal government. In addition, the advancement of impersonalism also decreased the sense of personal worth thought to exist in previous years. To a society reeling from crises beyond control, Reagan's words offered hope and direction that had all but vanished from contemporary life.

The irony of Reagan's message was that many people recognized in the tone of his remarks a familiar symbol: the cowboy of the American

West. Some assumed that his acting career had paralleled that of his longtime friend, John Wayne, who had come to personify the Western hero that anchors much of our national identity. Pictures of Reagan dressed as a cowboy appeared in newspapers, magazines, and on television screens throughout the 1980 campaign. Reporters could not get enough stories about the private life of Ron and Nancy on their ranch, and features covered such absurdities as the type of boots that the candidate fancied, or the awkwardness with which his wife accepted his love of the outdoors.

Beyond a handful of academics, movie critics, and Western film buffs, few Americans knew that Reagan had performed in only a half-dozen Westerns in his fifty-four-film career. But critics and supporters alike continued to equate his lifestyle and political philosophy with his outward embrace of the Western metaphor. Reaganites cheered their man as the sheriff riding into Washington to rid the town of bunco artists and thieves, while opponents in America and abroad saw in his blunt manner and simple homilies the limited nature of the cowboy mentality. This distorted Reagan's place in the history of Western film, and rendered public perception of his policies incomplete and contradictory.

The identification of Ronald Reagan with the West, to himself and to others, stems from two factors. Reagan's personal life was always directed toward the out-of-doors, whether with sports, nature, or recreation. In addition, Reagan imitated many other Americans in accepting the myths of the twentieth-century West. Using the rhetoric of the frontier, Reagan saw in California the "rich strike" that would provide a secure future amid the comfort of suburban surroundings. Thus when Reagan talked of mobility, freedom, and opportunity with voters, he spoke with a conviction born of his experiences as a lifeguard, football player, radio announcer, actor, and politician. America had been kind to Reagan, and the Western aura surrounding him from his movie career could only enhance the image already shaped in the public mind.

Ronald Reagan's direct link to the Western film genre consisted of several types of roles. In one he would play the standard cowboy hero, often a sheriff. These films included *The Bad Man* (1940), *Santa Fe Trail* (1940), *The Last Outpost* (1951), *Law and Order* (1953), *Tennessee's Partner* (1954), and *Cattle Queen of Montana* (1954). Reagan also appeared in several so-called "outdoor" pictures, such as *Sergeant Murphy* (1938), and *Stallion Road* (1947). In the former he portrayed a cavalry private in the twentieth-century U.S. Army, and in the latter a veterinarian tending to a champion horse. Less well-known were his parts in Western "spoofs," such as *Cowboy from Brooklyn* (1938), and *Boy Meets Girl* (1938). The first concerned a singing cowboy (Dick Powell) who was invited to perform in New York, while the second had Reagan play an announcer on a radio show that featured an aging cowboy star.[1]

These roles, plus Reagan's position as host of a popular 1960s television series, *Death Valley Days,* served as the nucleus of his public persona as a Western hero. But Reagan himself considered his interest in the genre to emanate from his youth in 1920s small-town Illinois. In his autobiography, *Where's the Rest of Me?* (1965), a title taken from Reagan's favorite line in his favorite film, *King's Row* (1941), he commented at length on the beauty of Midwestern nature. Speaking of Galesburg, Illinois, Reagan said: "The big green trees and dark red brick streets fitted into a picture of bright-colored peace, the way some primitive lithographs do." The imagery extended to pictures kept in the Reagan home: "Here, in the musty attic dust, I got my first scent of wind on peaks, pine needles in the rain, and visions of sunrise on the desert."[2]

The young Ronald Reagan could not avoid another 1920s window on the West: the ubiquitous double-feature films that played movie houses every weekend in towns across the Midwest. Like many of his peers in Dixon, Illinois, and elsewhere, the uncomplicated heroics of the silent-screen stars elicited strong visual responses from the adolescent Reagan. "There was the life (of the cowboy)," he said, "that has shaped my body and mind for all the years to come after." Young Reagan sat in the "Family Theatre" in Dixon, "watching the marvelous flickering antics of Tom Mix and William S. Hart as they foiled robbers and villains and escorted the beautiful girls to safety, waving back from their horses as they cantered into the sunset."[3]

The power of the Western over Ronald Reagan was no greater than that experienced by countless youths in America. The myths of the nineteenth-century West were harmless enough, but Reagan's biographers point to other imagery that reinforced the lessons he learned from the silver screen. These ideas stem from the literature of such "Lost Generation" novelists as Sinclair Lewis. Bill Boyarsky contended that the Midwest had more of an influence on Reagan in his formative years than any concepts he might have held of the West. Referring to the Babbitts of *Main Street,* Boyarsky described Reagan and his contemporaries as "conservative, materialistic, admiring the businessmen, intolerant of social service, foreigners and dissenters." Boyarsky concluded that Reagan disliked laws that "represented collective action through the state," preferring the unbridled individualism of the cowboy or the Midwestern entrepreneur.[4]

The films, stereopticon slides, and tree-lined streets of Reagan's youth offered him many opportunities to exercise his mind in fantasies of nature and the West. He sought certain values in his life that mirrored the qualities criticized by Sinclair Lewis and others, and he accepted that which Lewis considered unsavory about Midwestern life. In later years Reagan wrote that one of his favorite writers had been Edgar Rice Burroughs, author of the mythical "Tarzan" stories. "As I look back I realize," said Reagan in 1965, "that my reading left an abiding belief in the triumph of good over evil." Heroes such as Tarzan appealed to him because they "lived by standards of morality and fair play." This focus on the virtuous life would find its outlet in Reagan's wish to portray "good guys" who upheld the law and brought justice to whichever locale they represented on film.[5]

Despite this thorough grounding in an appreciation of the West and in the uplifting spirit of nature, Reagan's early career did not include Western roles of any sort. As a student at Eureka College, in his home state, he acted in stage productions and won an individual award at a prestigious competition at Northwestern University. Upon graduation in 1932 with a degree in economics, Reagan pursued employment as a sports announcer, eventually working for the 50,000-watt NBC station in Des Moines, Iowa.

While at WHO radio Reagan first cultivated his love for horses and horseback riding. This became a passion that would serve him well in his movie career and that prompted his ownership of several ranches in Southern California over the years. Among Reagan's friends in Des Moines were several young men who joined the Fourteenth Cavalry Regiment of the U.S. Army Reserves. Although this unit served primarily as an avenue for gentlemanly excursions on horseback, Reagan seized the chance to fulfill a lifelong ambition. "I loved horses," he confessed, even though he had "never been exposed to them . . . as a youngster." Reagan admitted that in his adolescence he "had only a yen to be like Tom Mix." But the afternoons spent riding on the outskirts of Des Moines confirmed his desire to own and raise horses someday, even if he did not act in films that included horseback riding.[6]

In the midst of his successful stint as a radio announcer, Reagan experienced a change of direction that united his love of horses with his childhood dreams of the West. Radio station WHO utilized Reagan's talents to broadcast the Chicago Cubs' baseball games to their large audience. In order to familiarize himself with the team, Reagan traveled to the Cubs' spring-training camp on Santa Catalina Island, one of the Channel Islands off the coast of Santa Barbara, California. While there in 1936 and 1937 Reagan became enamored of the warm winters and leisurely pace of Southern California, especially the lure of the beach.

When Reagan returned to Des Moines after the first westward trip, he accepted another post as announcer of a WHO country-dance program. One of the acts hired by the station was the "Oklahoma Outlaws," a group of local musicians with a substantial following. In the summer of 1936 the famed singing cowboy, Gene Autry, invited the Iowa band to appear in one of his musical Westerns. The Outlaws' stories of the movie business deeply affected Reagan, who remembered that their experiences "suddenly made acting and movies seem very close."[7]

Reagan's move to Hollywood was swift and successful, even by the abnormal standards of "Tinseltown." Good fortune dictated that a Des Moines singer named Joy Hodges met him before his 1937 visit to spring training, where she filled his head with stories of the opportunity in the movies for a handsome and athletic young man. Reagan managed to impress the executives at Warner Brothers Studios, who cast him in a series of light and breezy roles in the popular romances of the time. His second film, *Sergeant Murphy,* demonstrated Reagan's riding skills, and its location shooting unveiled to him more of the natural wonders of California. Quickly thereafter came *Cowboy from Brooklyn,* which parodied the Gene Autry musicals, and *Boy Meets Girl,* all within the space of several months in 1938.[8]

The talents Reagan polished in Des Moines were not limited to riding and announcing. He also joined a group of stars in the Warners' commissary who "roasted" each other by questioning their knowledge of a supposedly obscure subject. Reagan's friends knew of his love for horses and his service in the Army Reserve cavalry. In order to prepare himself for the good-natured ribbing at lunch, he spent many evenings reading about various aspects of horsemanship and troop maneuvers.

While Reagan, in his autobiography, treats his move to California as merely a stroke of luck, its symbolism for many Americans runs much deeper. One biographer likened Reagan's quest to that of the gold-rush prospectors of 1849. Reagan, said Lou Cannon of the *Washington Post,* "left the land of his boyhood for Hollywood to become an actor and strike it rich." This was a dream "shared vicariously by millions of Americans," a "fantasy which Reagan acted out in the real world." Cannon believed that it was at this point that Reagan's relationship to the West solidified. Americans of that generation needed the concept of the frontier "because it gave us something to conquer, something to settle, a place to strike it rich." Cannon's father cherished the same dream as Ronald Reagan, and Reagan's connection to this image only dramatized the idea that, as the columnist said, "many of us believe it still."[9]

The turning point of Reagan's acting career came with his portrayal in 1940 of the legendary Notre Dame football player, George Gipp. The film, *Knute Rockne—All American,* showcased Reagan's athletic ability and boyish charm. The day after a "sneak preview" of the film to Hollywood executives, Reagan received a call from his agent that he would play opposite Errol Flynn and Olivia De Havilland in the movie, *Santa Fe Trail.* The story would be set in the West, have many stars in its cast, and would focus on the violent Kansas border wars of the 1850s.

Much has been written about this particular film and of Reagan's role therein. It is undoubtedly the most famous of his Westerns and earned the highest praise for his acting in the genre. The major failing of the picture, however, was its blatant historical inaccuracy. The script had an "all-star" graduating class at West Point that included Jeb Stuart (Flynn) and George Custer (Reagan), who in reality were at least six years apart in age. The story utilized John Brown's anti-slavery raids as the dramatic angle, and came no closer to the town of Santa Fe than Topeka, Kansas. The *New York Times* recognized the film's ingredients for mass appeal, but warned: "For anyone who has the slightest regard for the spirit—not to mention the facts—of American history, it will prove exceedingly annoying."[10]

Reagan's portrayal of Custer has intrigued film buffs and Western historians for years. Instead of the racist, vainglorious megalomaniac of traditional folklore, the Custer character was jovial, handsome, and sensitive to the inherent wrongs of slavery. Reagan himself commented upon the inconsistencies of his part: "I discovered I would again be playing a biographical role, but with less attention to the truth this time." The plot vacillated between support of Army policies and sympathy for John Brown's crusade. Custer was merely an historical

Ronald Reagan, Olivia de Havilland, and Errol Flynn in
*Santa Fe Trail* (1940). *Michael E. Welsh*

appendage that viewers would recognize, yet one biographer noted
that Reagan "looked good on a horse," and that his mythical friendship
with Errol Flynn gave his career "another boost."[11]

One problem in Reagan's film career that he readily admitted was
his inability to capitalize on successive starring roles. This he attributed to the managerial style of Warner Brothers, where they selected
scripts that did not highlight his best qualities. Such was the case with
Reagan's next Western, *The Bad Man* (1940). He had achieved some
notoriety with *Santa Fe Trail,* and would soon appear in his most
famous role as Drake McHugh in *King's Row.* Warners then decided to
capitalize on Reagan's minor stardom by "loaning" him to Metro-
Goldwyn-Mayer (MGM) for a remake of the Pancho Villa story. Reviewers roundly scored *The Bad Man* for its poor plot and waste of
talent. Said the *New York Times:* "This is the most static and loqua-
cious Western we've encountered in a long time." *Scribner's* magazine
called it "sheer nickelodeon . . . as crude and primitive as anything

... in the old five-cent silent days." The *New York Times* called Reagan "an ineffectual hero," while *Time* magazine claimed that Reagan and his cohorts "seem to walk through their parts in a mechanical daze." Even Reagan recognized the failures of the film, saying: "Only MGM would cast a fellow (himself) in the role of a near-bankrupt rancher, and then wardrobe him in tailor-made Levis." The stagehands achieved the effect of poverty by "sandpapering and beating on the sidewalk" Reagan's $75 pair of pants.[12]

Following on the heels of the disappointing *Bad Man* was a second blow to Reagan's film career: enlistment in the Army in World War II. What he needed was more parts like Custer or Drake McHugh, and more visibility in successful ventures. But Reagan worried that his fans would not remember his achievements after the wartime hiatus. Of more significance was that public tastes had changed during and after the war. American moviegoers demanded more sophistication and content in their entertainment as a result of the nation's exposure to world affairs. Film makers responded to this desire for "realism" either through suggestive sex, as with *Duel in the Sun* (1945), or *The Outlaw* (1948), known for Jane Russell's physique and Howard Hughes's direction. Still other directions pursued in the postwar environment were contemplative pictures, such as *My Darling Clementine* (1948) or *Fort Apache* (1948), marked by their ambiguity and racial tension.[13]

Even though Reagan did not maintain his profile with the public, the war offered him the opportunity to make films for the Army Air Corps. Reagan first joined a cavalry unit in San Francisco because of his reserve status, but soon transferred to the First Motion Picture Unit of the Army, known as the "Culver City Commandoes." He narrated training and enlistment films, offering his dramatic style to enliven the storyline. Reagan also was detailed to Hollywood to appear in Irving Berlin's *This Is the Army* (1943), which offered its proceeds of $10 million to the war relief effort.

Reagan's service in wartime increased his sense of duty and patriotism, preparing him for a postwar era of reconciliation and, in his words, the "regeneration of mankind." But to his dismay the nation had become cynical and jaded about moral causes. Reagan vowed to wage a one-man campaign to right the nation's wrongs, and launched into his political involvement with the Screen Actors Guild and the anti-Communist purge in Hollywood. Perhaps because of this single-mindedness of purpose, Reagan was judged by casting agents as unsuited for the newer form of Western. He then accepted parts that did not flatter his image, although they did secure for him a comfortable niche in Hollywood.

The first film in which Reagan appeared after 1945 was an outdoor production, *Stallion Road* (1947). He played a veterinarian who became enamored of a wealthy young owner of a breeding farm. The plot did not inspire Reagan, but he enjoyed the opportunity to work with horses. In later years he considered *Stallion Road* as one of his favorite films because it introduced him to the "horsey set," and prompted his desire to own and raise a herd of horses. The *New York Times* viewed the Reagan part as delivered in "a conventionally stout-fellow style," and Reagan himself made little mention of this role in his autobiography.[14]

This lack of good parts disturbed Reagan, but not as much as the success of other actors in postwar Westerns. Audiences flocked to the John Ford-John Wayne epics, and Reagan petitioned Warner Brothers to give him a similar vehicle for public acclaim. He knew that the studio admired the script for *Ghost Mountain*, a popular novel by Alan LeMay. But the poor box-office returns on Reagan's previous film, *That Hagen Girl* (1949), with a teenaged Shirley Temple as his love interest, prompted Warners to offer the part to Errol Flynn.

When bypassed for the filming of *Ghost Mountain*, Reagan began to wonder about ever fulfilling his dream of Western stardom. "I thought then," Reagan remarked in 1965, "and think now, that the brief post-Civil War era when our blue-clad cavalry stayed on wartime footing against the plains and desert Indians was a phase of Americana rivaling the Kipling era for color and romance." Reagan lamented that "everyone rode into the sunset behind fluttering cavalry guidons," leaving him to venture to England to appear in a mediocre love story, *The Hasty Heart* (1951).[15]

By the early 1950s Reagan had suffered several reverses in his professional and private life, only one of which had been the denial of Western scripts. His marriage to Jane Wyman foundered on the rocks of Hollywood expectations, with her career eclipsing his when she won an Oscar in 1948 for *Johnny Belinda*. Reagan immersed himself in the political quagmire of Communist-hunting in Hollywood, and then had the misfortune of breaking his leg in a celebrity softball game. Lying in his hospital bed, Reagan reflected upon his fading dream. He "still wanted a crack at that outdoor stuff," but grew frustrated with the "certain knowledge that the cavalry-Indian cycle was wearing thin

due to overexposure." The presidential duties for the Screen Actors
Guild had, in his words, "identified (him) with the serious side of Hollywood's off-screen life," and Reagan ruefully commented that "if someone was casting a Western, I'd be the lawyer from the East."[16]

Reagan's absence from Western films finally ended with a succession of roles from 1951 to 1954. The advent of television threatened the
movie industry, which fought back with one of its perennial successes,
the Western. The studios cranked out dozens of B Westerns of uneven
quality to maintain the flow of customers to the box office. This meant
that actors such as Reagan could find employment if they were willing
to appear in films of lesser stature than they had before.

Reagan's Western "renaissance" occurred with his starring role in
*The Last Outpost* (1951). In typical self-deprecating fashion, he admitted that "it wasn't an epic." The story, which the *New York Times*
claimed was not "recorded in the history of the War between the
States," involved Confederate efforts to seize Union gold shipments in
the Arizona desert. The newspaper dismissed the whole affair as "ele-
mentary school stuff," and Reagan remembered it only for its color and
action. But film historian Tony Thomas saw something more in
Reagan's performance as a rebel cavalry captain. *The Last Outpost* was
Reagan's first "real" Western in his fourteen-year career, and Thomas
concluded that "in view of his love of horses, his life as a rancher, and
being an actor with a keen interest in the American West, his absence
from such (films) presents one of the ironies of life in Hollywood."
Thomas also believed that more roles like *Outpost* earlier in Reagan's
career could have given him "a better box office standing," from which
Reagan could have aged gracefully as did Jimmy Stewart and John
Wayne.[17]

To maintain this newfound momentum, Reagan turned immediately to another Western, *Law and Order* (1953). Not only was this the
third version of the film, but it was also the timeworn story of Wyatt
Earp and the gunfight at the OK corral. The film might have succeeded
in the more accepting 1930s, but the forty-two-year-old Reagan did not
look the part of the young, dashing lawman. Reagan had taken the role
out of his belief that the West was "recent enough to be real and old
enough to be romantic." But upon its release the reviewers politely
ignored the movie, and Reagan himself called it a picture that he could
excuse "only because it was a Western."[18]

The reviews of *Law and Order* did not keep Reagan from persisting
in his attempts to star in a major Western. The parts that he wanted,

Dorothy Malone and Ronald Reagan in *Law and Order*
(1953), a remake of the Wyatt Earp story. *Michael E. Welsh*

however, went to other more respected actors. He tried again in 1954
with *Cattle Queen of Montana,* where he had second billing to Barbara
Stanwyck. She was one of the few actresses to portray a Western
heroine, and the *New York Times* described her as "an intrepid citizen
who has known no fear of man, terrain or scripts over a long and illustrious career."[19]

Reagan knew that public attention would not rest on his character
in *Cattle Queen*. He consoled himself with the admission that "somehow working outdoors amid beautiful scenery and much of the time on
horseback never has seemed like work to me." His role was an undercover Army officer sent from Washington to investigate the twin evils of
cattle rustling and Indian unrest in Montana. The *New York Times*
analyzed Reagan's acting as "stalwart and obvious," and scored the film
itself for its insipid plot and "highly improbable" script. Reagan, however, came away from the production with an appreciation for Stanwyck's professionalism and charm. She had gained the respect of the

Blackfeet Indians who had participated in the film, and had been adopted as a blood sister of the tribe. The Blackfeet gave her the name, "Princess Many Victories," to honor her long and successful career, and whenever Reagan met her in later life he would greet her by her Indian name.[20]

By 1955 Reagan realized that his future would not include many more Hollywood films. He became the announcer and sometimes performer in a highly popular television series, the *General Electric Theatre*. He had married Nancy Davis several years before, and had begun raising a second family. That fall he closed out his Western film career with a mediocre version of Bret Harte's *Tennessee's Partner*. Reagan played the sidekick of John Payne, a conventional B-Western actor of the 1950s. In the film Reagan's part as "Cowpoke" was the same sort of breezy, unsophisticated character that had put him on the road

Ronald Reagan played an undercover agent in *Cattle Queen of Montana* (1954) with Barbara Stanwyck. *Michael E. Welsh*

to stardom in the late 1930s. But twenty years had taken their toll, and movie reviewers warned the public that Reagan was not believable as a young cowboy. Reagan himself made no mention of this film in his autobiography, or of the significance of closing out the Western phase of his career.[21]

*Tennessee's Partner* may have signaled the demise of Reagan as a Western film actor, but it did not eliminate the aura of the West that surrounded him. *GE Theatre* had several Western productions in its eight-year run, among them a remake of Charles Dickens's *A Christmas Carol* set in the West with Jimmy Stewart as a cowboy Scrooge. By 1961 *GE Theatre* dominated its time slot at 9 o'clock on Sunday evenings, and Reagan had gained much notoriety for his additional duties as a public speaker for the corporation. Then in an ironic twist, the show lost its top ranking in 1962 to the smash Western hit, *Bonanza*. Executives of General Electric believed that their program had outlived its usefulness. Reagan confessed that he too had shifted his viewing allegiance to the Cartwright family, and that *Bonanza* rated as one of his favorite shows.[22]

The demise of *GE Theatre* again left Reagan without a steady source of income. With two young children and a home in the Malibu hills, he needed to revitalize his career. Then, in one of the many strokes of luck that characterized Reagan's life, he gained the position as on-screen announcer, actor, and advertising pitchman for the U.S. Borax Corporation's Western series, *Death Valley Days*. The account executive for Borax at the McCann-Erickson advertising agency was Reagan's older brother, Neil "Moon" Reagan. When asked by Borax officials for recommendations for a suitable host, Neil suggested that they hire his brother, long experienced in television and in Westerns.

Reagan spent the next four years appearing weekly before a national audience in Western clothes and settings, gaining public attention that he never received in his feature film roles. Early in the series the Borax officials surveyed groups of housewives for their reaction to Reagan as company spokesman. The responses were almost uniformly positive, with the most common statement being that they would buy anything from him. Then the test audience stunned the researchers by volunteering that they would also vote for Reagan for public office, based on his manliness, sincerity, poise, and identification with the outdoors.[23]

This appeal to the sensibilities of the middle class became the springboard for Reagan's mid-life career change to politics. In his

youth and young adulthood Reagan had espoused New Deal Democratic beliefs, as much related to Franklin D. Roosevelt's personal
magnetism as to the tenets of the liberal faith. Yet after World War II
Reagan sensed a national mood to reject sacrifice and reduce the
involvement of government in people's lives. His Midwestern values of
individualism and opportunity led him to remain more conventional
than fellow Democrats who sought more radical solutions to the political, economic, and social questions of the day. His marriage to socialite
Nancy Davis suggested the degree of this shift, as did his speeches for a
major defense contractor, General Electric. All that remained was for
Reagan to leave the world of film and television for another medium of
entertainment, national politics.

When Reagan first tested the waters of the American political
scene, he found that he had carried with him the appeal of his relationship to the American West. He also spoke in the language of the
twentieth-century Western metaphor, addressing the conservative
wishes of the Sunbelt migrants for less government, fewer social programs, lower taxes, a strong defense (and the spending that
accompanied this), a return to the morality of the "good old days," and
access to the comforts of the postwar suburban West. Reagan caught
the eye of many voters with his stirring defense of the doomed 1964
presidential campaign of Barry Goldwater. Speaking on television
with the calm sincerity of a Gary Cooper, Reagan avoided the stridency
of the Arizona Republican that had unnerved many voters. Where
Goldwater had called the country to battle with his political jeremiads,
Reagan offered reasoned answers that brought the Republican ticket
more cash contributions than ever before.

Reagan's popularity among conservative power brokers in California was not limited to his gift for speechmaking. Two years later a
group of car dealers, bankers, and politicians convinced Reagan to seek
the governorship of California. His opponent, Edmund G. "Pat" Brown,
had been in the post for eight years, and had presided over much of
California's postwar prosperity. But voters were concerned about
campus unrest, rising taxes, and racial violence in the state's urban
centers. Brown dismissed Reagan as a washed-up actor, and tried to
link his *Death Valley Days* persona to the stereotype of the gunslinging
cowboy.

What Brown and many politicians failed to realize was that
although Reagan spoke and acted in the nineteenth-century style, his
ideas rang true with constituents enamored of the twentieth-century

Western myth. Rancho del Cielo, Reagan's home in the hills above Santa Barbara, was more like a suburban hideaway than a working ranch. Nancy Davis Reagan's Scottsdale roots were merely Gold-Coast Chicago transported to the Southwestern desert. The New Year's Eve parties in Palm Springs with Walter Annenberg and the visits to the Mexican retreats of John Wayne and William Holden were luxurious weekends that only happened to have Western locales. When Pat Brown's campaign staff plastered images of Reagan in cowboy clothes all over California they merely reinforced the positive feelings that many disaffected middle-class voters held for Reagan.

The "Reagan-as-cowboy" logic would dissipate during his two terms in the governor's mansion at Sacramento. Reagan's time in office showed him as a conservative-to-moderate politician who would not stand on principle if a compromise was needed. Yet the link to the West remained, surfacing in Reagan's campaign for president in 1980. Incumbent Jimmy Carter believed that he spoke for the same values and constituency as did Reagan. Carter wondered why Reagan's blunders at the public podium and his harsh language on social welfare and foreign policy could be forgiven so easily by the American public. More than once Carter accused Reagan of being a "warmonger" who could not be trusted to manage the nation's nuclear arsenal, and on one occasion Carter told reporters: "We are not dealing here with another shoot-out at the OK Corral."[24]

On Inauguration Day, 1981, Ronald Reagan awoke to find a copy of the *Washington Post* on his reading table. Inside was a fifty-page tabloid on his campaign and predictions for his presidency. The *Post* compiled dozens of stories and photographs about the new chief executive, attempting to reveal his deepest thoughts and secrets. On the cover of the section a photo showed a smiling Reagan wearing a cowboy hat and work shirt. Haynes Johnson, a two-time Pulitzer Prize-winning columnist for the *Post,* wrote the lead article. After introductory remarks, Johnson went to the heart of the matter. "Like a character out of one of his Western melodramas," said Johnson, "[Reagan] brings his white hat and cowboy boots into the weary East of Washington." The story utilized other examples of the nineteenth-century Western metaphor, and concluded that Reagan's greatest strengths were his optimism, energy, and uncomplicated view of life. None of these factors was necessarily the domain of the cowboy, but Johnson's portrayal signaled future journalistic pieces on Reagan and the West.

More insightful was the essay commissioned from Wallace Stegner, the noted Western novelist and writer. Entitled, "Will Reagan Ride with the Raiders?" the story took the more realistic approach of analyzing Reagan's appeal in the West and nationwide. Stegner immediately recognized the twentieth-century Western myth when he commented upon a sheriff's posse of horsemen scheduled to ride in the inauguration parade. Stegner noted their $10,000 horses, $25,000 saddles, and their relationship to the nostalgia of the bygone West. Then he studied Reagan's support of the "Sagebrush Rebellion," where developers and landowners sought more control of public acreage in the West. Reagan's choice of James Watt of Wyoming as his Secretary of the Interior also bothered Stegner, as did the lurking presence of beer baron Joseph Coors, auto dealer Holmes Tuttle, and other captains of Western industry among the President's closest advisors.

Stegner did not dwell very long on Reagan's clothes and gear. The writer's purpose was to explore the President's awareness of the history and culture of the region, of its beauty and fragility, and why federal policies had evolved to meet the crises of years past. Stegner suggested that Reagan was an "ersatz Westerner" who spoke more like a Chamber of Commerce booster than a student of the region. In doing so Stegner grasped the essence of Ronald Reagan and his attachment to the West. The President's youth in Illinois gave him the love of the outdoors that has remained all his life. The values of fair play and individualism that the Midwest inspired transferred to the silver screen, whether Reagan portrayed a cowboy, secret service agent, football player, or military man.

In later years, however, Reagan would speak for the desire for comfort, security, and freedom that brought not only himself but millions of other Americans to the shores of the Pacific and the open spaces of the mountain and desert West. Most likely his Western films did not solidify his cowboy image in the minds of his countrymen, especially the eighteen- to twenty-four-year-old age group of voters who supported him overwhelmingly in 1984. Reagan had not filmed a Western in their lifetimes, but the qualities of Gary Cooper, Jimmy Stewart, and John Wayne that gratified their parents had rubbed off on Reagan, allowing him to "get the girl" and "ride into the sunset" of real life even though he had rarely done so in the movies.[25]

NOTES

1. Tony Thomas, *The Films of Ronald Reagan* (Secaucus, N.J.: Citadel Press, 1980), pp. 40, 50, 54, 113, 116, 146, 148, 183, 203, 211.

2. Ronald Reagan with Richard G. Hubler, *Where's the Rest of Me?* (New York: Duell, Sloan and Pearce, 1965), p. 11.

3. *Where's the Rest of Me?* p. 11.

4. Bill Boyarsky, *The Rise of Ronald Reagan* (New York: Random House, 1968), pp. 27, 38.

5. Lou Cannon, *Reagan* (New York: Perigee Books, 1982, 1984), pp. 18–19.

6. *Where's the Rest of Me?* p. 67; Cannon, *Reagan,* p. 36.

7. *Where's the Rest of Me?* p. 71.

8. Thomas, *Films of Reagan,* pp. 48, 50, 54; Reagan, *Where's the Rest of Me?* p. 80.

9. Lou Cannon, "Reagan Brings Optimism for the Future, Rooted in Values of the Past," *Washington Post,* January 20, 1981.

10. "Santa Fe Trail," *New York Times,* December 21, 1940.

11. *Where's the Rest of Me?* pp. 95–96; Thomas, *Films of Reagan,* pp. 113–14; Cannon, *Reagan,* p. 56.

12. Boyarsky, *Rise of Reagan,* pp. 62–63; Cannon, *Reagan,* p. 116; *Where's the Rest of Me?* p. 99.

13. For a discussion of Hollywood in the years of World War II, see Gerald D. Nash, *The American West Transformed: The Impact of the Second World War* (Bloomington: Indiana University Press, 1985), pp. 178–98.

14. *Where's the Rest of Me?* p. 186; Thomas, *Films of Reagan,* pp. 146–48; "Stallion Road," *New York Times,* April 5, 1947.

15. *Where's the Rest of Me?* pp. 205–06, 212.

16. Ibid., pp. 215, 232.

17. Ibid., p. 216; "The Last Outpost," *New York Times,* June 22, 1951; Thomas, *Films of Reagan,* pp. 183–84.

18. *Where's the Rest of Me?* p. 242; Thomas, *Films of Reagan,* pp. 203–05.

19. "Cattle Queen of Montana," *New York Times,* January 26, 1955.

20. *Where's the Rest of Me?* p. 252; *New York Times,* January 26, 1955; Thomas, *Films of Reagan,* pp. 211–13.

21. "Tennessee's Partner," *New York Times,* November 5, 1955; Thomas, *Films of Reagan,* pp. 214–16.

22. *Where's the Rest of Me?* pp. 255, 272.

23. Boyarsky, *Rise of Reagan,* p. 104.

24. Cannon, *Reagan,* pp. 351–57.

25. Haynes Johnson, "Fresh Pledges and Familiar Frustrations," and Cannon, "Reagan Brings Optimism," both in *Washington Post,* January 20, 1981.

RICHARD C. ROBERTSON

# Just Dreamin' Out Loud:
# The Westerns of
# Burt Lancaster

Burt Lancaster's film career has spanned five decades and is studded with outstanding roles but movie fans do not automatically associate him with Westerns. In such films as *The Killers* (1946), *The Crimson Pirate* (1952), *From Here to Eternity* (1953), and *The Rose Tattoo* (1955), he showed an extraordinarily wide range in his early career. And with *Elmer Gantry* (1960), *Judgment at Nuremberg* (1961), and *Birdman of Alcatraz* (1962), he established himself as a talented actor as well as a dynamic screen personality. Of the sixty-six films Lancaster has made—which include costume dramas, spy thrillers, pirate adventures, and dramas—one fourth of them have been Westerns.

Lancaster came to Hollywood via a circuitous route. Son of a post office clerk, Burton Stephen Lancaster was born in New York City in 1913 and grew up in the working-class streets of East Harlem. He was energetic and athletic as a youth, although small. It was not until much later that he reached his full 6-foot 2-inch height. He acted in school and church plays early on but his real dream was the circus. With life-long friend and fellow street scrapper, Nick Cravat, he worked up a tumbling and acrobatic act. For more than seven years, the two played circuses and the vaudeville circuit. When this career appeared to be going nowhere, Lancaster quit and took a succession of jobs, including one as a furniture salesman at Marshall Field's in Chicago where he amused his fellow workers with acrobatic feats.

Drafted in 1942, Lancaster was assigned to Special Services where he wrote, directed, and acted in shows for G.I.s in North Africa, Sicily, Italy, and Austria. After the war, he returned to New York City. Through a wartime acquaintance, he landed a part in a short-lived play and attracted enough favorable attention to receive several offers from Hollywood. He was thirty-two when he signed a contract with producer Hal Wallis. Within three years, he was a rising star. Lancaster had made twelve films before he acted in a Western. Westerns are scattered throughout the next twenty-five years of his career, but nine of them were made in three clusters of three films each in the mid-1950s, mid-1960s, and early 1970s. Each of these groups can be seen as the heart of a period. They fall within the scope and boundaries set by other Westerns of their time and are not particularly innovative. Burt Lancaster's Westerns are, however, excellent examples of the films of their era and almost all of them are still enjoyable today.

In 1951, Lancaster made his first Western, *Vengeance Valley*. It was his thirteenth film. He took to the saddle well. His early athletic training proved valuable here as it did throughout his early and middle career. He appeared much younger than his thirty-eight years.

Set in the contemporary West and shot at the foot of the Rockies in Colorado, the story was simple and direct. Lancaster played the foster son of a rancher (Ray Collins). Robert Walker played the corrupt natural son who schemed to take over the ranch in a role foreshadowing Paul Newman's *Hud* a dozen years later. Walker is married to a good woman (Joanne Dru) who has long since given up on her philandering spouse. Lancaster and Walker's wife are drawn together while Walker pursues a local waitress.

The contrast between the no-good son and the upstanding foster son defines the moral dilemma. There can be but one denouement in a film made during this period. Lancaster is forced to shoot his evil foster brother, thus administering justice and incidentally also winning Walker's wife. Everything is neatly tied up at the end with morality satisfied through violence.

The film was written by Irving Rovetch from a Luke Short story. Director Richard Thorpe enriched the film with scenes from ranch life and the spring roundup, lending a feeling of realism which pointed the way to later films such as *The Last Hunt* (1956), *Cowboy* (1958), *Monte Walsh* (1970), and *The Culpepper Cattle Company* (1972). The cast included two future stars of the Western, John Ireland and Hugh O'Brian.

Burt Lancaster's first major Western came three years later in 1954. By then he had reached the level of major star with his swashbuckling, athletic performance in *The Crimson Pirate* (1952) and the critically acclaimed *Come Back, Little Sheba* (1952). In 1953, he received an Oscar nomination for his role as Sergeant Warden in *From Here to Eternity*. The independence brought by success allowed Lancaster to establish an independent film production company with Harold Hecht. He was the first Hollywood star to do so. One of their first films was a Western, *Apache,* with Lancaster in the title role.

The story begins in 1886 with the surrender of Geronimo and the end of organized Apache warfare. Supposedly based on a true incident, the film depicts the continued resistance to civilization by Massai, a single courageous and determined warrior. Along with scores of others, he is captured, handcuffed, and put on a train for reservation detention in Florida. As Massai boards the train, he looks longingly toward the mountains in the distance, a look familiar to Western afficionados. In this film, as in most Westerns, one of the uncredited major stars is the land itself. This is big country, big in every way, country which demands big men and makes men big. Massai's gaze to the mountains foreshadows Kirk Douglas in *Lonely Are the Brave* (1962) and Steve McQueen in *Tom Horn* (1980). In all three films, as in many others, the mountains represent freedom and safety to the heroes.

Freeing himself from his shackles, Massai escapes from the shuttered train somewhere in mid-continent. His arduous journey home is interrupted by two telling incidents. In the first, he finds himself in the midst of a large city, face to face with white civilization with all its bustle, confusion, and bigotry. Called a "dirty redskin," he flees in confusion.[1] In the second incident, he is sheltered and nursed back to health by a Cherokee family in Oklahoma. They live in a civilized house with curtains on the window, much to Massai's amazement. And the Indian patriarch teaches him about farming and the corn of Tahlequah. He takes a small amount with him when he continues his journey, along with the lesson that the Indian can only survive by adopting the white man's ways.

When Massai reaches his homeland, he is confronted by a hostile army and Indians forced to build roads. His initial advocacy of peace and civilization turns to open rebellion when he is betrayed and captured by Indian Police. He escapes and vows a single-handed war of revenge. "You fight only for yourself. There is nothing in (you) but hate," observes a fellow Apache. "I am the last rebel Apache left in this world," he says in another scene. At this point, the movie turns into an athletic romp for the former circus-performer-turned-actor as he sets fire to the fort and causes general pandemonium.

The last third of the film is a love story. Massai falls for an Apache maiden, Jean Peters, and tries to make a home for her as they hide out in the mountains. The story loses its direction at the end when Massai, because of paternal love, allows himself to be captured rather than die fighting. The weak ending was forced by fears that audiences would not like the original fatal finale at the hands of an Indian Policeman.

*Apache* was not a great Western. Mixed reviews praised Lancaster for the strength and vitality of his characterization while pointing out his starkly non-Indian appearance. The public apparently liked the film however. It was the top grossing Western of 1954, beating out John Wayne in *Hondo* and Joan Crawford in the Women's Western, *Johnny Guitar*.[2]

Burt Lancaster's piercing blue eyes and Aryan features did make it hard to believe him as an Indian but a white man playing an Indian was not new. They had done so at least as far back as Richard Dix in *The Vanishing American* (1925). *Apache* had no more of a burden to bear in this respect than did *Cheyenne Autumn* (1964) with the improbable pair of Ricardo Montalban and Gilbert Roland as Cheyenne chiefs, or *Broken Arrow* (1950) which cast Jeff Chandler as Cochise. For audiences of that era, "real Indians" were not required. In fact, the casting of leading men from other types of films as Indians probably did more to strengthen the Indian case than weaken it. By this time, Burt Lancaster had appeared in twenty pictures and had won a following as a hero in the spectacular *Crimson Pirate* (1952). The public had lifted him near the top rank of Hollywood stars after *From Here to Eternity* (1953). Merely to cast such a personality as the Indian protagonist in *Apache* already predisposed the audience to sympathize with his character and its race. It is an unmistakable indication of the film's leaning. And this was not the first time Lancaster had played an Indian. In *Jim Thorpe—All American* (1951), he had put his considerable athletic abilities to good use in portraying the tragic life story of America's greatest male athlete, a Sac and Fox from Oklahoma.

In these roles and in many other films of the 1950s, a new image of the American Indian, a more sympathetic and humane view was being crafted. In earlier films, the Indians were part of the dangerous environment, not unlike a pack of wolves. The newer Indian films went beyond even the noble savage of *Ramona* (1936 and 1910). *Broken Arrow* (1950), was the precursor of these new films. It elicited our sympathy for the *Apache* as a group and beyond that for Indians as a race. Many such films were to follow: *Battle of Apache Pass* (1952), *The Battles of Chief Pontiac* (1953), *White Feather* (1955), *The Last Hunt* (1956), *Walk the Proud Land* (1956), and many others.[3]

*Apache* is a part of this new sympathetic treatment of the Indian. It differs in its emphasis on the story of a single person. It is a biography, not a history. Massai is the focus throughout and this puts the burden on Lancaster. Despite all the obstacles, he succeeds in making us believe in and care about Massai. And through Massai we see that Indians are individuals caught up and swept along by forces greater than any one person can resist or even comprehend. In this sense, Apache can even be compared with the *Man In the Gray Flannel Suit* (1956) and *The Apartment* (1960) and finally with our own lives.

Lancaster immediately followed *Apache* with *Vera Cruz* (1954), an even bigger and more successful Western. Gary Cooper received top billing in this story of greed and intrigue set in the revolutionary Mexico of 1866. A wide-screen Technicolor extravaganza, the film sees Cooper's hero and Lancaster's villain paired to escort a pretty lady (Denise Darcel) and a shipment of gold through rebel territory. When Cooper decides that the gold should go to the Mexican people, Lancaster plays his villainous part to the hilt. The film was big and beautiful and made a lot of money for everyone involved.

*The Kentuckian* (1955) was Lancaster's third Western in a row and his first attempt at directing. The film is a frontier love story set in early Kentucky and Indiana. A.B. Guthrie, Jr., wrote the screenplay based on a Janice Holt Giles novel, *The Gabriel Horn*. Perhaps because of Lancaster's inexperience as a director or because of his double duty as actor and director, the film is slow and plodding. The only real action is generated by a villainous Walter Matthau in his screen debut. The film was not a box-office success.

Following *The Kentuckian*, Burt Lancaster made three dramatic films before returning to a full-fledged Western. In *The Rose Tattoo* (1955), he played opposite the fiery Anna Magnani, assisting her in an Oscar-winning performance as he had Shirley Booth in *Come Back, Little Sheba* (1952). He followed this with the role for which his youth as a circus performer had prepared him, *Trapeze* (1956). And in the same year, Lancaster starred opposite Katherine Hepburn in a Western of the farm frontier, *The Rainmaker* (1956), a play transposed to film. It is rare for Westerns to feature farmers. When they do, it is usually as a counterpoint to the cowboy or cattleman. There is no flamboyant violence in this film. The emphasis is on ideas and characterization rather than action and setting. Katherine Hepburn plays a frustrated and skittish middle-aged Kansas spinster who takes care of her father and several younger brothers while longing to marry. During a summer drought, all their lives are transformed by the unexpected arrival of a snake oil salesman-con man who promises to conjure up rain for a hundred dollar fee. Lancaster is perfect as Starbuck, the rainmaker. His energy and poetic vision shoot off sparks that ignite the vague romantic longings of the spinster, Lizzie. He is a charlatan, she knows that, but he brings her to life. Like Lancaster's later *Elmer Gantry* (1960) the audience likes Starbuck even though he is a fraud.

*The Rainmaker* is a fine film with a strong supporting cast including Lloyd Bridges, Wendell Corey, and a boyish Earl Holliman. It is unusual not just because it offers views of some unusual frontier types but also because the central focus of the film is a woman. The Western genre almost invariably puts the hero at center stage. Women and their concerns are usually peripheral. Lancaster and Hepburn complement each other beautifully in *The Rainmaker* and the part of Starbuck led directly to Lancaster's best-known Western role.

Hal Wallis, who had brought Burt Lancaster to Hollywood, asked him to play Wyatt Earp in *Gunfight at the O.K. Corral* in 1957. Lancaster agreed in exchange for the part of Starbuck. Opposite Lancaster, Wallis cast Kirk Douglas, another of his discoveries who had become a star, as the consumptive alcoholic Doc Holliday. By this point in their careers, both actors reportedly were difficult to work with, "The Terrible Twins" as Sheilah Graham called them.[4] The filming was difficult because Douglas and Lancaster pushed Wallis and director John Sturges for changes in Leon Uris's screenplay. What emerged was a classic Western that has stood the test of time.

The story of the clash of the Earps and the Clantons has been told often on the screen, including John Ford's *My Darling Clementine* (1946)—still the best—*Hour of the Gun* (1967) and *Doc* (1971). Each of these later adaptations makes the story more squalid and less heroic. *Gunfight at the O.K. Corral* is based on the importance of family and personal loyalty and culminates in an exciting and deadly gun battle.

Burt Lancaster plays a stiffly upright and humorless Wyatt Earp who first meets Doc Holliday at Fort Griffin, Texas. Neither likes the

Burt Lancaster and Kirk
Douglas in *Gunfight at
the O.K. Corral* (1957).
*The Museum of Modern
Art/Film Stills Archive*

other but Wyatt saves Doc's life by telling him of a hidden gun carried
by one of Doc's adversaries. Doc kills the man and leaves town pursued
by a lynch mob.

Later Doc reciprocates, in Dodge City, by saving Wyatt's life. They
become friends but their relationship is rocky because of Doc's hard
drinking and gambling on the one hand and Wyatt's stiff Puritanism
on the other. The final showdown in Tombstone follows a call for help by
one of Wyatt's brothers. Wyatt responds to the call for family solidarity
and is accompanied by Holliday. After Wyatt unsuccessfully attempts
to salvage one of the evil Clantons and his brother Jimmy Earp is
murdered, the fateful showdown foreshadowed in the film's title takes
place. All the good guys survive and all the bad guys perish in an exciting and elaborately choreographed gunfight. At the end of the fight,
Wyatt, who is disgusted with the orgy of killing, takes off his badge and
drops it along with his gun in the dust by the body of the youngest
Clanton. Wyatt rides off for California at the end, leaving Doc Holliday
to a lingering but certain death over cards and whiskey.

This version of the Earp story stresses family values, the law, and friendship just as John Ford's earlier film had. But there is a certain ambivalence and uncertainty in this film which reflects the questioning of traditional values so prevalent in the 1950s. Wyatt and Doc uphold the law and triumph over evil but the lines are not so clearly drawn. The Earps are driven by ambition and revenge. Doc is not an admirable man, particularly in his relations with Kate Fisher, a bar girl. The good are not so pure and the bad are similarly alloyed. Billy Clanton is misguided and might have been saved if Wyatt had had more time to redeem him. These complexities and the doubts that arise from them lead to Wyatt's rejection of the law and violence as symbolized by the badge and gun in the dust.[5] *Gunfight at the O.K. Corral* is a major Western, probably the most memorable of Burt Lancaster's career.

*The Unforgiven* (1960) was Lancaster's next Western. With a cast that included Audie Murphy, Charles Bickford, and Lillian Gish, and direction by John Huston, this big-budget film would seem to have everything going for it. It failed principally for two reasons: The story is improbable and Audrey Hepburn makes an impossible Indian. Rarely has a part been so miscast.[6]

Burt Lancaster plays Ben Zachary, head of a frontier family that had long ago adopted a foundling girl who is now grown. Without warning a band of Kiowa Indians arrives to claim her as their own. The family refuses to give her up, even in the face of urging by their white neighbors. The resultant siege and slaughter occupies the remainder of the film with the hero and heroine left free to marry at the end but faced with a life filled with racial prejudice.

Director Huston and Lancaster clashed during the film. Huston wanted a message picture while Lancaster sought an action-adventure story. What resulted was a good example of neither. The civil rights era concern for racial harmony in the face of violent bigotry is a major underlying theme in *The Unforgiven*.[7]

Five years passed before Lancaster made another Western, *The Hallelujah Trail* (1965). In the intervening years he had made ten films, including *Elmer Gantry* (1960), *Judgment at Nuremberg* (1961), *Birdman of Alcatraz* (1962), *The Leopard* (1963), and *Seven Days in May* (1964). These roles were the most memorable of his career. Lancaster at fifty-two was at the height of his acting powers.

*The Hallelujah Trail* is a spoof of Westerns, one of a long line stretching back at least to Buster Keaton's *The Paleface* (1922) and *Go West* (1926). In this film, Lancaster plays the commander of a cavalry unit in post-Civil War Colorado. He is caught up in an swirl of absurd activity. Denver, facing the possibility of a long winter without whiskey, contrives a rescue convoy of forty wagon loads of hooch. Out to spoil their plans are Indians, who want the liquor for themselves and a group of feisty female temperance workers who are determined that no one get a drop. Lancaster is caught in the middle.

Originally conceived as a comic epic long enough to require an intermission, the film was shortened for restless audiences. Still, it did disappointing business. It has its moments, as when the temperance leader (Lee Remick) storms into Lancaster's bath to deliver a tirade at him in his tub. He calmly puts his newspaper aside, takes his cigar from his mouth and delivers a deadpan line, "You'll excuse me if I don't stand up?" The film ends with the kind of free-for-all where no one gets hurt that highlighted so many John Wayne frontier farces.

Western films vary considerably but they do so within a recognizable range. Similar plots are so common that they seem to run together in our minds. This is characteristic of any genre, including gangster films, musicals, and police stories. All rely on variations of only a few plots. How many basic Western plots there are is debatable. Burt Lancaster's next Western, *The Professionals,* represents one of the best of a new plot line that emerged in the 1960s.[8]

For sheer entertainment and excitement, *The Professionals* (1966) is hard to beat. Audiences seem to have agreed; it was the second highest grossing Western of that year, after *Nevada Smith*. Lancaster was joined by Lee Marvin, in one of his first starring roles after *Cat Ballou,* and supported by Woody Strode, Robert Ryan, Jack Palance, and Claudia Cardinale. The plot involves a rescue attempt into the revolution-torn Mexico of Pancho Villa. Marvin and Lancaster played munitions and dynamite experts who are recruited by a wealthy American to go into Mexico and rescue his kidnapped wife (Cardinale) from one of Villa's warlord allies, Raza (Palance). They recruit an embittered horse breeder (Ryan) and an expert with bow, rope, and knife (Strode). Together they set out to steal back the girl and all for money—$10,000 each. Four major battles later, they have defeated their adversaries at every turn while earning each other's respect.

But the girl does not want to be rescued because she loves Raza. Our heroes have to decide whether to turn her over to her husband for the money or reunite her with her lover. The decision is made without consultation, so deep is their understanding of each other and their own personal code of honor. They ride off into the desert together, poorer but happier than when they began the adventure. A group of professional specialists had been seen in *The Magnificent Seven* (1960) and would be seen again in *The Wild Bunch* (1969).

Lancaster, dashing about and flinging sticks of dynamite, was at his athletic best in *The Professionals*. Not since *The Crimson Pirate* (1952) had he had so much fun. The professional plot line emerged in the 1960s during the Vietnam era and parallels the military platoon specialties of the United States Army. The subgenre copied Kurasawa's *Seven Samurai* (1954). In the background of the film is the Mexican Revolution. The Mexican people are seen as helpless before the arms of the professionals, the Mexican Army, and Raza's guerrillas. The corrupt Army is composed of mercenaries. Raza's men, while closer to the people, are uncouth and brutal. Only the professionals can be admired. They have expert knowledge, personal honor, and group loyalty. In the end it is this group loyalty, even in the face of death or the loss of their reward, that fulfills them. They ride off into the sunset, like Massai and Wyatt Earp, secure in their own personal integrity.

In *The Scalphunters* (1968) Burt Lancaster returned to Western farce. Lancaster is a mountain man-fur trapper whose pelts are stolen by a band of Kiowa Indians. In exchange they leave behind an escaped slave (Ossie Davis). Their comic escapades make up most of the film. Along the way they run into a band of scalphunters led by Telly Savalas and his mistress (Shelley Winters). Besides the heavy-handed humor we are pointedly taught racial equality by Lancaster and Davis, as when they emerge both the same color from a fight in a mud puddle.[9]

Vengeance and age are the twin themes of *Valdez Is Coming* (1971). For the third time in his career, Lancaster began three Westerns in a row. Lancaster played another professional, a local constable who had been a military policeman. Valdez is Mexican-American and lives in a small town just the other side of the border where he is the only remnant of law and order. The film is not a major Western, but we can see several elements of the Western of the 1970s in it.

The violence in *Valdez Is Coming* is graphic and of the masochistic variety traceable back to *One-Eyed Jacks* (1961) and seen in its contemporary, *The Wild Bunch* (1969). Near the film's beginning Valdez is beaten almost to death and tied to a long pole. He drags himself through the cactus-covered desert to his lonely shack. The visual analogy to crucifixion is unmistakable.

Then an old convention of Westerns shows up. Valdez, hardly alive, struggles to pull a trunk from under his bed, digs down to the bottom, and takes out a paper-wrapped package. Untying it, he reveals his old army uniform, his "sacred duds." Donning these clothes he is magically transformed and healed. He stands upright and sends a message to his tormentors. "Tell them, Valdez is coming."[10]

Valdez abducts the evil gang leader's girl friend. They pursue but soon discover that Valdez is no ordinary man. His old skills return and with his big-bore Hawken rifle he picks off his enemies like bottles on a fence. Valdez does not get the girl—Lancaster said he was "too old to get the girl any more"—but he proves the quality of even an aging Western hero.[11]

Sabbath, an arid, sleepy Western town, where every day is a day of rest is the setting for *Lawman* (1971) directed by Michael Winner. The local sheriff is a shadow of his former self. Robert Ryan plays the part perfectly. He was not always a "kicked dog," says the local ranching magnate (Lee J. Cobb). "In his day you could not walk in the same sun as him."

In rides Jared Maddox (Burt Lancaster), marshal from the distant town of Bannock. He carries warrants for several men, including the son of the local magnate. They had gotten drunk and shot up Bannock, killing one of the citizens, and Maddox is there to take them back to face the law. Sheriff Ryan does not welcome the lawman. He tells Maddox that Sabbath is in rancher Bronson's pocket, and he is there too. Maddox gives him a message for Bronson and the men he seeks. "I'm going to take these men back with me or kill them where they stand." The sheriff delivers the message as well as his impression of Maddox. "Some men just go to a thing in a straight line, Mr. Bronson, they do not bend and they do not trade. He's got the mark."

Sheriff Ryan and Maddox represent the alternative futures that faced Wyatt Earp when he rode off at the end of *Gunfight at O.K. Corral*. On the one hand he could, through old age and a failure of nerve become like Ryan, a shadow of his former self, a broken toady to the local cattle baron. On the other hand, he could hold fast to his principles and find himself isolated, hated, and alone. When town leaders plead with him to leave he responds, "You want me out of your town, what happened some other time, some other place ain't your trouble. I've seen men like you in every town in the West. You want the law but you want it to walk quiet, you don't want it to put a hole in your pocket." Although Ryan is corrupt he sympathizes with Maddox, and the two develop a kind of mutual respect. They understand each other.

Rancher Bronson believes that he can buy off Maddox or frighten him away. He thinks the old days of settling things with guns are all past, but he is wrong. Maddox has a simple but direct philosophy: "I never drew first on a man in my life. That's the only way to stay clean. You play it by the rules. Without the rules you are nothing." This is not new. It has been seen in hundreds of Westerns. But here the terrible loneliness and isolation is made apparent. The scene is reminiscent of Gregory Peck in *The Gunfighter* (1950) leaning back in his chair in the saloon, hands under the table, alone. The lawman is just as alone and just as much a killer. "I'm a lawman," Maddox tells one of the men he seeks. "You know what a lawman is, Crow? He's a killer of men. That's what the job calls for." His former girl friend says it best: "Do you known what they call you, Jared? The Widowmaker!" The end of the film confirms her report.

Just before the shoot-out, Maddox, feeling his age and loneliness, wavers for a moment. "Soon there will be no more towns like Bannock, towns that need a gun like mine. I guess yours is the right way, Cotton, sit out the years. Find a nice quiet town." But Ryan objects, "Don't do it my way Maddox, quit clean." Bronson and his men arrive and call Maddox out into that familiar dusty street. He leaves to face them with a parting word to Ryan: "You can't change what you are and if you try, somethin' always calls you back."

In the shoot-out, four men face him and four men die. Bronson, seeing his son dead in the street, turns his six-shooter on himself and blows his brains out in one of the most shockingly graphic scenes on film. Maddox rides out without a glance.

*Ulzana's Raid* (1972), Lancaster's third Western in two years returns to the desert world of the Apache. Director Robert Aldrich had worked with Lancaster in *Apache* nearly two decades earlier. This time Lancaster is a grizzled calvary scout named McIntosh, who acts as fulcrum for the story of two cultures in conflict. Set in the 1880s, Ulzana (Joaquin Martinez) is an escaped Apache leader who leads a small band in an orgy of revenge and reprisal against white society. The scenes of violence are almost too graphic to view. At one point two Apaches cut the heart from a soldier and toss it between them. McIntosh explains their cruelty as an attitude of mind which makes life in this harsh environment possible. When the young calvary officer, Lieutenant DeBuin (Bruce Davison), expresses his hatred for the Apache, McIntosh equates them with the landscape itself: "Hatin' the Apache would be like hatin' the desert because there ain't no water on it."

The Apache are not the only ones who turn to violence and brutality. DeBuin is revolted to find his own men mutilating the dead body of

Burt Lancaster and Joaquin Martinez in *Ulzana's Raid*
(1972). *The Musem of Modern Art/Film Stills Archive*

Ulzana's son. McIntosh comments, "What bothers you, Lieutenant, is
that you don't like to think of white men behaving like Indians; it kind
of confuses the issue." The issue here is that both societies have merit
but also possess fallible people. Both can commit atrocities. As
McIntosh says, "Hell, ain't none of us right." Thus Lancaster plays the
role of the voice of reason, the man who stands between the two cultures, who wears the cavalry shirt and Apache boots.

Lancaster dominates the film but in a different way than he had
two decades earlier in *Apache*. There is no leaping from rock to rock
here, although the film contains a scene in which a horse is shot from
under Lancaster and he comes up with his rifle blazing. McIntosh is an
old man, even older than Lancaster at the time the film was made. But
he is a wise man at peace with himself, with the desert and the two cul-

tures. He is a mature man, like so many other Western heroes of the 1960s and 1970s.[12]

Robert Altman's *Buffalo Bill and the Indians or Sitting Bull's History Lesson* (1976) defies easy analysis. There may never have been such a self-consciously didactic Western. It came at the end of the modern Western movie era, in the year of John Bernard Book, John Wayne's Western finale as *The Shootist*. And, in its own way, *Buffalo Bill* illustrates the end of the Western movie. It is confused and confusing, a play within a play, a farce and a fantasy, a black comedy without humor.

In the title role Paul Newman plays the Wild West Show star as a man without an identity. He is overwhelmed by the theatrical legend that has been constructed around him. Bill alludes to this contrast between fiction and reality when he welcomes Sitting Bull to his show: "You'll find it ain't all that different than real life." The focus is always on the fabricated legend versus reality. "Goddam it, where's my real jacket," yells Bill. Cody looks longingly at the portrait of Buffalo Bill as though wishing he really were the hero.

Burt Lancaster plays Ned Buntline, the publicist and dime novelist who invented and embroidered the legend of Buffalo Bill. Like a cross between the calm wisdom of McIntosh and the wiliness of the con man Starbuck, Buntline sits on the sideline and comments on the significance of what he sees. Lancaster's character is the best part of the film, perhaps because it is the only realistic character on screen. At one point he toasts Bill, "Buffalo Bill, the thrill of my life to have invented ya." Although Buntline had created Buffalo Bill, he does admire Bill's vision. "No ordinary man could realize what tremendous profits could be made by telling a pack of lies in front of witnesses like it was the truth." Perhaps that is what legends and movies are. In the final analysis movies are not history, not reality recreated.

*Cattle Annie and Little Britches* (1981) was Burt Lancaster's last Western to this date. Coming out at the same time as *Local Hero*, it was not a success. There is a nice connection between *Buffalo Bill* and *Cattle Annie*. In the former, Lancaster is Ned Buntline, the dime novelist who made Buffalo Bill famous. In this film, two young girls from the East travel to the West in search of the "desperado heroes" they had read about in Buntline's novels. They discover the burned-out and decidedly nonheroic remnants of the Dalton gang led by "tired old Bill Doolin" (Lancaster). The film chronicles their sometimes comic adventures as they come to grips with reality.[13] His last Western was not Lancaster's best.

Burt Lancaster as Ned
Buntline in *Buffalo Bill
and the Indians or
Sitting Bull's History
Lesson* (1976). *The
Museum of Modern Art/
Film Stills Archive*

Burt Lancaster's Westerns span a period of three decades and fall
into roughly three groups. The first period from 1951 to 1960 is remarkable for its diversity. He played a contemporary cowboy, an Indian, a
frontiersman, a con man, and a lawman. This variety in Westerns was
a reflection of his professional drive to prove himself capable of diverse
roles in all kinds of films. His Westerns show no consistent pattern,
though the later ones, especially *Gunfight at the O.K. Corral* and *The
Unforgiven*, show growing sensitivity to the anxiety and social consciousness of the later 1950s. *Apache* had been one of the earliest such
films, although not the first. Lancaster's Westerns of the 1950s were entertaining examples of their genre but only *Gunfight at the O.K. Corral*
is still viewed as a defining example of the period.

In the 1960s, Lancaster made only three Westerns. Two of these
were farces. *The Scalphunters* is chiefly significant for its clumsy
attempts at racial commentary. *The Professionals* is an important
Western because it is one of the best of a new subgenre. Looking at the
films of the 1960s, however, it is hard to discern a constant theme.
When we turn to the Lancaster Westerns of the period from 1971 to
1980, however there is one consistent and overarching theme—

maturity. Each of the characters that Lancaster plays during this decade is a man who has confronted his growing old and come to terms with it. Valdez is far past his prime but still takes pride in his skills and faces death with a calm assurance. Marshal Maddox accepts his mortality and his lonely fight for the law. The scout McIntosh, like Ned Buntline, views life from a detached perspective. They all accept the limits of human nature. It is not that Bill Doolin and Valdez and McIntosh welcome death but that they face up to life and accept it for what it is.

Other Westerns with other stars dealt with age in the same way. John Wayne, Kirk Douglas, Robert Ryan, Steve McQueen, and Charlton Heston played such parts in the 1970s. The theme emerged in Peckinpah's *Ride the High Country* (1962) with Randolph Scott and Joel McCrea at the end of their careers. Kirk Douglas embodied the same theme in *Lonely Are the Brave* that same year. His character was not old but he had outlived his time. The aging theme runs through all the major Westerns of the 1960s and 1970s, and the films of Burt Lancaster illustrate it well.

Writing about the several stages of life, Erik Erikson, discusses the final stage, maturity, in terms of two opposite tendencies. Facing up to the limited achievements of remaining life and the ultimate death which awaits all of us, one alternative is despair. But giving in and giving up are not acceptable or admirable solutions. The alternative is what Erikson calls "integrity," a kind of calm self-assurance and acceptance of life's limits. This "informed and detached concern with life itself in the face of death itself" he calls "wisdom."[14]

The aging and aged Western characters played by Burt Lancaster in the 1970s were a far cry from his bounding heroes of the 1950s. In all his early films, and not just the Westerns, Lancaster was known for the energy and animal aggressiveness he exuded on screen. In mid-career, he won praise for his restrained and controlled performances, in which he kept that dynamic energy on a tight leash. His Westerns of the 1970s were notable for the calm, assured integrity of his portrayals of mature and aging men, not heroes but ordinary men who had faced obstacles and were now at peace with life and unafraid of death.

Burt Lancaster's fourteen Western roles over four decades of movie making covered a wide spectrum of frontier types. Along with the films of the other major Western stars in this volume, he helped carry the burden of the American Western movie genre. And, if all movies are myth, the Western movie is the best myth of all, as Lancaster's Ned

Buntline puts it in *Buffalo Bill and the Indians,* "just dreamin' out loud."

NOTES

1. John H. Lenihan, *Showdown: Confronting Modern America in the Western Film* (Urbana: University of Illinois Press, 1980), p. 65.
2. Will Wright, *Six Guns and Society: A Structural Study of the Western* (Berkeley: University of California Press, 1975) p. 31.
3. Lenihan, *Showdown,* p. 46; Peter Biskind, *Seeing is Believing: How Hollywood Taught Us to Stop Worrying and Love the Fifties* (New York: Pantheon Books, 1983) p. 240.
4. These paragraphs on *Gunfight at the O.K. Corral* are based primarily on three sources: Tony Thomas, *Burt Lancaster* (New York: Pyramid Publications, 1975), pp. 73–75; and Robert Windeler, *Burt Lancaster* (New York: St. Martin's Press, 1984), pp. 95–97; *Gunfight at the O.K. Corral* in Frank N. Magill, ed., *Magill's Survey of Cinema: English Language Films,* Second Series (Englewood Cliffs, N.J.: Salem Press, 1981), Vol. II, pp. 952–55.
5. A similar symbolic act takes place in *High Noon* (1952) and in the urban Western, *Dirty Harry* (1971).
6. The film was also a physical disaster for Audrey Hepburn. When she was thrown from a horse, she broke four bones that required weeks to heal and delayed the film's completion. Ian Woodward, *Audrey Hepburn* (New York: St. Martin's Press, 1984), pp. 176–80. That same year, Elvis did a creditable job as an Indian half-breed in *Flaming Star.*
7. John Tuska thinks this is Audie Murphy's best film, *The Filming of the West* (Garden City, N.Y.: Doubleday and Company, Inc., 1976). And, of course, any glimpse of Lillian Gish that we have justifies the film by itself.
8. Will Wright, in *Sixguns and Society: A Structural Study of the Western* (Berkeley: University of California Press, 1975) argues that there are four basic plots, one of which he names "The Professional Plot."
9. Lenihan, *Showdown,* p. 85; Philip French, *Westerns: Aspects of a Movie Genre* (New York: Oxford University Press, 1977), pp. 88, 96.
10. The "sacred duds" convention at its most obvious may be found in *The Lone Ranger* and *Zorro* films. But it is not unknown in even classic Westerns such as *Shane* (1953), in which Shane's actions in getting out his guns are very similar to Valdez's. In *Rio Bravo* (1956) Chance (John Wayne) returns to Dude (Dean Martin) his old gun belt and guns from the time when he was an unbeatable gunman, and they have a visible effect on Dude.
11. Windeler, *Burt Lancaster,* p. 151.
12. Jack Nachbar, *Ulzana's Raid* (1972), in *Western Movies,* ed. William T. Pilkington and Don Graham (Albuquerque: University of New Mexico Press, 1979), pp. 139–47; Lenihan, *Showdown,* pp. 47, 48, 81; French, *Westerns,* p. 170.
13. Vincent Canby, *New York Times,* May 24, 1981.
14. Erik Erikson, *The Life Cycle Completed: A Review* (New York: W. W. Norton and Company, 1982), pp. 61–72.

JIM   MILLER

# Clint Eastwood:
# A Different Kind of
# Western Hero

Over the years Clint Eastwood has become known to his fans as
Rowdy Yates, The Man With No Name, and more recently as "Dirty
Harry" Callahan. These screen heroes have different personas, but being American heroes, they are fiercely independent, which also applies
to Clint Eastwood, the actor who has portrayed them. It can also be said
of other actors who portrayed stalwart heroes on the screen—Gary
Cooper, Burt Lancaster, and John Wayne, for example—but none, with
the exception of Wayne, has affected American moviegoers as Eastwood has. And perhaps the oddity here is that Eastwood's emergence as
the star of Sergio Leone's Man With No Name trilogy in the 1960s is
largely responsible for putting him on the road to challenging the
image of John Wayne as America's supreme cowboy. Eastwood will admit that a lot of good luck allowed him to become a successful actor, but
it is also true that he gave America a look at a different kind of Western
hero.

The average moviegoer probably sees three separate entities in
the roles that have brought Eastwood to the peak of his profession but
three slender threads tie these heroes with one another and to Eastwood himself. One is the fierce independence of each, a characteristic
trait Americans always have looked for in their heroes—and anti-
heroes as well—whether they're mythical/legendary or real, seen on

television or in the movie theatre, or read about in the books of Charles Dickens, Louis L'Amour, or Mickey Spillane. The second bond involves an instinct about what the public is looking for at the box office. This is evident and an important factor in Eastwood's career when one considers that America's social turmoil during the late 1960s and early 1970s coincided with the emergence on the screen of The Man With No Name and a renegade cop named "Dirty Harry," both of whom did as much outside the law as they did within it. Such films would have been financial disasters rather than successes at an earlier time. Eastwood trusted his good luck when he embarked on such speculative ventures. The third bond takes the form of individual privacy, although in Eastwood it is viewed as shyness. In any of the more than two dozen films he has made since 1964, his last year on the Rawhide set, the character he portrays is one who would just as soon be left alone once he gets outside his professional life. This can be dismissed as Eastwood acting out Eastwood, much in the same way critics viewed John Wayne as acting the role of John Wayne in any movie in which he starred. The truth of this statement is substantiated by the effect these two film giants had on the American public through the roles they played: Wayne as a super-patriot in both the military men and western frontiersmen he portrayed, and Eastwood in the role of a cynical loner at a time when the mood of the country was shaped in much the same line of thought. Few other actors have had as great an impact.

Eastwood's first success came with his role as a traditional cowboy, Rowdy Yates, in the television series Rawhide, but his earlier years are no less interesting. Born in San Francisco on May 31, 1930, he was named after his father, who spent a good deal of his time looking for a job, like most of the rest of America during the Great Depression. In the decade preceding World War II the Eastwood family had to move about once a year while the senior Eastwood held jobs that ranged from an accountant to a gas station attendant in the northern California area. Young Eastwood was never in any one place long enough to make friends, a factor that played a part in the development of the outsider in his personality. Occasionally Eastwood stayed with his grandmother in Livermore, California, while his father looked for a job. She was a self-sufficient woman who owned a chicken farm, and he learned much from her, including how to ride a horse, a skill that came in handy when he began to act in Westerns.[1]

At the age of fifteen Eastwood had grown to nearly his 6-foot 4-inch adult frame, but he was still an introverted high school student. He excelled in sports and became proficient in playing the piano and the trumpet by the time he was graduated.[2]

An admiration for the kind of person who knew what they wanted in life led Eastwood to strike out on his own after graduation. He worked in Oregon for a year as a lumberjack and then at a pulp mill. After his family joined him in Oregon, he took a job stoking a furnace for Bethlehem Steel. He later worked as a truck driver and lifeguard before being drafted into the Army during the Korean Conflict. He spent his two-year hitch at Fort Ord, California. By the time of his discharge he had decided that there were three things he wanted in life. The first was a marriage to Maggie Johnson, a young student at Berkeley he had begun dating while stationed at Fort Ord, and they married on December 19, 1953. The second thing he wanted was to live in Carmel, California, if he could ever afford it. The third thing he wanted was to become an actor.[3]

Part of the decision to take up such an unstable career grew from experience with location shooting that Universal Studios had done on his base. An assistant director told him that he had the right looks for being in movies. During his years in the service he met David Jansen, who became one of his best friends, and Martin Milner, both of whom committed themselves to acting careers. So after his military service ended he moved to Los Angeles and used his GI Bill benefit to attend Los Angeles City College. He also worked as a swimming pool installer and later as a lifeguard before Universal hired him in 1954 for six months at $75 a week.[4]

His contract was renewed in 1955, and he had small parts in such forgettable features as *Revenge of the Creature* (1955) and *Tarantula* (1955), but he (and his friends David Jansen and John Saxon) were dropped in 1956. For the next three years Eastwood free-lanced. He did minor roles for RKO in 1956 and played the heavy in his first Western, *Ambush at Cimarron Pass* (1957). He made more money digging swimming pools than he did by acting in 1957–1958, and if ever he had second thoughts about finding another line of work it must have been in those lean years. But he persevered and in 1959 his star began to rise.[5]

*Gunsmoke* was then the most popular Western on television and Charles Marquis Warren, its creator and considered the dean of the television Western, had another series in the works. The lead had been cast but there was a part for a young man in his twenties who would co-star in the program. Eastwood was interviewed by Warren for the part, but a group of CBS executives in New York made the decision to cast Eastwood in the role, even after the director had made his own choice from the screen tests. Thus Clint Eastwood was cast as Rowdy Yates.[6]

Popular Western author Louis L'Amour has stated that he thought *Gunsmoke* was the most authentic Western series on television. Credit for this must go to Warren and his producers for their detailed accuracy in depicting the Old West. The same can be said of *Rawhide*. The first episodes of *Rawhide* were filmed on location in Arizona. Real rodeo cowboys were used in action sequences with the herd of cattle during shooting, and Eastwood, who was quick to pick up on the ways of the old-time cowhand, improved his own horsemanship. He loved outdoor work and later claimed that the years he worked on his only television series were among the most rewarding of his career.[7]

The concept of using a trail drive as a format for a Western series was not original. Howard Hanks had done so on the big screen with his 1948 production of *Red River*. In fact, *Rawhide*'s trail boss, Gil Favor, and his ramrod, Rowdy Yates, were patterned closely after the characters played by John Wayne and Montgomery Clift in the movie. For CBS that was the series' only drawback, because even with a big-name guest star in many of the episodes, Eric Fleming and Clint Eastwood were virtual unknowns to the television audience. The first dozen episodes were filmed in the fall of 1958, but soon afterwood CBS began to wonder if it had been a mistake. This news upset the cast, but as Christmas approached Eastwood received a telegram from his agent informing him that network executives had decided to broadcast the program. *Rawhide* premiered on January 9, 1959, as a replacement series, ran until it was cancelled on January 4, 1966, almost seven years exactly to the day.[8]

As the continuous story of a cattle drive on its way to Sedalia, Missouri, intermixed with guest stars and their stories each week, the show was an immediate success. One reviewer called it the cattleman's answer to *Wagon Train*, but as long as it made money the studio did not mind. It was Eastwood's first steady job as an actor and he liked the work. At first he described it as fun, but he soon was immersed in learning how a director and the crew worked on a set. This was beneficial to him when he put together his own production company a decade later. Eastwood received large amounts of fan mail and the fame that goes with being a television star, but he seldom spoke with the press about his private life as other stars did.[9]

The trouble with being a television star, he soon found out, was that he was locked into the series and could not accept outside single features or guest appearances on other shows. In addition to this frustration he developed a keen desire to direct an episode to see if he could do it, but was given no more than trailers to do. The management did not have confidence in his proposals. When he voiced his complaints, the studio gave him the permission to do guest appearances and make a motion picture or two, but the movies could only be made during the summer break of the series. Whether it was luck or gall that got him his break—it likely was a bit of both—Eastwood had the foresight to broaden his acting career, especially after the fourth year when plots became rather thin on the series. But even the next step in his acting career had a touch of what can only be called the Eastwood luck to it.[10]

To say that Clint Eastwood fell into the role of The Man With No Name would not be inaccurate, for at the time he was chosen for the role, Sergio Leone, the Italian director who was putting his first Western film together, already had asked Steve Reeves, Richard Harris, and James Coburn to be the lead and had been turned down. Harris suggested Eastwood for the part, and after viewing an episode of *Rawhide*, Leone asked the young actor to join his cast. The other actors would not accept the role because it paid less than $25,000 for a starring part. Although Eastwood at first was cool to the idea of shooting a Western in Europe, he accepted because he had never traveled to Europe. In May 1964 he arrived in Almeria in the south of Spain, a desolate-looking area where he filmed *A Fistful of Dollars* (1966), as well as two other Westerns that featured The Man With No Name.[11]

Like the successful *Magnificent Seven* (1960), *A Fistful of Dollars* was based on a Japanese film pitting good against evil and the devastating affect a stranger has on two warring factions when he comes to town. In fact, the hero in *Yojimbo* (1961) (played by Toshiro Mifune, one of Japan's finest actors) was referred to as the Stranger With No Name, accounting for Eastwood's role as The Man With No Name.[12] Although the storyline remained much the same in *Fistful* as it had in *Yojimbo*, a man alone playing both sides against each other, the end result of Clint Eastwood's role brought about a whole new look at the Western hero as a lone wolf, anti-hero that was totally different from characters John Wayne had played. The anti-hero had been done before and been well received by the American public in the role of Bret Maverick (James Garner), but the public had always been aware that Bret Maverick was a parody of the traditional Western hero. The Man

With No Name was a Western anti-hero who had not yet been viewed by American moviegoers, and that made the character and the actor who played him a different kind of Western hero.

By the time he was offered the part of No Name, Eastwood was well aware that television stars tended to be typecast in their roles so he determined to be the antithesis of the easygoing, friendly Rowdy Yates in this role. In so doing he wisely drew on what he had learned as a co-star of *Rawhide*, borrowing the cool efficiency of Eric Fleming's Gil Favor and adding to it a laconic vocabulary that had seldom been heard from any previous Western film hero.[13] Unlike the John Wayne version of the Western hero, No Name had no strict moral code and did not fight to save the land or the little guy; he looked out for himself first, regardless of the consequences, and if the little guy was able to pick up the pieces after the gunsmoke had cleared ... well, that's how it was. In portraying The Man With No Name Eastwood shattered what has been called "the myth of the West," "the code of the West," and "the cowboy code," in which the hero was always kind to women and children, usually fell in love with a good woman, and nearly *always* let the bad guy draw first in the final showdown, if for no other reason than to justify self-defense and prove once again to the audience that right wins out over wrong. In the No Name trilogy women are treated as sex objects who, although they may have a short sexual affair with the hero, never fall in love with him. Children play an even lesser role. And if No Name comes anywhere close to having a code to live by, it is that of the survival of the fittest. When a slightly prejudiced comparison was made between the "spaghetti" Westerns and the traditional Westerns after his films were released in America, Eastwood took a stand in defense of the realism those films portrayed. "People don't believe in heroes," he said. "Everybody knows that nobody ever stood in the street and let the heavy draw first. It's him or me. To me that's practical and that's where I disagree with the Wayne concept. I do all the stuff Wayne would never do. I play bigger than life characters but I'd shoot the guy in the back."[14]

Had *A Fistful of Dollars* opened in America in 1964, the year it was filmed, it would have been a flop. Instead it opened in Europe first and became such a huge box-office success that it sparked a series of imitation "spaghetti Westerns" that established a cult following. When the film was released in the United States in 1966, Eastwood had made his second No Name film with Leone, *For a Few Dollars More*, and was finishing the third of the trilogy, *The Good, the Bad, and the Ugly*, and both were also hugely successful in Europe. These two films were released in the United States in 1967 and 1968, and although they seldom received good reviews, they were as successful as they had been in Europe. The Man With No Name trilogy was re-released fifteen times in America. Part of its success can be attributed to the Eastwood luck, but a good share of it must also be given to its timing, an important entertainment factor.

Setting aside the fact that they both played bigger-than-life characters on the screen, the greatest parallel between the careers of John Wayne and Clint Eastwood is the timing of their careers. After John Ford's *Stagecoach* (1939), John Wayne's film career was given a boost by World War II, when he played not only Western heroes but also military heroes—usually in the service of the Marine Corps or Navy—who did their patriotic duty in fighting the war in the Pacific. Some of these films were classics and others have been described as B-grade pictures, but moviegoers flocked to see these pro-America films because patriotism was the mood of the country at the time. In much the same way Clint Eastwood benefited in his rise to stardom from the popularity of The Man With No Name. At the time these films were released the United States was engaged in a war that, if anything, gave patriotism a bad name with many. The boldness of portraying an atypical movie hero at that time, especially in a Western film, mirrored the beliefs of a significant segment of the population with regard to international affairs. Just how widely No Name's character affected its viewers' ideas about their country is another matter, but one thing is clear: Eastwood assured himself and the public that he would never again be stereotyped. He would reprise the cynical, flint-eyed, no-nonsense character he created in the No Name trilogy, but his fans would remember less and less about Rowdy Yates and the less memorable films made before he became a star as the years went by.

By 1968 Eastwood had starred in two moderately successful American-made Westerns, *Hang 'Em High* (1967) and *Coogan's Bluff* (1968). He also gained enough popularity—and money—to form Malpaso, his own production company.[15] The word itself is a combination of two Spanish words meaning "bad idea," but Malpaso turned out to be a good idea for Clint Eastwood. With the exception of *Escape from Alcatraz* (1978), which was made by Paramount, all of Eastwood's films from 1971 to the present have been produced by Malpaso in coordination with either Warner Brothers or Universal Studios. All those years on the *Rawhide* set and the interest he had taken in the behind-the-scenes process of film making began to pay off. His initial production company was made up of many of those who had helped get him started in his early years on television. In the early 1970s Eastwood again tried his hand at directing. Although his debut as a director in a more modern film, *Play Misty for Me* (1971), was successful, the first Western that he both directed and starred in became a minor classic. *High Plains Drifter* (1972) has been described as a "moody . . . self-conscious" film,[16] but for Eastwood fans it was a *tour de force*. Reprising his Man With No Name role—this time referred to as The Stranger—Eastwood expanded it somewhat. Once again his character is a loner who can be more than a little violent when the occasion calls for it, but at the end of the film, when The Stranger identifies himself as a former lawman of the town whose unmarked grave is now sporting full identification, the viewer has experienced The Man With No Name with a new, added dimension. Whether he is a ghost, the dead marshal come back to life, or a stranger passing through who just happens to save the town from outlaws, there is a bit of Gary Cooper's Will Kane in the hero. In fact, *Drifter* might be described as *High Noon* with a reverse twist, for where Gary Cooper's hero felt a certain dedication to duty in protecting a town that would not support him, Eastwood's hero puts the town folk through the wringer as he takes on the outlaws single-handedly, never letting them forget what cowards they really are. If there were any truth to the claim that John Wayne played John Wayne in his many movie roles, nearly the same could be said of Eastwood with the release of *High Plains Drifter*, for although Eastwood kept a low profile off screen, his on-screen performance of life on the American frontier as one of pure survival rather than high morals paralleled his own beliefs on the subject.

The Western genre was not the only one in which he'd presented this type of anti-hero. In 1971 a rather unique oddball inspector on the San Francisco Police Department named "Dirty Harry" Callahan appeared for the first time. Eastwood fans, many of them middle-class blue-collar workers, saw this new Eastwood character as the symbol of justice as it should be dispensed, at least in their two hours of escape in movie theatres. Critics, on the other hand, saw the film in a different light. To them Callahan was as immoral and even as fascistic as the bad guys in the film. "Dirty Harry" could be seen as a modernized version of The Man With No Name, a cop who was gutsy enough to jeopardize his job by going just one step beyond the law and getting away with it simply because he was willing to take the chance. Callahan is as glib, no-nonsense a character as was No Name. He has little social life and he is constantly embroiled in some aspect of his chosen profession. No matter what obstacles fall in his pathway, Callahan, just like No Name, gets his man, the only difference being that "Dirty Harry" does not shoot them in the back. He will shoot them while running away, perhaps, but seldom in the manner No Name used.

Four films featuring "Dirty Harry" Callahan, *Dirty Harry* (1971), *Magnum Force* (1973), *The Enforcer* (1975), and *Sudden Impact* (1984) have appeared. All have been successful, but *Dirty Harry*, the original, must be classified as a minor classic in filmmaking for its excellent pacing throughout as opposed to the constant slambang action sequences of such films as *Raiders of the Lost Ark* and *The Temple of Doom*.

Despite the declining interest in the Western film in 1976—even the stalwart and ever popular John Wayne did not do that well at the box office—Eastwood's *The Outlaw Josey Wales* drew large audiences that year. The story followed the traditional Western theme: Josey Wales, a farmer, comes home one day to find his family killed by guerrillas during the Civil War and sets out to find the men who did it. He becomes no better than those he is pursuing.[17] The growing Eastwood mystique drew moviegoers to see the film. Josey Wales was not The Man With No Name, but the star went through the same mannerisms, killing his opponents with a dedication that convinces the audience that the bad guys will die. As with other movies of that era, justice was served without the benefit of the law.

From a historical point of view, the films of John Wayne and Clint Eastwood have a certain amount of truth in relationship to how life in frontier America was really lived. The real West was not the sex-laden bloody era depicted in so-called "adult Western" novels, and did indeed have a code as portrayed in many of the Wayne Westerns. But until law enforcement became well established a man was often his own law when it came to defending himself and his property. In more than one case a cattle- or horse-rustler was caught in the act and hanged on the spot, more for convenience than any kind of vengeance. The rancher who caught the culprit knew that it would take a day or two to get the thief into town and possibly another week for the circuit judge to arrive and a trial to take place. This required time he could not afford to lose from his ranch, so he hanged the thief in anticipation of the inevitable outcome, considered himself as having done the community a favor, and got back to ranching. Seldom was his judgment questioned. It is

Clint Eastwood in *The Outlaw Josey Wales* (1976). *Malpaso Production Company*

this aspect of character portrayal that has made Clint Eastwood a different kind of Western hero. John Wayne played a strong, independent Westerner who was his own man in the way most Americans like to picture themselves, and he did so with the idealism that the world viewed as a part of the "cowboy era" of American history. It is a viewpoint with more than just a hint of myth and legend to it, but one we have cherished since the first dime novel appeared. It is the way that America is symbolized in the world—the one independent loner who has the strength to go up against the odds and still come out a winner.

The Eastwood Westerner is equally as strong, independent, and self-sufficient as Wayne's, but he is portrayed in a more realistic manner than the Wayne hero and is often more violent than previous screen heroes. From the appearance of The Man With No Name this difference pitted Eastwood's critics against his fans who have flocked to see his movies, particularly his Westerns. Just as John Wayne's hero lent credibility to the importance of myth and legend at a time when the nation had reached the zenith of its accomplishments—the winning of World War II—so did Clint Eastwood's version of that same hero give credibility to the questioning of some of our legends at a time when we were gravely questioning our own values as well.

In the decade that followed the making of *The Outlaw Josey Wales* Eastwood has gained fame not only as an actor but as the head of a production company that seldom goes over budget on its pictures. In Eastwood, Malpaso Productions has its own producer, director, and star, a combination that is hard to beat. In the spring of 1985 Hollywood producers anxiously awaited the debut of *Pale Rider*, Clint Eastwood's first Western in nearly ten years. It was also the first quality production of a film in the Western genre since John Wayne's *The Shootist* and Eastwood's *Josey Wales*, both of which appeared in 1976. The anxiety surrounding this event centered on whether the Western had a chance to make a comeback, both in print and on the silver screen, after a decade of taking a backseat to the occult and outer space themes that

Clint Eastwood. *Malpaso Production Company*

proved so popular in the late 1970s and early 1980s. Could yet another variation of The Man With No Name replace Luke Skywalker and Indiana Jones as the box-office hero of the 1980s? Veteran character actor John Russell, who co-starred as the bad guy with Eastwood in *Pale Rider* stated that he thought the *Star Wars* movies were nothing more than Westerns in outer space. The success of *Pale Rider* proved that Eastwood is a groundbreaker in Hollywood, for within six weeks after it premiered producers had optioned ten more Westerns for future motion pictures.

Not seeing Clint Eastwood in a Western portraying what is essentially the character of The Man With No Name is now nearly as unthinkable as not seeing John Wayne in a Western portraying the likes of John Chisum or Davy Crockett. Both men have known what their fans want. *Pale Rider* is more a contemporary Western than Eastwood's "spaghetti" Westerns in that it has a definite setting and place in 1850 in California during the Gold Rush days. The plot centers around independent miners who are fighting their takeover by a big corporation mining outfit. This is more in line with what Americans have conceived as a traditional Western story. Perhaps this will give Hollywood the incentive it needs to bring out more Westerns, but the main attraction of *Pale Rider* is Eastwood, once again reprising his role as a man who comes to town and is known only as The Stranger. He sides with the independent miners and faces a half-dozen gunmen in what has come to be known as the classic *High Noon* gunfight. No matter what the film critics will say, the film will be another money-maker for Clint Eastwood and Malpaso Productions.

Eastwood once stated that he thought the kind of movies his fans wanted to see were ones with a lot of action and in which the good guy won out in the end.[18] Such a comment is certainly not a new one, for it has been the formula for many successful and popular movies. It must be taken into consideration when evaluating the career of an actor who is as shy and modest today about his accomplishments, fame, and fortune as he was thirty-five years ago when he struck out on his own with virtually nothing of material value. At the age of fifty-seven, Clint Eastwood has achieved success as a producer and director and has been and likely will be one of the most popular entertainment figures in the United States for some time to come. After years of criticism he has come into his own as a respected producer whose films set trends. His fans are many, not only in the United States but throughout the world, and few of his pictures have lost money. His films and career have had a definite effect on how we view the Western in film, in book form, and in reality. Some might claim that it was the Eastwood luck which brought all this success. Others would say it was brought about by hard work and being in the right place at the right time.

Luck, hard work, and proper timing have played a significant role in the success of more than one person in the film industry. In the case of Clint Eastwood the road to success began over twenty years ago when, in a desperate move to keep from being stereotyped as a television cowboy, he ventured to the plains of Almeria, Spain, and dared to be a different kind of Western hero.

BIBLIOGRAPHY

The term "full-scale biography" has always seemed more suited to those people who have retired or passed on in life, and since Mister Eastwood has done neither it would be superfluous to indicate any such book as being written about him. However, I am grateful to Iain Johnstone's *Man With No Name* (New York: Morrow Quill, 1981), which supplied me with much of the background on my subject and is perhaps the most complete biography of Eastwood to date. David Downing and Gary Herman, *Clint Eastwood* (New York: Music Sales, 1978), and Frank Allan, *Screen Greats: Clint Eastwood* (New York: Bookthrift, 1982), are less thorough.

Filmographies featuring photos and plot lines of Eastwood's films include Lee Pfeiffer, *Films of Clint Eastwood* (Secaucus, N.J.: Citadel, 1983); Boris Vnijewski, *Films of Clint Eastwood* (Secaucus, N.J.: Citadel, 1982), and Mark Whitman, *The Films of Clint Eastwood* (St. Paul, Minn.: Greenhaven, 1978).

Film histories and analyses of Westerns that feature Eastwood include Jon Tuska, *The Filming of the West* (Garden City, N.Y.: Doubleday, 1976); George N. Fennin and William K. Everson, *The Western: From Silents to the Seventies* (New York: Penguin, 1973); and John Lenihan, *Showdown: Confronting Modern America in the Western Film* (Urbana: University of Illinois Press, 1980).

NOTES

1. Iain Johnstone, *The Man With No Name* (New York: Morrow Quill, 1981), p. 11.
2. Ibid., pp. 11–12.
3. Ibid., pp. 11–14.
4. Ibid., pp. 14–16.
5. Ibid., p. 23.
6. Ibid., pp. 25–26.
7. Ibid., p. 25.
8. Ibid., p. 26.
9. Ibid., p. 31.
10. Ibid., p. 32.
11. Ibid., pp. 35, 38.
12. Ibid., p. 36.
13. Ibid., p. 40.
14. Ibid., p. 51.
15. Ibid., p. 64.
16. Ibid., p. 101.
17. Ibid., p. 113.
18. Ibid., p. 138.

SANDRA KAY SCHACKEL

# Women in Western Films: The Civilizer, the Saloon Singer, and Their Modern Sister

ALTHOUGH WOMEN HAVE been visible in Western films from the silents to the present, the male hero has dominated the genre. This is not to say that women have not played important roles in Westerns: think of Dallas in *Stagecoach* (1939), Vienna in *Johnny Guitar* (1954), or Etta Place in *Butch Cassidy and the Sundance Kid* (1969). Nevertheless, the male hero has usually overshadowed the female role because Westerns have so heavily stressed masculinity. Therefore, to analyze women's roles it is necessary to view them through the context of the male characters. In addition, since men have written and directed Western films almost exclusively, women's roles tend to reflect a male perspective. As such, women's roles are imbued with traits traditionally considered feminine: passivity, dependence, gentleness, and sensitivity, among others. If women are given strong characters, they must ultimately depend on a man for their happiness and security. The male perspective thus dominates the genre in ways in which women's roles are played out in accordance with male expectations of female behavior.

Just as importantly, films reflect changing social and cultural values of the period in which they are made. Several authors have likened movies to mirrors that reflect the social and cultural milieu of their times.[1] From the simplicity of *The Great Train Robbery* of 1903 to the complex, psychosocial movies of the 1980s, films have clearly responded to specific political, economic, and social events in American society. Westerns are no exception. The early silent films of D. W. Griffith and W. S. Hart depicted a romantic, nostalgic, and sentimental West, while those of John Ford and Howard Hawks in the 1930s and 1940s celebrated the arrival of civilization and the last showdown between the independent westerner and the forces of progress. This version, or formula, of the Western held audiences' attention until the 1940s. After World War II, however, variations on the standard Western saga began to appear.

The postwar years were a time of critical reevaluation in America as social and political values and institutions were questioned. The direction of foreign policy, the assimilation of ethnic minorities, and the growing clash between the corporate welfare state and individual rights, for instance, were issues that crept into Western films in the 1940s and 1950s.[2] Howard Hawks's *Red River* (1948), for example, pitted the self-interest of an aging cattleman, Tom Dunson (John Wayne), against the welfare of the larger society, while the 1952 classic, *High Noon*, is often seen in the light of anti-Communist fears that the McCarthy hearings generated.

Westerns made during the 1960s and 1970s displayed even more biting social commentary, paralleling the unrest of that decade caused by Vietnam, civil rights issues, campus unrest, and the re-emerging women's movement. In this era a change occurred in women's movie images that reflected society's growing awareness of female capabilities. At the same time, sex and violence began to dominate many Westerns. The films of Sam Peckinpah (*The Wild Bunch*, 1969; *Pat Garrett and Billy the Kid*, 1973) and the "spaghetti" Westerns of Sergio Leone starring Clint Eastwood (*A Fistful of Dollars*, 1966; *For A Few Dollars More*, 1967; *The Good, the Bad, and the Ugly*, 1967) are vivid examples of this trend. These sex and violence-ridden films marked the beginning of "adult" Westerns, many of them branded with an R rating. Along with such emphases, these decades mark a turning point for women's roles away from traditional stereotypes that had characterized the genre since the silents.

The stereotypes are not hard to spot, nor are they particularly imaginative. They include woman as nurturer/civilizer and woman as femme fatale/vamp. Two stars of the silent era, Lillian Gish in *The*

*Battle of Elderbush Gulch* (1913) and Mae Marsh in the non-Western, *Birth of a Nation* (1915), idealized women as gentle, dependent creatures reminiscent of Victorian times. Marlene Dietrich in *Destry Rides Again* (1939) represents the wickedly daring vamp, while Mae West personified the ultimate femme fatale in *My Little Chickadee* (1940), a woman who is out "to get her man" at any cost. The rancher's wife, the army officer's lady, and the pioneer mother all served to soften the savagery of the West as nurturers and civilizers; even Etta Place was a schoolteacher before she joined forces with Butch and Sundance.

The vamp, usually a prostitute, was the other stereotype most often depicted in Westerns. She could be a whore with a heart of gold (Frenchy in *Destry*), a bad woman turned good (Dallas in *Stagecoach*), or a shrewd businesswoman looking out for her own interest (Mrs. Miller in *McCabe and Mrs. Miller*, 1971). Or she could be one of the common prostitutes that littered the script of *The Wild Bunch*. Thus, traditionally, women in Westerns have most often been scarlet-clad saloon singers, ever ready to die for the hero, or Eastern-born embodiments of the civilized graces that the West urgently needed.[3]

Stereotypes are an integral part of the formula Western that developed in the early years of the film industry. An example of such a Western is described by John D. Weaver in "Destry Rides Again and Again and Again."

> The West was won for the gunslingers of television by the hard-riding, quick-drawing heroes of an earlier, less complicated day, when Good (clean-shaven, white hat) pursued Evil (mustache, black hat) across a silent screen to the piano accompaniment of the William Tell Overture. Greed, buttoned into the town banker's black frock coat, preyed on Innocence, an orphan in calico. Lust worked the saloon beat, hustling drinks in her spangled finery, and Death waited off-stage for justice to be served by the traditional shootout.[4]

This simplistic scenario illustrates the standard formula many Westerns employed from the earliest films until the 1960s. As John Cawelti notes in *The Six-Gun Mystique*, the formula Western centers around an "epic moment" of confrontation between the pioneer and the wilderness.[5] The hero, who is squared off against nature and savages, represents civilization, as does the homestead, ranch, and town. The heroine is often a spirited rancher's daughter or a refined Easterner who represents the moral fiber of the community as well as its susceptibility to danger. The final union of hero and heroine in many Westerns meant that the spiritual strength and physical durability of American society would continue.[6]

The star of the Western has traditionally been the male hero, though his horse often shared the screen with him in the popular B Westerns. His feminine counterpart was a wife or a "civilizing agent" who became a wife by the picture's end. This scenario clearly reflects a male perspective that it is men who selflessly face danger and subdue nature while women impart the civilizing graces. Jenni Calder demonstrates this point in *There Must Be a Lone Ranger* when she describes two basic types of heroines: the "chocolate box type," associated with civilization, domesticity, the schoolhouse, and the church; and the spunky heroine who can ride the range and face danger but is tamed enough to marry the hero.[7] Grace Kelly as Amy Kane in *High Noon* embodies the essence of the chocolate box type, while Barbara Stan-

Barbara Stanwyck in
*The Great Man's Lady.*
S. K. Schackel

wyck more than once played a feisty ranchwoman heroine (*The Great Man's Lady*, 1942; *The Cattle Queen of Montana*, 1954). However, the hero did not always wind up with the woman. Witness the many times John Wayne rode off into the distance just as he had arrived, alone, as in *The Searchers* (1956), for example. This was the final scene for *Shane* (Alan Ladd) also, since the woman he loved was married to another man.

It was important to have a wife to serve as helpmate in conquering the West, but not an absolute necessity. Or was it? A recent movie, *Heartland* (1979), presents a more believable scenario that is closely tied to frontier reality. The film centers around a single man, Clyde Stewart (Rip Torn), who advertises for a housekeeper. The woman who answers the ad, Elinor Pruitt (Conchata Ferrell), eventually marries her employer for pragmatic reasons. They need each other to battle the forces of nature and share the work of ranching; romance plays a negligible role in this film. While Ferrell fits the heroine-as-wife stereotype, the film transcends it in the portrayal of two people who share equally in the business of day-to-day living and meet every challenge with courage.[8]

Clearly a new stereotype has appeared in the past twenty-five years that differs from the two traditional images of women. This new image is the strong, independent woman who can take care of herself in most situations and expects to do so. The best examples, in addition to the female role in *Heartland*, are Candace Bergen's role in *Soldier Blue* (1970), Kathleen Lloyd's in *The Missouri Breaks* 1970, and Jane Fonda's in *Comes a Horseman* (1978). The appearance of this long overdue heroine parallels current historical research that illustrates women with these characteristics, sometimes living alone and sometimes working beside a man. Recent works by Julie Roy Jeffrey, Joanna Stratton, Sandra Myres, and Theresa Jordan recount many stories of settlement in the West by women with and without husbands, sons, and brothers, women who managed to lead productive and satisfying lives.[9] The acknowledgment of independent women in film clearly reflects the shifting social and cultural climate of the past decades that recognizes women in more equitable roles, both on and off screen.

Nevertheless, women's film roles were fairly well defined, and limited, in the early days of the industry. Many Westerns were based on the films of W. S. Hart (*Hell's Hinges*, 1916; *Tumbleweeds*, 1926) and books by Zane Grey (*The Vanishing American*, 1925; *Wild Horse Mesa*,

1926) in which women and men filled traditional roles as part of the pattern of heroic virtue. In these years Westerns were often grand, sweeping spectacles that depicted the taming of the West, acted out in gunfights, cattle stampedes, Indian attacks, cavalry charges, gold and silver rushes, and innumerable saloon fights. These grand-scale Westerns of 1910 to 1930 utilized Victorian ideas that divided womanhood into either good woman (the civilizer) or bad woman (the prostitute).

Lillian Gish and Mae Marsh were two actresses who personified the former image. In *The Battle of Elderbush Gulch* (1913), Gish and Marsh play two young Eastern women who come to live in the West, encounter Indians on the warpath, and are rescued when the hero arrives with the cavalry. A Buck Jones movie, *Timber Wolf* (1925), set in a South Carolina lumber camp but utilizing a traditional Western format, carries out the then-popular theme of "taming" the heroine before allowing her to marry the hero, a variation of the spunky heroine idea.[10] By the late 1920s, however, sexless and saintly images appeared oddly out of step with the lively Jazz Age.

A remarkable exception to such Victorian-inspired roles was the rise to fame of femme fatale Mae West and her explicit sexuality in stage and screen performances. In the 1920s and 1930s, sex was not an uncommon ingredient in movies—as in the successes of siren Jean Harlow and the "It" girl, Clara Bow—but West took sexuality to new and outrageous heights with her caricatures of sexiness. Sometimes hailed as the "first lady of liberation" on the screen, West was a woman in control of her own destiny; she wrote her own material, was usually self-supporting, and guarded her independence.[11] At age forty-seven, West starred in *My Little Chickadee* (1940) with W. C. Fields, a comic Western in which West makes the alcoholic actor look like a buffoon. Conveying her sexuality through suggestive mannerisms and drawled speech, West always "got her man." Even before *Chickadee*, however, the censors disapproved of her screen behavior. As a result of pressure from the newly established Legion of Decency, West was forced to soften the innuendoes and eliminate outright suggestive material by the mid-1930s. A few short years later, Jane Russell even more brazenly portrayed female sexuality in *The Outlaw* (1943).

In 1939, sex and comedy highlighted another Western, using a fading femme fatale, Marlene Dietrich, in the leading role in an attempt to boost her flagging career.[12] In *Destry Rides Again*, Dietrich plays Frenchy, a "tough cookie" and proprietress of the Last Chance Saloon. Frenchy is a saloon singer in love with a local gambler, but she falls for

Sheriff Destry (James Stewart), when he is called in to clean up the town. Her talents in this saga including wisecracking, singing, and a dramatic fistfight with another woman, but the bad woman heroine meets her fate by dying in Destry's arms.

*My Little Chickadee* and *Destry Rides Again* were major Westerns that reflected the newly revised censorship code. The Western, even more than other genres, such as the gangster film and the risqué comedy, responded to the reform movement by adopting a more conventional format.[13] One effect of this development was the rise of the B Western and its emphases on fighting cowboys, singing cowboys, and comic sidekicks. These cheaply made formula films focused on action—fistfights, chases, and riding stunts—and made heroes of Tex Ritter, Hopalong Cassidy, Lash LaRue, the Lone Ranger, and the singing cowboys, Gene Autry and Roy Rogers. In the B Western, romance was kept to a minimum, often sublimated through comedy directed at the hero's male sidekick, such as Smiley Burnett, Gabby Hayes, or Pat Buttram. The heroine usually was a passive permanent-waved civilizer whose main function in these horse operas was to provide motivation for the action: it was her ranch or cattle the villains coveted.

In the 1940s, female roles in B Westerns expanded somewhat as women became more self-reliant, often portraying capable ranchers. In the singing Westerns the heroine provided a pretty (non-sexual) object for Rogers's or Autry's songs. One of Rogers's leading ladies, Dale Evans, lived out the "cowboy wins the lady" cliché; after playing opposite him for two years, they were married in 1946.[14] Other B Western heroines include Linda Stirling, Peggy Stewart, Gail Davies, and Vera Ralston. The B Westerns remained popular for their simple formula of fast action and good-overcomes-evil theme until competition from television in the 1950s relegated them to near obscurity. In the meantime Hollywood began to capitalize on the use of sex to sell movies.

During the 1940s, sex became a major theme in films. The wartime boom put money in people's pockets and going to the movies was a popular way to spend it. Overseas, American men wanted sex symbols in bathing suits and tight sweaters. Women at home, many of whom had jobs and new responsibilities and values, wanted to see women in more fulfilling roles.[15] The result, for women in film, was sexual exploitation. Two Westerns of this decade are notable for their treatment of sexuality in this way.

*The Outlaw* was an especially degrading film for Jane Russell in which she is raped, abused, and regarded primarily as a sex object for

Billy the Kid. Indeed, when Billy and Doc Holliday have to decide between Russell and a horse as a prize in a poker game, they choose the horse! The message in this movie is clearly that Rio, a Mexican spitfire stereotype, is unimportant except for her large bosom that producer/director Howard Hughes exploits at every opportunity. The film, and accompanying publicity posters, was so daring that the film was held back for three years because of censorship problems.

 *Duel in the Sun* (1946) followed on the heels of *The Outlaw* and its heavy breathing and sensuous scenes quickly earned it the nickname "Lust in the Dust." Jennifer Jones played Pearl, a half-breed girl who was torn between good and evil and succumbed to her passions. Lillian Gish plays foster mother to flirtatious Pearl, who drives the men around her mad with desire. In the final tempestuous scene between Pearl and

Claire Trevor and John Wayne in *Stagecoach*. *S. K. Schackel*

Lewt (Gregory Peck), they die in each other's arms after a shoot-out. *Outlaw* and *Duel* are but two of many movies made during the 1940s that treated sexuality in an exploitative and sensational manner.

Meanwhile, John Wayne continued to make movies for John Ford, a director whose Irish Catholic background largely shaped his ideas of female behavior. Ford was intent on constructing a value system that would reaffirm a belief in the continuity of traditional values in a rapidly changing world.[16] Marriage, home, and family were basic to his concept of civilization. Since sexual love was not a value in itself, he tended to sublimate sexual attraction in favor of gallantry or heartiness. Ford's heroines tend to be strong, supporting women who exemplify goodness and virtue. For example, Claire Trevor, who played Dallas in the 1939 classic, *Stagecoach*, overcomes her tainted past as the town's bad woman, and is redeemed through her compassion and unselfishness toward the other female passenger and the drummer and by the Ringo Kid's growing respect and love for her. Similar virtuous roles are played by Shirley Temple, Joanne Dru, and Maureen O'Hara, the female leads in the Ford-Wayne trilogy—*Fort Apache* (1948), *She Wore a Yellow Ribbon* (1949), and *Rio Grande* (1950). Vera Miles, the long-suffering woman waiting for her man to return in *The Searchers* (1956), displays the passive, patient nature prevalent in Ford's female characters.

The female roles in Ford's *My Darling Clementine* (1946) clearly portray the dichotomy between the good woman and the bad woman. Fair, virginal Clementine Carter (Cathy Downs) follows Doc Holliday (Victor Mature) to the West, but when he refuses to return to the East with her, she stays on in Tombstone and becomes the schoolmarm, the classic stereotype of the civilizer. In contrast, dark, exotic Chihuahua (Linda Darnell) is a Mexican (or Apache) woman who becomes Doc's mistress. She plays an important role in his life as lover and moral supporter, yet her fate is ambiguous. In *Clementine*, Ford's women possess predictable qualities that determine their behavior. As in other films, Ford brings a male perspective to the screen that places women in an unrealistic either/or category.

Unlike Ford, Howard Hawks's work shows little sense of the family as a basic unit, and only a minor interest in romantic love.[17] His movies tend to reflect the intimate relationships between hard, determined men with women playing roles peripheral to the male characters. Nevertheless, Hawks's female roles are important in his Westerns, and they embody a strength and independence lacking in Ford's

women. Angie Dickinson, as Feathers in *Rio Bravo* (1959), plays a
saloon girl, but she is a far cry from the whore with a heart of gold
willing to die for the hero.[18] Instead she exhibits qualities typical of
Hawks's women—she is intelligent, resilient, and responsive. She allows John T. Chance (John Wayne) to establish authority over her, but
this clearly represents a voluntary surrender on her part.[19]

Despite Hawks's ability to invest his female characters with such
admirable qualities, his male-female relationships are not carried to
their logical conclusions. In *Red River* (1948), Tess Malay (Joanne Dru)
plays the lead female role, but her romance with Matthew Garth
(Montgomery Clift) is never fully developed. Yet Dru affects the reconciliation between Wayne and Clift at the film's end. As Jack Nachbar
points out, Dru's role is a key element in the formula Western for, in
*Red River* as well as in *She Wore A Yellow Ribbon*, she unites the older
hero with the younger one to preserve peace on the newly settled
frontier.[20] In this way Dru plays the familiar female role of mediator.

Two other important movies of the 1950s highlight women in
stereotypical fashion. In *High Noon* (1952), Grace Kelly plays a loyal
wife who stands by her husband when all others have deserted him. In
the same film, Katy Jurado plays the Mexican woman of questionable
virtue, Helen Ramirez. In this film, however, the traditional bad
woman/good woman contrast is given a new twist. Of the two, Jurado is
stronger, more independent, and appears to be Will Kane's (Gary
Cooper) emotional equal. Amy does not seem to understand Will's need
to face down the outlaws; she is acting out of her Quaker belief in non-
violence without considering the code of honor that compels him to
finish a task he began five years earlier. Helen recognizes the moral
responsibility Will feels to confront Frank Miller and, accordingly,
advises Amy to "stand by her man," just as she recognizes that her own
future depends on taking the noon train out of Hadleyville. Yet the film
has a traditional ending, befitting the moral climate of the 1950s. Amy
puts aside her personal beliefs and runs to her husband's side at the
last moment; the tainted woman leaves town.

In *Shane* (1953), Jean Arthur plays the traditional, loyal wife common to this era. She is a gentle, hardworking homesteader's wife raising a son to be honest, polite, and responsible. Unexpectedly, however,
Marian develops feelings for drifter Shane (Alan Ladd) that set up conflicts she must resolve. When she tells Joey (Brandon DeWilde) not to
love Shane too much, knowing Shane will move on out of their lives,
she is cautioning herself against the same emotion. At the same time,

Lloyd Bridges, Katy Jurado, Gary Cooper, and Grace Kelly
in *High Noon. S. K. Schackel*

Marian, like Joey, is drawn to Shane for his quietly heroic qualities.
Her husband (Van Heflin) is sensitive to her feelings for Shane and is
able to reassure her of his love when she reaches out to him. Ultimately
Marian chooses to stay with her son and husband whose love implies
unquestioning trust. The pastoral quality of this and other movies of
the 1950s reflects the quiet conservatism of the Eisenhower years, a
quiet that would be shattered abruptly by events in the next decade.

   Two variations on the woman-as-civilizer stereotype warrant discussion. One occurs in the musical Westerns that came into vogue
briefly in this period. *The Harvey Girls* (1946), starring Judy Garland,
is a story of hardy young women who follow the railroad West, serving
as waitresses in the Harvey hotels while seeking adventure on the
frontier. Two of the better musicals focused on female "hell-raisers":
Annie Oakley (*Annie Get Your Gun*, 1950) and *Calamity Jane* (1953).
The basic story line in these movies was "how to get a man without
besting him at his own game." To do so, Betty Hutton (Annie) and Doris

Jean Arthur, Alan Ladd, and Brandon DeWilde in *Shane*.
*S. K. Schackel*

Day (Jane) mute their independence and disguise their sharpshooting
skills to soothe male egos and win husbands.

Seven Brides for Seven Brothers (1954) is a flashy extravanganza
based on the highly dubious premise that women want to be abducted.[21]
In this film Jane Powell and the other six women are expected to
civilize and educate Howard Keel and his uncouth brothers, the classic
female role, even in this sub-genre. And in *Oklahoma* (1955) Laurie
(Shirley Jones) plays off the attentions of cowboy Curley (Gordon
MacRae) against farmhand Judd Fry (Rod Steiger) over the burning
issue of who will escort her to the box social. Musical Westerns further
limited women as domestic, submissive characters who were willing to
accommodate themselves to male demands.

The second variation of woman as civilizer is the heroine as a
spunky ranchwoman, often portrayed by Barbara Stanwyck. Usually,
the lady struggles to hold on to her ranch in the face of great odds despite the loss of a father or husband. This scenario provided the plot for

*The Cattle Queen of Montana* (1954) in which Stanwyck, with the help of a government agent (Ronald Reagan), brings to justice a gang of cattle rustlers. But winning back her herd also gains her a husband, allowing her to continue the family dynasty according to prevailing values.

Stanwyck also plays strong, determined, and competent women in other roles. In *Union Pacific* (1939) she is the Irish engineer's athletic "spitfire" daughter and postmistress of the town, while *The Great Man's Lady* (1942) turns on the theme of self-sacrifice with Stanwyck the "power behind the throne," helping her husband (Joel McCrea) build an empire in the West, enduring hardships, and giving up whatever she must in order to provide him with what he needs.[22] *Forty Guns* (1957) finds her running the county with the help of forty gunmen and a crooked sheriff, but in *Maverick Queen* (1956) she plays an outlaw queen who dies to save the hero (Barry Sullivan). In these Westerns Stanwyck brought to the screen an appealing quality related to her ability to carry out adventurous, demanding tasks.

The ranchwoman stereotype differed from other Western heroines in the way she dressed. In *The American West in Film*, Jon Tuska notes that women dressed in pants and blouses when doing chores or hard riding but wore dresses to "fall in love" or manipulate men.[23] This is manipulation of women (actresses) by men (directors) who wished to depict certain female behavior in prescribed ways through clothing. Jenni Calder points out that the woman who wears jeans and rides horses can be an appealing kind of heroine, her femininity intact irregardless of masculine clothing and behavior.[24] Stanwyck is such a heroine, and despite the fact that her adventures usually were manipulated in such a way as to enlarge the hero, her roles allowed female action in an otherwise male world.[25]

In addition to woman as civilizer, the other most common stereotype prevalent in Westerns is the saloon singer, often a step away from a prostitute. Marlene Dietrich is the "grande dame" of the type stemming from her roles as Frenchy, a saloon owner in *Destry Rides Again*; the beautiful, manipulative Cherry Malotte in *The Spoilers* (1942); and as the owner of a gambling saloon on the Mexican border in *Rancho Notorious* (1952). Variations on the standard bad woman role include the tainted woman winning the hero, as Dietrich won John Wayne in *The Spoilers*. Similarly, saloon singer Marilyn Monroe in *River of No Return* (1954) wins the love and respect of Robert Mitchum after they make a treacherous raft trip together, and Angie Dickinson's gambler

James Stewart and
Marlene Dietrich in
*Destry Rides Again.*
*S. K. Schackel*

role in *Rio Bravo* allows her to chase John Wayne until he catches her. This theme also permits Claire Trevor to transcend her questionable past in *Stagecoach*, although, in part, Ringo's love and respect redeem her. The saloon girl, then, is not always confined to a loveless ending, despite the many times she dies in the hero's arms.

Sometimes this stereotypical role allows women to be "heroes." In *Johnny Guitar* (1954) Joan Crawford plays a tough, determined saloon owner in competition with another woman, Mercedes McCambridge, for the love of a man (Sterling Hayden) and railroad lands. This film, variously labeled an anti-McCarthy Western, a lesbian Western, and a neurotic Western, is about a conflict based on sexual jealousy and greed and culminates in a gunfight between the two women.[26] Finally, in a highly implausible film, gambling queen Marie Windsor and her "dance and gun" girls in *Outlaw Women* (1952) control the town of Las

Mujeres until Marshal Richard Rober and his men take over. The conclusion, however, finds the town still run by the women, although they
have become the wives of their "captors." This film seems to be saying
that women could be "in charge" if they had husbands to back them up,
a male perspective. Overall, the saloon singer stereotype and its variations is important in illuminating how men see women in roles apart
from the good woman/civilizer image.

Until the 1960s, little variation occurred in female ethnic roles in
Westerns. A white female usually acted the good woman stereotype;
often the saloon singer was a Mexican or Hispanic woman. The Latin
woman, especially, was stereotyped as hot-blooded, exotic, passionate,
and not quite acceptable in "white" society. Katy Jurado fulfilled this
image in countless screen roles. In *High Noon* (1952), Jurado's strong
character overshadows Grace Kelly's colorless Quaker wife role, yet
the Latina is forced to leave town because of her past association with
the outlaw and the hero. In *Broken Lance* (1954), she plays a Comanche
"princess" who acts as peacemaker between her husband (Spencer

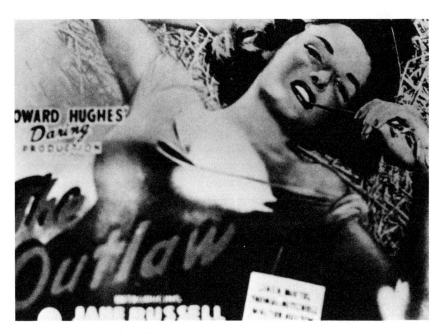

Jane Russell in *The Outlaw*. *S. K. Schackel*

Tracy) and their four sons. Sometimes white women fulfill the Mexican whore/half-breed image as Jane Russell does in *The Outlaw* and Jennifer Jones in *Duel in the Sun*. Jones's unrepressed sexuality in *Duel* is a reflection of director King Vidor's idea of the sexual freedom of the lower classes or darkskinned races.[27] As a result, Pearl is perceived as a sexually possessed woman who has to reassure others that she is a "good girl." It is no coincidence that she dies at the end of the film, however, which is Hollywood's convenient way to banish bad women.

Women and Indians have not fared well, either. Since the early days of the industry, anti-Indian attitudes have affected women (white and Indian) in two ways. As objects of "the red man's lust" white women often received the scorn of their peers if they survived captivity by Indians. On the other hand, Indian women were never "good enough" to make wives for white men in white civilization. This double standard was implicit in many films; a white man might take an Indian wife but Indian men did not marry white women. And if a white man married an Indian and lived in her culture, he carried the derogatory label "squaw man." Not until the 1960s did attitudes change sufficiently to allow a white woman, Shelley Winters, to pair up with an Indian male, as she did in *The Scalphunters* (1968).[28]

The 1950 film, *Broken Arrow*, is often cited as a trend setter in its treatment of Indians as sympathetic human beings with genuine grievances.[29] Yet the story line for the female lead, Debra Paget, is strikingly familiar. Wed to frontiersman James Stewart in a romantic wedding ceremony, Paget is killed shortly thereafter in a skirmish with white settlers. *Broken Arrow* prompted many imitators that used dark-eyed Paget look-alikes, but most Indian brides of white men did not live through the final reel.

The fear of miscegenation is present in many Westerns. This theme is made starkly clear in *The Searchers* (1956), the story of Ethan Edwards's (John Wayne) obsessive five-year search for his niece Debby, captured by Comanches. Edwards is so consumed with racism and blind hatred toward the Comanches that he is determined, until a last minute change of heart, to kill Debby for having become a "squaw."[30] Most films of this genre do not consider the captured woman's feelings regarding her ordeal but instead, following the "you-know-what-they-do-to-white-women" approach, it is expected that she will take her life rather than endure or submit to sexual relations with an Indian. It comes as a shock to whites that a white captive might become acculturated into Indian society and prefer to remain in that environment.

This is Debby's preference when Edwards finds her, but though she is spared a bullet, she is, nevertheless, removed from her Indian family and returned to her white relatives. The white male's way prevails.

In *Trooper Hook* (1957), Barbara Stanwyck is captured by Indians and subsequently gives birth to a son whom she refuses to leave behind when Sergeant Hook (Joel McCrea) comes to rescue her. Because she is condemned by townspeople for sleeping with her Indian mate rather than committing suicide, this movie reflects society's refusal to accept and appreciate a woman who has been strong and brave enough to survive rape.[31] This theme continues into the 1960s in *Two Rode Together* (1961), *Duel at Diablo* (1966), and *The Stalking Moon* (1969). The 1960s and 1970s were a time of political activism for civil rights and these movies attempt to portray a sympathetic attitude toward Native Americans. Nevertheless, it seems society was not yet ready to sympathize with raped women.

*Tell Them Willie Boy Is Here* (1969) is another "pro-Indian" movie with Katherine Ross playing an important role. As Lola, an educated Paiute, she "elopes" with Willie Boy (Robert Blake), who is wanted for the murder of her father. She tries unsuccessfully to reason with Willie Boy, to convince him to give himself up to his white pursuers, but feeling she has become a liability to him, she takes her life. In this Indian-woman-as-civilizer role, Ross's suicide is a drastic action, one which suggests her white-inspired attitudes were incompatible with Paiute ways.

Compared to Native Americans and Hispanics, black women have been nearly invisible in Westerns. According to George N. Fenin and William K. Everson, horse operas with all-black casts served black audiences in Chicago, New York, and in the South during the 1930s and 1940s but gradually went the way of the more orthodox B Westerns.[32] Three decades later, when Hollywood began to acknowledge the emphasis on black pride, black males (but not females) began to appear in leading roles. For example, Sidney Poitier starred in *Duel at Diablo* and co-starred with Harry Belafonte in *Buck and the Preacher* (1972); Fred Williamson starred in *The Legend of Nigger Charley* (1972); and Cleavon Little appeared in *Blazing Saddles* (1974). Despite society's growing concern with racial discrimination, things did not change significantly for black women in Western roles.

One exception to this development is Lena Horne's somewhat confusing role in *Death of a Gunfighter* (1969). In stereotypical fashion, the woman-of-color, bearing the Hispanic name of Quintana, runs a bordello and is mistress to Marshal Frank Patch (Richard Widmark). Uncharacteristic of this stereotype Quintana marries the hero by the film's end. It is significant that in this film Horne represents both major stereotypes—she is the tainted woman who defends her man against the townspeople and is "rewarded" with marriage to the hero, a white hero at that.

Since the 1960s, roles for women in film have changed in two ways: the exclusion of women from the scene of action and the development of a new stereotype, the strong, determined "modern" woman. In addition, violence, often directed at women, played a major role, particularly in the films of Sam Peckinpah and the "spaghetti" Westerns of Sergio Leone that starred Clint Eastwood. Many of these Westerns emphasized the relationships between male heroes and subjects other than women, such as nature, relegating female roles to the background.

For example, the men of *The Wild Bunch* (1969) use women as sexual objects and bullet shields. In *The Life and Times of Judge Roy Bean* (1972), the love objects are a live-in, barefoot Mexican girl (Victoria Principal) and Bean's fantasy lover, actress Lily Langtry, but a major theme of the film is Bean's fanaticism for hanging and otherwise killing men and his pleasure at setting the town on fire. *Jeremiah Johnson* (1972), on the other hand, played by Robert Redford, has a love affair with nature, and *Butch Cassidy and the Sundance Kid* (1969) is a story of love between two men that sometimes includes Sundance's girl friend, Etta Place. Other Westerns stress this theme of male camaraderie as well—*Two Rode Together* (1961), *Ride the High Country* (1962), *Pat Garrett and Billy the Kid* (1973), and *The Long Riders* (1980). It is interesting to speculate on the relationship between fantasy and reality in these movies. As American women demand equal rights, are men (on the screen) retreating into male relationships in defense? While this is not easy to determine, these Westerns suggest a questioning of traditional values in a period of social and political upheaval.

Other films in this period show a decided improvement in roles for women, a change that does reflect society's rising consciousness of female equality. In a spoof of the traditional Western, Jane Fonda is cast as the "hero" in *Cat Ballou* (1964). The ambivalent Cat, caught between the two worlds of dependence and independence, is determined to avenge her father's death and retain the family land, yet she often falls back on feminine wiles to get her way. Although she turns to men for help, she demonstrates a plucky courage that carries her exploits to a successful conclusion.

Similarly, Julie Christie, in *McCabe and Mrs. Miller* (1971), is a self-sufficient, capable woman in her business dealings with small-town operator McCabe (Warren Beatty). As a shrew business-minded madam with ambition, Christie proves to be the stronger of the two, although the price she pays for success precludes her ability to develop a warm, loving relationship with McCabe. At his death she resorts to the solace of opium.

Jane Fonda plays the heroine in two other 1970s Westerns. In *Comes A Horseman* (1978), she and James Caan are two small ranchers united in their fight against encroaching oil companies. Fonda is also fighting against memories of a past seduction by the land-owner she is challenging. In a successful resolution, she finds, as did Dallas in *Stagecoach*, that she does not forfeit the chance for future happiness in payment for past sexual activities.[33]

Opposite Robert Redford in *The Electric Horseman* (1979), Fonda

Jane Fonda in *Comes A Horseman*. S K. Schackel

plays a greenhorn reporter hoping to scoop a story on a faded rodeo-star-turned-breakfast-cereal promoter. In this movie about ecology and liberation, citified Hallie gradually comes to understand Sonny's need to free his horse in order to redeem himself. In turn she earns Sonny's respect for her endurance in the wilderness and together they achieve a spiritual liberation by setting the horse free.

Fonda is an important figure in the 1960s and 1970s for her roles both on and off screen. Her screen roles mirror, to some degree, part of the trauma taking place in America in those chaotic years. Fonda's ability to offend, however, especially in regard to her position on the Vietnam war, dampened her reputation as an actress in the 1970s. Nevertheless, her acting ability has remained of a high caliber and she continues to be a role model for the development of more complex roles for women in film.

In this survey, it is not possible to discuss all the films that reflect women's changing image in the film industry, but two important themes stand out. First, because men have most often written and directed Westerns, the films view women from a male perspective that emphasizes the male hero. The lack of a female counterpart to John Wayne is a reminder that the frontier West was perceived by many as a masculine experience. Second, since movies tend to reflect the changing social and cultural climate in which they are created, the chaotic social and political events of the 1960s and 1970s resulted in a new direction for women's roles in Westerns. No longer are women limited to the stereotypical roles of good woman/civilizer or bad woman/prostitute. Increased public awareness of women's rights as well as changes in scholarship have finally recognized the complexity of women's roles on the frontier. As women's and men's roles change, the predominantly male Western no longer fits today's values. And as the genre moves away from roles men thought women ought to play and toward roles they actually did play, Western films will more realistically reflect women's role in the celluloid winning of the West.

NOTES

1. See John G. Cawelti, *The Six-Gun Mystique* (Bowling Green, Ohio: Bowling Green University Popular Press, 1971); Molly Haskell, *From Reverence to Rape: The Treatment of Women in the Movies* (New York: Holt, Rinehart and Winston, 1973); John H. Lenihan, *Showdown: Confronting Modern America in the Western Film* (Urbana: University of Illinois Press, 1980); and Richard W. Etulain, "Changing Images: The Cowboy in Western Films" in *Colorado Heritage* I (1981):37–55.

2. Lenihan, *Showdown*, p. 5.

3. Roy Armes, "Peckinpah and the Changing West" in *London Magazine* 9 (March 1970):101–06.

4. John D. Weaver, "Destry Rides Again and Again and Again," in *Holiday* 34 (August 1963):77–80.

5. Cawelti, *Six-Gun Mystique*, pp. 38–39.

6. Lenihan, *Showdown*, p. 13.

7. Jenni Calder, *There Must Be a Lone Ranger* (New York: Taplinger Publishing Co., 1974), p. 170.

8. Cheryl J. Foote, "Changing Images of Women in the Western Film," *Journal of the West* (October 1983):64–71. This article is one of the few written on this topic, pointing up the need for further research in the field.

9. Julie Roy Jeffrey, *Frontier Women: The Trans-Mississippi West 1840–1880* (New York: Hill and Wang, 1979); New York, 1979); Joanna Stratton, *Pioneer Women: Voices from the Kansas Frontier* (New York, 1981); Sandra L. Myres, *Westering Women and the Frontier Experience 1800–1915* (Albuquerque: University of New Mexico Press, 1982); and Theresa Jordan, *Cowgirls: Women of the American West* (Garden City, N.Y.: Anchor Press/Doubleday & Company, 1982).

10. George N. Fenin and William K. Everson, *The Western: From Silents to the Seventies*, rev. ed. (New York: Grossman, 1973), 151.

11. Marjorie Rosen, *Popcorn Venus: Women, Movies & the American Dream* (New York: Coward, McCann & Geoghegan, 1973), 153.

12. Alexander Walker, *The Celluloid Sacrifice: Aspects of Sex in the Movies* (London: Michael Joseph, 1966), 88.

13. Fenin and Everson, *The Western*, p. 200.

14. Jon Tuska, *The Filming of the West* (Garden City, N.Y.: Doubleday and Co., 1976), 462.

15. Jay Hyams, *The Life and Times of the Western Movie* (New York: Gallery Books, 1983), 58.

16. Robin Wood, "Shall we Gather at the River? The Late Films of John Ford," in *Film Comment* 71 (Fall 1971):8–17.

17. Tuska, *The Filming of the West*, p. 513.

18. William T. Pilkington and Don Graham, eds., *Western Movies* (Albuquerque: University of New Mexico Press, 1979), 87.

19. Ibid., p. 94.

20. Jack Nachbar, "Riding Shotgun: The Scattered Formula in Contemporary Western Movies," in Jack Nachbar, ed., *Focus on the Western* (Englewood Cliffs, N.J.: Prentice-Hall, Inc., 1974), 101–12.

21. Phil Hardy, *The Western: The Film Encyclopedia* (New York: William Morrow and Company, Inc., 1983), 234.

22. Ibid., p. 62.

23. Jon Tuska, *The American West in Film: Critical Approaches to the Western* (Westport, Conn.: Greenwood Press, 1985), 228.

24. Calder, *Lone Ranger*, p. 169.

25. Ibid., p. 169.

26. Hyams, *Life and Times*, p. 119.

27. Haskell, *From Reverence to Rape*, p. 200.

28. Philip French, *Westerns: Aspects of a Movie Genre* (New York: Oxford University Press, 1977), 88.

29. Fenin and Everson, *The Western*, p. 281.

30. Lenihan, *Showdown*, p. 73.

31. Ibid., p. 75.

32. Fenin and Everson, *The Western*, p. 283.

33. Foote, "Changing Images," p. 70.

G A R Y   A.   Y O G G Y

# When Television
# Wore Six-Guns:
# Cowboy Heroes On TV

ALTHOUGH RADIO WAS late in developing that unique American entertainment genre, the Western, two of the first heroes to ride across the television screen were cowboys—Hopalong Cassidy and the Lone Ranger. And in the years that followed "Hoppy's" first appearance in 1948, well over 150 "oaters" rode into countless millions of American living rooms—more than any other program format except situation comedies.

Nearly half of these series first aired between 1955 and 1960. Eighteen Western series debuted in 1958 when twelve of the top twenty-five Nielsen-rated shows were Westerns, including a phenomenal seven of the top ten.[1] The following season, their peak year, thirty-two Westerns were broadcast nationally each week in prime time.

The early television Westerns were usually made with a juvenile audience in mind. The plots were simple and to the point. Good always triumphed over evil, crime did not pay, and the hero was invariably brave, just, kind, smart, and tough. Television shows modeled after the old B Westerns that were such an integral part of those Saturday matinees of the 1940s became a sensation on television in the 1950s. "Good guys" such as Gene Autry, Roy Rogers, the "Range Rider," Wild Bill Hickok, "Hoppy," and the Lone Ranger never shot first and rarely killed the "bad guys." They simply incapacitated them by expertly shooting pistols out of their hands and turned them over to the law for punishment.

Hopalong Cassidy, television's first cowboy hero, was a natural. Originally a pulp novel character created by Clarence Mulford, Cassidy was a ragged, illiterate, "tobacco-chewin', hard-drinkin', able-swearin' son of the Old West who got his nickname because of a limp." As William Boyd portrayed him on the screen, however, "Hoppy" did not drink, smoke, swear, or kiss girls, and, in fact, even his limp had healed up by the second film.

Boyd was quite an unlikely choice to portray such a paragon of virtue. Born in Hendrysburg, Ohio, to a poor farm laborer, Boyd quit school after the sixth grade and went to work. Drifting to Hollywood in the 1920s, he went from a $30 a week extra in Cecil B. DeMille extravaganzas to one of the romantic matinee idols of the silent screen.

Dazzled by success, he spent freely, gambled heavily, and lived lavishly. He married and divorced three beautiful actresses. In 1932, due to a case of mistaken identity, his career suffered a setback. A Broadway actor named Boyd was arrested at a gambling, drinking orgy and a picture of the Hollywood Boyd was published by mistake. Although the newspapers later printed a retraction, the damage had been done and Boyd's career plunged downward.

Boyd was a thirty-seven-year-old has-been in 1935 when Paramount offered to star him in a series of cowboy films based on Mulford's fictional character. Boyd, who could not ride a horse, asked for changes in the script that studio executives felt would make Hopalong too much of a gentleman. Boyd persisted and his portrayal of the "good guy" who always wore a black hat became the longest-running characterization in Hollywood history.

Between 1935 and 1948, sixty-six Hopalong Cassidy films were made. In 1947 Boyd bought up the rights to his Westerns and released them on television. The following year, when no more than one American in ten had even seen a television program, Hoppy syndicated his films. The first *Hopalong Cassidy* TV shows were simply condensed versions of these feature-length films.

The response was so great that Boyd made a new series of thirty-minute shows expecially for the new medium that ran on NBC for several years before going into syndication. The plots were similar to the old films, with the silver-haired Hoppy dressed in black chasing villains to their doom on his trusty white horse, Topper.

William Boyd as *Hop-along Cassidy. Stephen Sally*

Within two years of his debut on television William Boyd was a national hero. Cassidy was President Harry S Truman's guest of honor in 1950 for "I Am an American Day." He drew the largest circus attendance in history at the Chicago stadium, headlined Macy's Thanksgiving Day Parade, and greeted 80,000 people who crowded through a Brooklyn department store to catch a momentary glimpse of him.

Boyd became a millionaire through the sale of school lunchboxes, gun and holster sets, cowboy outfits, and dozens of other items emblazoned with the "Hoppy" brand. He founded a club called "Hoppy's Troopers" that rivaled the Boy Scouts in membership for a while. It had a Hopalong Code of Conduct that emphasized loyalty, honesty, ambition, kindness, and other virtues. Boyd also donated thousands of dollars to childrens' hospitals and homes, saying, "The way I figure it, if it weren't for the kids, I'd be a bum today. They're the ones who've made my success possible. They're the ones that should benefit from it."[2]

Soon joining Hoppy in the new medium was another Western hero from the B-Western mold, the Lone Ranger, a character originally created for radio. *The Lone Ranger* premiered on Detroit radio station WXYZ on January 31, 1933. The brainchild of station owner George W. Trendle and writer Fran Striker, the series began as a local show but quickly spread to a nationwide hookup over the Mutual Radio Network. It was an immediate success and was adapted for the screen in 1938 as a fifteen-chapter serial, *The Lone Ranger*, starring Lee Powell. A year later, another serial, *The Lone Ranger Rides Again*, was released with Bob Livingston in the lead.

In 1949, "the masked rider of the plains" was brought to TV in a series of half-hour films made especially for the new medium. General Mills, long-time sponsor of the radio series, footed the bill, but the casting, writing, and directing of the series were handled by Trendle.

Clayton Moore and Jay Silverheels played the title role and his faithful Indian companion, Tonto. Brace Beemer, whose voice had symbolized the Lone Ranger to millions of radio listeners for so many years, apparently was never seriously considered for the part because he had no experience as a film actor. Moore, a veteran of nine movie serials, including *Perils of Nyoka* (1942), *Jesse James Rides Again* (1947), and *Ghost of Zorro* (1949), played the role for the first three seasons. After asking for a substantial salary increase in 1952, Moore was replaced by John Hart who previously had played only one film lead in the Columbia serial *Jack Armstrong* (1947). Moore returned to the role two years later and remained until the series ended first-run production in 1957.

Tonto was played throughout the entire series by Jay Silverheels, a mixed-blood Mohawk Indian. He had appeared in several outstanding films including *Yellow Sky* in 1948 and *Broken Arrow* in 1950. Both Moore and Silverheels appeared in the two color Ranger films, *The Lone Ranger* (1956) and *The Lone Ranger and the Lost City of Gold* (1958).

The opening television episode of the series, broadcast on September 15, 1949, told the familiar story of how the Lone Ranger received his name and his mission in life. He had been one of a posse of six Texas Rangers tracking a gang of desperadoes. The Rangers were ambushed in a canyon and five of them were killed. The sixth, young John Reid, was left for dead. Reid was found and nursed back to health by Tonto, an Indian he had once befriended. Reid buried his past with the graves of the five dead Rangers, donned a mask, and set out with Tonto to avenge wrongs throughout the Old West.

Clayton Moore as *The Lone Ranger. Stephen Sally*

*The Lone Ranger* was ABC's biggest hit in its early years. In the first national television poll taken by the A.C. Nielsen Company in 1950 it was that network's only program to rank in the top fifteen, coming in seventh. One of the reasons for its success with younger viewers was the abundance of action. Parents enjoyed the show also because of the lack of overt killing and the high moral code by which the Ranger lived.

The purpose of the program was good, clean entertainment, and although right invariably triumphed, the stories did not preach to their viewers. Much like the Cassidy series, the masked rider of the plains taught his lessons of morality and citizenship by example. According to a strict writer's guide established by Trendle, the Ranger:

> ... never smokes, never uses profanity, and never uses intoxicating beverages.

... is a man who can fight great odds, yet takes time to treat a bird with a broken wing.

... believes that our sacred American heritage provides that every individual has the right to worship God as he desires.

... at all times uses precise speech, without slang, or dialect. ...

... never shoots to kill. When he has to use guns, he aims to maim as painlessly as possible.[3]

An unswerving adherence to this mythical "code of the West" gave the Lone Ranger such lasting popularity that even today the programs are being rerun on countless television stations all over the world.

Following on the heels of "Hoppy" and "the masked rider of the plains" came "America's favorite cowboy," Gene Autry, who was both a top B Western film hero at Republic Studios and a successful radio star with his popular, long-running *Melody Ranch* show. Autry's thirty-minute TV series premiered on CBS on July 23, 1950. For six seasons he and his sidekick, Pat Buttram, rode through the Southwest maintaining law and order. Each episode provided an opportunity for Autry to sing, Buttram to get into some silly predicament, and Autry's talented horse, Champion, to show off his training by coming to the hero's rescue.

Autry shot the series at Pioneer Town, near Palm Springs, California, during the first season. Within a year, however, he could afford his own Hollywood studio facilities and he launched his own production company, Flying A Productions, with the debut of *The Range Rider*.

*The Range Rider* starred former stunt man Jock Mahoney, best-known for his outstanding work in the Charles Starrett Durango Kid films. This valiant defender of justice on the range thrilled viewers with his acrobatic mounts, dismounts, flying leaps, and gracefully choreographed fisticuffs. Dick Jones was featured in the series as Dick West, the Rider's young "all-American" sidekick. Later Autry gave Jones his own show, *Buffalo Bill, Jr.*, also produced by Flying A. These programs were among the first original TV Westerns that were not based on a radio series, film, or novel.

Autry's Flying A Productions also developed the first female Western TV star, Gail Davis. Davis appeared with Autry in several of his films and was a regular on *The Gene Autry Show*. In 1954 she became

*Annie Oakley*, a character who shared only the name and shooting skills of Buffalo Bill's real life protégée. Set in the fictional town of Diablo during the 1860s where a woman rancher, who happened to be an expert sharpshooter, attempted to maintain law and order, the series had a successful five-year run on ABC on Saturday mornings.

Champion, Autry's "wonder horse," was even given a television show of his own. *The Adventures of Champion*, which premiered on CBS in September 1955, focused on the stallion's twelve-year-old owner, Ricky North (Barry Curtis), and co-starred the former cowboy star of a series of Red Ryder films, Jim Bannon, who played Ricky's uncle, Sandy North. Autry did not appear in the shows. Their major attractions were the miraculous feats performed by the "wonder horse" and Ricky's pet German shepherd, Rebel, in saving the young hero from evildoers or natural disasters.

Another singing cowboy star from B Westerns and radio, Roy Rogers, soon joined his rival on TV. On December 30, 1951, *The Roy Rogers Show* made its debut over NBC. "The King of the Cowboys" was joined in the series by his wife Dale Evans ("Queen of the West"), and Pat Brady, who played his bumbling sidekick. Rogers's palomino, Trigger, who had been billed as "the smartest horse in the movies," his German shepherd, Bullet, and Brady's cantankerous jeep, Nellybelle, completed the key ingredients of the successful series.

The stories were set in a contemporary West where Roy owned the Double R Bar Ranch near the fictional community of Mineral City. Despite his constant struggle to promote law and order, there was always time for a song or two from Rogers, Evans, and the Sons of the Pioneers. The series ran in prime time for six years, then moved to Saturday mornings where it remained a popular fixture for another seven years.

Rogers was not a native of the West. Born Leonard Slye, near Cincinnati, Ohio, he arrived in Hollywood at the age of nineteen in 1931. After working in a factory, on a farm, and in road construction, he began his singing career in a Los Angeles theatre for a dollar a performance. Assorted radio spots interspersed with more days of manual labor followed.

By chance, a Republic executive, Sol Siegel, gave him an audition. Slye, by then known as Roy Rogers, was on his way to stardom. He became the studio's wartime replacement for Gene Autry and by 1943 he was the leading box office attraction. In 1947 he married his current leading lady, Dale Evans, and together they made movies—and money.

Roy Rogers and Trigger.
*Stephen Sally*

Within a few years of Rogers's TV debut, merchandise bearing his name or likeness earned manufacturers millions of dollars.

Another juvenile Western hero who made a successful transition from radio and films to the television screen was "The Cisco Kid." Based on the exploits of a character created by O. Henry, this series had more "staying power" than most of its contemporaries. "The Robin Hood of the Old West" made his syndicated debut in 1951 and still drew a substantial viewing audience more than a decade later. In 1956, the show was dubbed and distributed to twenty countries, including France, Italy, Belgium, and Argentina, and by 1959 it had grossed a total of $11 million.[4]

No less a figure of heroic qualities than the Lone Ranger or Hopalong Cassidy, the Cisco Kid was not as deadly serious about the world as most other TV cowboys. He was a man who liked to talk to his horse, Diablo, joke with his sidekick, Pancho—a character who loved food and sleep above all else and rode a mount appropriately called Loco—and

flirt with women. Generally an amiable fellow, the Kid could be provoked by an act of gross injustice.

*The Cisco Kid* proved popular partly because it was one of the first
television programs to be filmed in color and partly because of the
chemistry of its two stars. Warner Baxter, César Romero, and Gilbert
Roland had all portrayed Cisco in films, but the actor best remembered
as the broad-humored swashbuckler was Duncan Renaldo. Born in
Camden, New Jersey, but raised in Versailles, France, Renaldo
appeared in such prestigious films as *For Whom the Bell Tolls* (1943)
and *The Bridge at San Luis Rey* (1944) before donning the black outfit
of "The Cisco Kid." He was forty-seven years of age when be began filming the 176 episodes that comprised the TV series. Leo Carrillo was
already in his seventies when he was fitted for Pancho's sombrero to
become Renaldo's sidekick. Even today, somewhere in syndicated reruns, he can still be heard imploring, "Cisco, let's went!"

One of the most sophisticated juvenile Western heroes, *Sky King*,
also debuted in 1951. Another immigrant from radio, Schyler King
used a twin-engine Cessna, the Songbird, in lieu of horses to patrol his
southwestern holdings known as the Flying Crown Ranch. With the
aid of his teenage niece, Penny, and nephew, Clipper, Sky brought
many an evildoer to justice in the contemporary West. The stories dealt
with human interest, cops 'n' robbers, and ecological themes, often
employing electronic gadgetry and modern science. Devices that are
commonplace today, such as Geiger counters, tape recorders, and dish
antennas frequently were utilized to solve a crime or bring a criminal
to justice.

Kirby Grant, who played "Sky King," was uniquely qualified for
the role. Born in Montana, he was also a real cowboy. In World War II
he served as an Air Force flight instructor and was well prepared to fly
the Songbird.

Although he was considered a musical child prodigy on the violin,
Grant's interests shifted to baseball and acting as he grew older. After
performing with a Midwest stock company in 1937, he entered a "Gate-
way to Hollywood" talent contest and won the prize of a six-month
RKO film contract. Grant appeared in the 1940s in a string of musicals,
comedies, singing-cowboy films, and Canadian Mounted Police features before taking the controls of the Songbird. *Sky King* was Grant's
most successful role. It kept the cowboy-aviator hero flying into American living rooms for nearly two decades.

*Wild Bill Hickok* was another early television Western with longevity. The syndicated, thirty-minute show premiered in 1952 and was carried at various times during the next six years on both CBS and ABC networks. This series, like *Annie Oakley*, borrowed only the name and occupation of a real-life character and had no basis in historical fact. Wild Bill was depicted as a U.S. Marshal who traveled around the West of the 1870s with his sidekick, Jingles Jones, hunting outlaws. Like many other successful children's Westerns, this show also enjoyed a popular run on radio.

Two years after its premiere *Wild Bill Hickok* was so successful that one New York station ran it a second time each week without charging the sponsor for air time. Station officials realized that if they could cut one minute from each episode and fill it with a new commercial, they would still make a profit.[5]

The stars of the show were an unlikely pair of Hollywood actors. The title role was played by the slender, handsome Guy Madison, who spoke in a tenor voice. His sidekick, Jingles, was portrayed by the overweight, ever-giggling Andy Devine, who spoke in a gravelly, rasping voice due to a childhood injury.

Madison first caught the attention of the public when he charmed bobby-soxers in *Since You Went Away* (1944). Roles in *Till the End of Time* (1946) and *Honeymoon* (1947) followed. He also appeared in several films while he was playing Wild Bill on TV.

Devine had appeared in films before his television co-star was old enough to ride a horse. In the silent film era Universal had planned to make him a romantic star, but with the coming of sound, directors wisely saw that comedy was his forte. Thereafter, he appeared in dozens of memorable movies such as *Yellow Jack* (1938), *Stagecoach* (1939), and *Sudan* (1945) and in a succession of mid-1940s Republic Westerns as Roy Rogers' sidekick. In 1954 NBC saw Devine as the heir-apparent to the late Smilin' Ed McConnell and made him the host of *Andy's Gang*.

In the same mold, but not nearly as successful, came *The Adventures of Kit Carson*. A thirty-minute weekly series, it related the exciting exploits of Christopher "Kit" Carson, frontiersman and Indian scout, and his Mexican sidekick, El Toro, on the Western frontier of the 1880s. Starring former swimmer Bill Williams and veteran supporting actor Don Diamond, some 104 episodes were filmed by MCA-TV between 1952 and 1955. All but forgotten now, *Kit Carson*, according to *Variety*, reached more children's homes in 1954 (3.5 million) than any other juvenile program of any type.[6]

Yet another successful refugee from radio starred one of the most famous canines ever to grace the silver screen. *The Adventures of Rin Tin Tin* premiered on ABC on October 15, 1954, and ran for seven years. CBS later reprised the series and the show went into a long and profitable syndication.

Despite some similarities to another popular show that featured a heroic dog with a young boy as his companion, there were considerable differences between the two shows. *Rin Tin Tin* was set in the Old West and was packed with violent action, including rampaging Indians, thrilling chases, and bloody gunfights. The boy Rusty (Lee Aaker) had been orphaned in an Indian raid and he and his dog ("Rinty") were adopted by the 101st Calvary soldiers at Fort Apache, Arizona. Both were made honorary troopers and proceeded to assist the cavalry and townspeople of nearby Mesa Grande establish law and order on the frontier.

Three different German shepherds played the title role in the TV series, two of them descendants of the original Rin Tin Tin who had died in 1932 after appearing in twenty-two movies. The third stand-in for Rinty was the offspring of another movie canine, Flame, Jr.

A review of juvenile TV Westerns would be incomplete without including the champion of all animal series, *Fury*. *Fury* was set in the contemporary West and dealt with issues that were identifiable to young audiences. The show focused on a tough orphan named Joey (Bobby Diamond), who was adopted by widower Jim Newton (Peter Graves), owner of the Broken Wheel Ranch and a magnificent black mustang named Fury.

Each episode dramatized a simple lesson about civil defense, bicycle safety, wildlife preservation, freedom of the press, family responsibilities, or fire prevention. The show won awards from the National Education Association, the Junior Achievement program, the U.S. Civil Defense agency, the United Fund, the Red Cross, the Boy Scouts, and the National PTA.[7]

Much of the credit for the show's success belonged to Beauty, the beautiful fifteen-hands high, coal-black stallion that "played" Fury. He appeared in a number of movies before gaining stardom on the small screen. The stallion carried Clark Gable in *Lone Star* (1952), Joan Crawford in *Johnny Guitar* (1954), and Elizabeth Taylor in *Giant* (1956). Peter Graves rode *Fury* to national prominence until dismounting for the starring role in "Mission Impossible."

Television's most innovative juvenile Western lasted for only one season. *Cowboy G-Men* was a forerunner of the much more popular and longer running series, *The Wild Wild West*, without the sophisticated humor and modern gadgets of the latter. The stories concerned the adventures of two "hard-riding, fast-shooting" government agents, Pat Gallagher and his bumbling partner Stony Crockett, who "worked undercover on dangerous, special assignments" in the Old West. Former Hopalong Cassidy sidekick Russell Hayden starred as the upright and handsome Pat Gallagher, while his comic sidekick Stoney Crockett was played by former child actor, Jackie Coogan.

Film historian Don Miller points out that the series "was happily without the condescending attitude that becomes the bane of the majority of juvenile programming." This, and the fact that "Hayden and Coogan worked smoothly as a team with the latter's comedy not too broad and astutely valued,"[8] made *Cowboy G-Men* one of the better Westerns on TV at the time.

Throughout the 1950s Westerns became more popular than most other juvenile shows by adhering to a successful formula that had been established in years of B Westerns and several dozen kid-oriented shows from the golden age of radio. The brave, infallible hero to uphold the mythical "Code of the West," the comic sidekick to break the "monotony" of nonstop action with a few laughs, children in supporting roles to give young viewers a sense of involvement in the stories, and a noble and trusted steed to carry the hero out of harm's way were all essential ingredients. There were, of course notable exceptions. Tonto was certainly not an intentionally humorous character, for example, but there was little comedy of any sort on *The Lone Ranger*.

Women rarely appeared as continuing characters in juvenile Westerns. When various female characters did appear in these shows they were usually in trouble and needed assistance from the hero. They were in stories to be rescued, but never kissed. The most romantic treatment women might expect was an occasional song from Gene Autry. Again, there were a couple of significant exceptions—*Annie Oakley* and Dale Evans in *The Roy Rogers Show*.

Without exception, however, the hero of a juvenile Western lived by a strict code. As Western TV historian Ralph Brauer states, the hero presented "values which Americans believe are typically theirs and theirs alone. The hero was clean living and clean thinking—clean in thought, word and deed." These values "were personified by the star . . . and each week their essential goodness was demonstrated by the downfall of the villain, who was, in every way, the antithesis of the hero."[9]

The Western hero in many ways resembled a medieval knight. He was a champion of the oppressed, the weak, the less fortunate, and those in need of help such as widows, orphans, and the elderly. He brought law, order, and justice to the frontier. He was a model of honesty, integrity, fairness, courage, hard work, mental alertness, mercy, tolerance, and patriotism, and he attempted to instill these qualities in his young viewers.

With the development of programs designed for adult viewers, scheduled during prime-time viewing hours, the Western craze was under way. Many factors added momentum to this trend. President Eisenhower's fondness for Western novels stimulated interest in the historic West. Westerns offered an escape from the confusing complex problems of the present to a simpler time when the good guys always won and the bad guys always lost. In Cold War America, we were searching for heroes.

Westerns reflected the average American's conception of the East-West struggle. According to broadcast historian J. Fred MacDonald,

> they were social allegories in which honest, hard-working American folk were threatened, without good reason, by evil forces.... The honest folk never asked for trouble, never did anything to precipitate it. But it was now upon them, and it called for heroic intervention by a brave soul.[10]

David Shea Teeple writing in *American Mercury* (April 1958) argued that American diplomats could benefit greatly from viewing TV Westerns. According to Teeple the popularity of these programs proved that "the American public ... wants to abandon the grey philosophies of fuzzy minds and return to the days when things were either black or white—right or wrong." To prove his point Teeple summoned an array of TV Western heroes:

> Would a Wyatt Earp stop at the 38th Parallel, Korea when the rustlers were escaping with the herd? Ridiculous! Would Marshal Dillon refuse to allow his deputies to use shotguns for their own defense because of the terrible nature of the weapon itself? Ha! Would the Lone Ranger *under any circumstance*, allow himself to be bullied and threatened by those who sought to destroy the principles by which he lives? Would Jim Hardy of "Wells Fargo" attempt to buy his friends who would fight for the right ... ?[11]

Most television historians cite 1955 as the year when the adult

Western made its initial appearance on the home screen. But *Death Valley Days*, a refugee from radio where it had thrived for some fifteen years (1930–45), preceded the landmark series *Gunsmoke* and *The Life and Legend of Wyatt Earp* by over three years. *Death Valley Days* presented an anthology of tales set in various locations in or near Death Valley, California, during the latter half of the nineteenth century. These dramatizations of purportedly true incidents in the struggle of the Western pioneers to establish a new homeland, starred veteran actors and actresses who were already well established on the Hollywood scene such as Ronald Reagan, Robert Taylor, and Yvonne DeCarlo and newcomers who were soon to make their mark such as Clint Eastwood and Bethel Leslie.

Although the series could not be considered among television's best, the acting usually was competent and the stories interesting. For example, the first woman judge fights against corruption in a rough and tumble frontier town; an ex-cop from New York tries to maintain law and order in a rowdy Western town without a sixgun; a woman struggles to establish a medical practice in a dusty desert town.

The show's most memorable feature was its host who introduced and closed each story. The first and longest running was Stanley Andrews, the Old Ranger (twelve years), followed by the most memorable, Ronald Reagan (three years), Robert Taylor (two years), and Dale Robertson (three years). Only *Gunsmoke* rivaled this syndicated series in longevity.

By the mid-1950s, the assumption that Westerns were "just kid stuff" began to change as theatrical films such as *High Noon* (1952) and *Shane* (1953) placed more serious plots in Western settings. These films, which were acclaimed critically as well as box-office successes, became known as adult Westerns. In its waning years, radio drama also had experimented with Western stories aimed at a mature audience and although, with the exception of *Gunsmoke*, the shows were short-lived, most critics agreed that several were among the highest quality dramatic programs ever broadcast.

The adult Western is a difficult genre to define. Ralph Brauer, in *The Horse, The Gun and The Piece or Property* concludes that the network's idea of "adultness" simply meant that the shows must have more violence.[12] While Roy Rogers merely shot the gun out of the villain's hand, the adult Western hero would usually either kill him or beat him senseless.

Violence was, of course, a real part of the Western experience and

adult Westerns made no attempt to minimize it. But there was sub-
stance to the adult Western hero as well. Here one found a hero who was
more human and consequently was more believable than the one-
dimensional stars of the kiddie Westerns—a complex mixture of good
and evil, strength and weakness. The hero of the adult Western could
have doubts, make mistakes, and have misgivings about what he had
to do.

The "bad guys" in adult Westerns also were a different breed. Not
totally evil and cowardly characters motivated solely by greed or a lust
for power, as was so often the case in juvenile Westerns, the villain
could be the victim of circumstances beyond his or her control. Frequently psychological problems and social conditions were motiva-
tional factors influencing evildoers in adult Westerns.

It was not unusual to find controversial themes in adult Westerns
that were scrupulously avoided in juvenile Westerns. In addition to
excessive violence, stories dealing with sex, religion, and racial discrimination—especially concerning the American Indian—were
presented effectively in a number of successful adult Westerns. There
was also a much greater attempt at historical accuracy in these programs, although "literary license" was employed liberally when the
producers did not find the truth to be "more exciting than fiction."

*The Life and Legend of Wyatt Earp*, which made its network debut
for ABC on September 6, 1955, was somewhat unique in the previously
make-believe world of TV Westerns. Not only was it more or less based
on fact, it developed its characters over a period of six years in a continuing story involving politics and family relationships as well as standard Western action. In many ways it resembled a serial drama.

Most of the early episodes allegedly were based on historical
events in the life of the West's most famous lawman. Wyatt Earp was
portrayed on the show as a character who was more interesting than
one-dimensional heroes such as Hopalong Cassidy and the Lone
Ranger.

The conflict between a previously lawless town and an effective,
dedicated lawman provided a strong basis for the weekly stories, and
according to television historians Harry Castleman and Walter J.
Podrazik, "the program was well executed and avoided obvious Western film cliches even within the obligatory fights, chases, and shoot-
outs."[13]

Every effort was made to create sets and costumes that were accurate even to the make of Earp's gun, the Buntline Special. The scripts

followed Earp from his arrival in Ellsworth City, Kansas, through his career in Dodge City and Tombstone, Arizona, concluding with a five-part dramatization of the famous gunfight at the OK corral.

The show brought actor Hugh O'Brian from obscurity to fame. O'Brian, who was a Marine Corp drill instructor at the age of eighteen, began his television career by working for nothing during the period when the medium was new and did not pay its actors. He gambled that some day producers would be able to pay performers who had prior experience. When this situation came about in the late 1940s, O'Brian found steady employment.

Taking his role seriously, O'Brian did extensive research on Wyatt Earp and developed an empathy for him. In an interview he said:

> He's a controversial character who has been depicted as everything from saint to devil, lawman to bully, loquacious to taciturn. So I devoted seven months to reading about Earp, and I'm convinced that he was a thoroughly honest man, righteous and utterly fearless. He was also just. In two hundred gunfights, he killed only four men. He had a wonderfully subtle sense of humor, and was essentially an easy moving, relaxed type of guy. But he could tense up like a coiled spring, and he had fabulous reflexes. You stay alive through two hundred gunfights, and you've got to have fabulous reflexes.[14]

From the start, *The Life and Legend of Wyatt Earp* was a ratings success. It was ranked in the Nielsen Top Twenty for three out of its six years, and reached sixth during the 1957–58 season.

The most successful of all adult TV Westerns, "Gunsmoke," premiered only four days after the Wyatt Earp series. When John Wayne introduced "Gunsmoke" to the television public on September 10, 1955, many viewers were already familiar with the show. The creation of producer Norman MacDonnell and writer John Meston, *Gunsmoke* had its genesis on CBS radio in the spring of 1952. William Conrad played the resolute, determined Marshal Matt Dillon. Their intent had been to transfer the radio cast to television, but the series TV director, Charles Marquis Warren, felt that the stocky Conrad, who remained the radio voice of Matt Dillon for nine years and later starred in television's successful *Cannon*, did not project the proper physical presence for the visual medium.

The first choice for the role was John Wayne, who probably would have done well in the part, but he did not want to commit himself to a weekly series. Wayne suggested James Arness, a young, relatively unknown actor friend. Arness had limited film experience in *The*

*Farmer's Daughter* (1947) and *The Thing* (1951), but his most important qualification was his size. At 6-feet 7-inches, Arness was even bigger than Wayne and proved to be perfect for the role of the heroic marshal.

*Gunsmoke* was set in Dodge City, Kansas, around 1880. Other key characters included crusty old Doc Adams (Milburn Stone, the only cast member besides Arness who stayed with the show during its entire run), the kindly sympathetic town physician; softhearted but businesslike Kitty Russell (Amanda Blake, an actress with some previous screen experience) who started out as one of the hostesses of the Longbranch Saloon and eventually became its owner; and Matt's loyal, well-meaning deputy, Chester Goode (Dennis Weaver, until he left the series for a starring vehicle in 1964), who walked with a pronounced limp, talked with a twang, and "brewed a mean pot of coffee." Later, Festus Haggen (Ken Curtis), a scruffy hillbilly deputy, and Newly O'Brien (Buck Taylor), a refined, former medical student-turned-gunsmith, were added to the cast as regulars.

Former *Gunsmoke* production assistant Kristine Fredriksson points out that to watch the 640 episodes of the series, a total of 521½ hours of film, "would take twenty-three days of around-the-clock viewing or, translated to prime-time programming, five years of daily three-hour sessions."[15] The show, the longest running dramatic series on television, was broadcast on Saturday and later Monday evenings over a twenty-year period.

The series changed the course of the TV Western. The plots were mature and generally avoided the action sequences so crucial to the juvenile and B Westerns. Later Western heroes on television owed more to Marshal Matt Dillon than to Gene Autry or Roy Rogers.

Dillon had to reason as often as fight or shoot and he did both rather well. Faced with such problems as having to amputate a friend's leg, or deal with a retarded youth on a murderous rampage, the marshal acted with sensitivity and tact and used his gun only as a last resort.

During the first six seasons, when the program was thirty minutes long, the show used stories from the successful radio series and most were written by its creator, John Meston, or by Les Crutchfield. Each episode incorporated the tight combination of inevitable violence and compelling slices of human interest that had worked so well in the audio medium.

After the series was expanded to an hour in 1961, more of the

James Arness as Matt Dillon in *Gunsmoke*. *Art Fernandez*

shows revolved around the supporting cast members while Dillon was "out of town." Later programs often featured guest stars who carried the dramatic development of the stories with the regular characters becoming plot catalysts. From the beginning, however, the list of actors appearing on the program read like a "Who's Who" of Western TV stars. James Drury (*The Virginian*), Charles Bronson (*Empire, The Travels of Jaimie McPheeters*), Chuck Connors (*The Rifleman, Branded*), Stuart Whitman (*Cimarron Strip*), Andrew Duggan (*Lancer*), Jack Kelly (*Maverick*), Pernell Roberts (*Bonanza*), Pat Conway (*Tombstone Territory*), Dan Blocker (*Bonanza*), Jack Elam (*The Dakotas, Temple Houston*), and Alan Case (*The Deputy*), gained valuable experience on *Gunsmoke* before starring in their own Western TV series.

As a Saturday-night television institution, "Gunsmoke" ranked in the Nielsen Top Twenty shows from its second season until 1965, reaching number one from 1957 thru 1961. After moving to Monday evenings in 1967, the series returned to the Top Ten and remained there until its final season on the air. It was an achievement unmatched by any other television program.

The Western hit, *Cheyenne*, also premiered in 1955. The off-screen story of this troubled series is almost as interesting as the dramatized stories. Each episode depicted the exploits of frontier scout Cheyenne Bodie, a man of Indian descent and learned in both the ways of the white man and the Cheyenne. Drifting from job to job, he encountered villains, beautiful girls, and gunfights. He might appear in one episode as the foreman of a ranch, in another as trail scout for a wagon train, and in yet another as a recently deputized lawman.

When *Cheyenne* first appeared it was one of three alternating segments on *Warner Brothers Presents*. All three were based on successful movies. *Cheyenne* was a 1947 film starring Dennis Morgan; the other two were *Casablanca (1942) and King's Row* (1941).

The shows were produced lavishly by Warner Brothers, but the main reason that *Cheyenne* succeeded while the others failed was its star, Clint Walker. At six feet, six inches, Walker stretched to just an inch less than James Arness, with broad shoulders and a magnificent physique to match. The series stressed plot and action rather than dialogue and character development, as did so many of the popular adult Westerns.

Within two years, as much fighting was occurring off camera as on. Walker demanded the same percentage deals—participation in the program's profits—as James Arness and Hugh O'Brian enjoyed on their shows. He also wanted to make public appearances without having to give the studio half of his income. The studio refused, feeling that since they had made him a star they were entitled to the money. Unable to come to terms, Walker left the show.

The studio replaced him with Ty Hardin in the role of "Bronco" Layne, and Walker finally returned. *Cheyenne* now rotated between a humorous Western called *Sugarfoot*, starring Will Hutchins, and *Bronco*, and steadily declined in the ratings. Although it appeared in the Top Twenty consistently from 1958 to 1960, it was canceled after the 1962–63 season.

The hero of yet another of the new breed of Westerns of the 1950s was more unusual than those of most television "oaters." Paladin of *Have Gun, Will Travel* was, by profession, a gunman, a mercenary who sold his services to those who could afford them. TV's Western soldier of fortune was also a man of culture, refinement, and impeccable taste who resided in elegance in a fine San Francisco hotel. Paladin, a former army officer, usually sold his gun and his experience to people who were unable to protect themselves from the hostile elements of the society in which they lived.

Paladin, dressed all in black, was distinguished by two trademarks: a black leather holster that bore the symbol of the white chess knight (called a Paladin), and a calling card that read, "Have Gun—Will Travel. Wire Paladin, San Francisco." The program was unique among television Westerns in another remarkable way. The series was so popular that a radio version was developed, reversing the usual trend of successful radio shows that were adapted for television. It was broadcast from 1958 to 1960.

Paladin was similar to other Western heroes in that he possessed a strict sense of ethics that dictated what he would and would not do.

Richard Boone as Paladin in *Have Gun, Will Travel. Stephen Sally*

This occasionally led him to turn against the people who had hired him, if they were on the wrong side of fairness and justice. By definition, a paladin is one who undertakes a noble cause.

To play the title role CBS selected the rugged 6-foot 2-inch Richard Boone, a former ordnance man in the U.S. Navy, who was right at home working with Paladin's belt derringer, six-shooter, saddle rifle, and self-styled machine gun. Although of limited acting experience, Boone had completed two successful seasons as the star of NBC's *Medic*. He played the role of Paladin with relish, explaining that "he's an intriguing sort of a guy with an air of mystery about him."[16]

Endowed with action and interesting plots by such distinguished writers as Sam Peckinpah, *Have Gun Will Travel* was an overnight hit, ranking in the top five programs during its first season on the air. From 1958–61 it was the number three program on television, behind two other Westerns—*Gunsmoke* and *Wagon Train*. Even the show's theme song, "The Ballad of Paladin," was a hit record during the early 1960s.

Premiering on September 18, 1957, just four days after *Have Gun, Will Travel*, *Wagon Train* became one of the most popular Western series during the golden age of television Westerns. Television historians Tim Brooks and Earle March claim that "it was big in scope (the whole American West, it seemed), big in cast (many top-name guests), and big in format (sixty minutes most seasons, ninety minutes in one)."[17]

*Wagon Train* was an adult Western that successfully combined the elements of a drama anthology series with a stable cast of regulars. Each week a new group of characters (guest stars) joined the wagon train or wandered in off the plains on its run from St. Joseph, Missouri, across a treacherous expanse of Western territory to California. Some were settlers, others adventurers, and still others scroundrels. The regulars in the cast—the wagonmaster, the frontier scout, the cook, and their assistants—were seen in co-starring or sometimes even supporting roles.

Inspired by John Ford's epic film, *Wagonmaster* (1950), and given authenticity by the supervision of Western historian and novelist Dwight B. Newton, this series had a simple, loose formula. Ward Bond was featured as the show's original wagonmaster (Major Seth Adams). Bond, a veteran of over 200 Western films, including Ford's *Wagonmaster*, died in 1961 and was replaced by another experienced actor, John McIntyre, in the newly created role of Chris Hale. Newcomer

Robert Horton played Flint McCullough, the scout, during the first five seasons.

The regulars acted as protectors and counselors to the traveling party as they fought outlaws, hostile Indians, and the extremes of nature, often stepping aside and allowing the traumas and complications affecting the passengers to carry the episodes. This permitted scriptwriters a wide range of plots dealing with character development and kept the program consistently sophisticated and engrossing.

Produced at the then staggering cost of $100,000 per episode, the list of guests who appeared on the series included such Hollywood stars as John Wayne, Bette Davis, Mickey Rooney, and Mercedes McCambridge. This format managed to keep *Wagon Train* rolling for eight seasons and provided a pattern that was followed successfully later by two other Western blockbusters, *Bonanza* and *The Virginian.*

The series took a year to become popular, but in its second season it made the Nielsen's Top Ten. After three years of placing a close second to *Gunsmoke*, it became the number one program on television during the 1961–62 season.

The third hit Western of the 1957–58 season introduced a different brand of hero to television–the maverick, or anti-hero. "Maverick," a term of "Western" invention, appropriately means "one who does not conform to the practices of his group." It was probably coined after S. Maverick, a Texan who did not brand his cattle. The Maverick brothers roamed the West, not in the classic tradition of the cowboy hero upholding the mythical "code of the West," but as gambler-playboys who were more interested in lining their own pockets than in promoting law and order. As *TV Guide* noted, the brothers had none of the "rugged, individualism, lofty moral principles, lack of humor, fanatical courage, mechanical marksmanship, physical perfection, unflinching honesty, commendable generosity, and all the other attributes of the Western hero."[18]

Bret and Bart Maverick supported their expensive habits and tastes with clever schemes and con games. Their one concession to morality was to save their most outlandish exploits for overblown figures of authority, usually in defense of hopeless causes and mistreated underdogs. The brothers occasionally worked as a team, but usually went their separate ways in search of high stakes and beautiful women.

Among the high points of the series were periodic spoofs of other

TV Westerns. In an episode entitled "Gunshy," Bret outwitted Marshal Mort Dooley, his lame deputy, Clyde Deffendorfer, his dance hall girl-friend, Amy, and Doc Stukey. In a wild parody of *Bonanza* called "Three Queens Full," the leading characters were Joe Wheelright and his three sons, Moose, Henry, and Small Paul, owners of the vast Subrosa Ranch. There were also satires of other popular television shows such as *Dragnet* in which Bret turned in a Joe-Friday-like dead-pan narration, and *The Untouchables* where Lancelot Vest came West to battle Frank Nifty, Captain Scarface, Slugs Moran, and Jake Goose-neck.

In every episode the viewer could be certain that when it came time for a showdown, the Mavericks would try to "talk things over" and, failing in that, would slip quietly out of town. Bret was fond of quoting advice given him by his "Pappy": "He who fights and runs away, lives to run away another day" (from "Greenbacks" broadcast on March 13, 1960); "A coward dies a thousand deaths, a brave man only once. A thousand to one's a pretty good advantage" (from "Two Tickets to Ten-Strike" broadcast on March 15, 1959); and "All men are equal

James Garner and Jack Kelly as Bret and Bart Maverick. *Stephen Sally*

before the law, but what kind of odds are those?" (from "Last Wire from Stop Gap" broadcast on October 16, 1960).[19]

*Maverick*'s producer explained during the series' second season: "What we set out to do was create a character that deliberately broke all the rules of the traditional Western hero. He's a little bit of a coward, he's not solemn, he's greedy, and not above cheating a little. He's indifferent to the problems of other people. He's something of a gentle grafter."[20]

Cast as the lead in television's first Western series not to take itself too seriously was an actor who did not take himself too seriously. James Garner came to the show directly from five appearances as a "heavy" in another TV Western, *Cheyenne*. "Bret Maverick is lazy," said Garner. "I'm lazy. And I *like* being lazy!"[21] Jack Kelly as Bart Maverick joined the cast about two months after the series first aired. His fairly straight character was written into the series to keep from straying too far from the traditional Western mold.

Although the show had a cult of loyal followers, *Maverick* broke into the Top Twenty only once during its five seasons on the air. It might have lasted longer were it not for the fact that the popular Garner, who was more visible and clearly had the juicier role, left the series over a contract dispute after the third season. Cousin Beauregard Maverick, played by Roger Moore before his James Bond roles, was added for one season and then still another brother, Brent, appeared during the final year. None of this worked well and the show was canceled in July 1962.

Only one other series of the sixteen Westerns that debuted in 1957 lasted more than a couple of seasons. *Tales of Wells Fargo* lasted five years, long enough to expand from thirty minutes to an hour. Described as "an entertaining throwback to the simpleminded days of Hopalong Cassidy,"[22] it had a single regular cast member, Jim Hardy, who was a special investigator for the Wells Fargo stagecoach company. Hardy's troubleshooting ranged from helping company employees out of personal jams to functioning as an unofficial lawman by fighting outlaws who preyed on Wells Fargo shipments and passengers.

One of the benefits enjoyed by this series was that its originator and the writer of many episodes was Frank Gruber. Gruber had been a Western novelist during the 1930s and 1940s and had written *The Kansan* (1943), *Rawhide* (1951), and *Broken Lance* (1954) for the screen.

Dale Robertson played the lead. He became so interested in the subject matter of the stories that long after the series disappeared, he authored a book, *Wells Fargo, the Legend* (1975), that included true stories of "the Concord stage, Black Bart, the intrepid stage drivers and shotgun messengers, the California gold rush, and Nevada silver strike." His contributions to and support of the National Cowboy Hall of Fame in Oklahoma City is another indication of Robertson's genuine respect for the West.

During the show's final season (1961–62), both its length and regular cast were expanded. Although still a Wells Fargo agent, Jim Hardy was now also the owner of a ranch just outside of San Francisco. He had acquired a young assistant and a ranch foreman and lived next door to a widow who had two beautiful daughters. During this final season practically all of the stories took place on the ranch or in San Francisco. These changes obviously did not sit well with the viewers, for the series, which had been ranked as high as third during its first season, disappeared from the Nielsen rankings and was canceled in 1962.

The peak season in the great Western boom came in 1958, when eighteen new series made their appearance on the TV screen. The networks exploited almost every possible aspect of the old West and at one point seven of the top ten shows were Westerns: *Wagon Train*, *Gunsmoke*, *Maverick*, *Sugarfoot*, *The Rifleman*, *Cheyenne*, and *Have Gun, Will Travel*. Most of the new shows lasted only a season or two and only three, *Wanted: Dead or Alive*, *The Rifleman*, and *Rawhide* outlived the fad.

The first of these to appear was *Wanted: Dead or Alive*. The fictional hero of this series was a professional bounty hunter named Josh Randall. TV Westerns had now fully developed the anti-hero. Randall was a man who checked the wanted posters wherever he happened to be, tracked down and captured the culprit, and returned to claim the reward. Less interested in upholding the law than in collecting a sizable reward, Randall seemed to be a man who was motivated by nothing except his own self-interest.

Randall felt little apparent emotion and was a man of few words. He was also adept at using his gun, not a normal pistol but a unique cross between a handgun and a rifle. His "Mare's Leg" was a 30-40 sawed-off carbine that could be handled like a pistol but had much more explosive impact.

Since bounty hunters were common in the West during the last half of the nineteenth century, the stories had some historical basis. Because it did not matter if the criminals were captured alive, the opportunity for bloodshed and violence in the plots was great. This, coupled with the charisma of series lead Steve McQueen, provided a winning formula.

McQueen came to the role following such films as *Never Love a Stranger* (1958) and *The Blob* (1959). Although only 5-feet 11-inches tall, he held his own by maintaining an image of rugged unflappability. The show catapulted McQueen to cinematic superstardom.

The series had a meteoric rise and equally rapid tumble in the ratings. In its first season it was ranked sixteenth, and by the second year it reached ninth position in the Nielsen ratings. During its third season, however, it was nowhere to be found in the top twenty-five shows and was canceled. Steve McQueen, however, went on to bigger and better projects.

*The Rifleman*, 1958's second hit Western, survived two seasons longer than *Wanted: Dead or Alive*. On the surface this series appeared to be another gimmick Western, emphasizing the hero's use of a rifle in place of the traditional six-shooter. The program's real attraction, however, was the warm relationship between Lucas McCain, a homesteader struggling to make a living off his ranch, and Mark, his young son.

The stories were set in the town of North Fork, New Mexico, where Lucas constantly was called upon to help the marshal bring the countless bullies, drunks, rustlers, and killers that popped up in each episode to justice. The series took its name from the trick rifle that Lucas always carried, a modified Winchester with a large ring that cocked it as he twirled it. According to the scripts, he could fire off a round in three-tenths of a second.

The shooting was played down and Lucas's attempt to make a man of Mark gave the hero more credibility than most other television Western heroes. While Lucas lacked the impenetrable emotional shell of a Josh Randall, he was a more human hero. And in every episode of *The Rifleman*, Mark learned something about life on his own or from his father, making the series an adult Western with genuine family appeal.

Chuck Connors, a 6-foot 5-inch ex-major league baseball player, played Lucas McCain with strength and sincerity, while young Johnny Crawford was launched on the way to a successful acting career in the role of Mark. *The Rifleman* was an immediate success. It reached fourth in the ratings in its first season, but slipped to fourteenth the second year. Some minor changes were made in the show's supporting cast during the third season, but it was never able to regain its former popularity and left the air in 1963.

*Rawhide*, like *Gunsmoke*, is considered one of the best dramatic series of any genre to appear on television. It was the closest television came to creating an authentic "sweat and blood" Western. The series, which premiered in January 1959, as a mid-season replacement, made no attempt to embellish the basic format of man-against-the-West, and it achieved a rugged documentary realism.

The program was the creation of veteran Hollywood writer-director Charles Marquis Warren, who had been instrumental in developing the TV version of *Gunsmoke* and recently had finished directing the film *Cattle Empire* (1958). This project gave Warren the idea for a television Western based on the great cattle drives of the 1870s. Originally entitled *Cattle Drive*, the series followed the men on a drive as they moved cattle from Texas to the railroads in the Midwest.

Although it was described by some as "the cattleman's answer to

Paul Brinegar, Clint Eastwood, and Eric Fleming in *Rawhide*. *Stephen Sally*

*Wagon Train*," *Rawhide* was more than simply a drama set in the American West that concentrated on the harsher aspects of life on the frontier. Warren set out to depict the "working West" of the Cattle Kingdom and the men and women who inhabited it. Discussing how his show was different from the other TV Westerns, Warren said,

> With us, the herd is primary. We're always up against the elements, and we never leave them entirely behind. For instance, the "Wagon Train" people come across their exploits and suddenly, the wagon train disappears while they tell their story . . . With the acute beef shortage, and a nation starving after the Civil War, if it came to a choice between men and beeves, the beeves won.[23]

Seeking authenticity, Warren based much of his detail for the stories on a diary written by George Duffield, who had served as a drover on a cattle drive from San Antonio, Texas, to Sedalia, Missouri, in 1866. From Duffield's diary came the unique terminology that gave the series much of its realism. Terms such as "beeves" (a collection of cattle), "drover" (a working member of the drive), "trail boss" (head of the drive with complete authority over his men), "ramrod" (second in command on a drive), "drag" (member of the drive whose job was to ride behind the herd and "eat dust"), and "point" (member of the drive who rode ahead of the herd scouting the terrain) were used extensively in the series.[24]

Warren sometimes even invented terminology to cover aspects of the drive not defined in Duffield's diary such as "swing" to describe the drovers who rode along the sides of the herd. He also authored the lines used to close each episode, "Head 'em up! Move 'em out!" Later a cattleman told him that that was what cowhands had been saying for years.[25]

Warren also was responsible for the beautiful monologues which set the scene for each episode during the first season:

> Ridin' herd over a long trail may be a headache, but I can tell you that it's never boresome even when it's goin' smooth. When there's plenty of sweet grass, blue skies, clear spring water, you can ride lazy, thinkin' of what you left behind, dreamin' of what's ahead. But ridin' easy doesn't come often on a drive when you're pushin' 3,000 head and twenty hands. There's always something about to happen. Whatever it is and whenever it comes up, I got ta meet it. That's my job. I'm Gil Favor, trail boss.[26]

The leads in the series were cast for the most part with unknown actors. The major role was that of trail boss Gil Favor, "a tough man of action who possessed good judgment, compassion, and an iron will."

Eric Fleming, whose prior acting credits consisted mainly of low-budget science fiction films (*Conquest of Space*, 1955; *The Queen of Outer Space*, 1958), proved an excellent choice because he was tall and possessed a deep, resonant voice.

Second in command to Favor was ramrod Rowdy Yates. He often let his emotions get him into trouble, especially when a pretty girl was involved. Clint Eastwood, another unknown, was selected for the role—a break that launched him on a career that made him one of Hollywood's true superstars. At the time Eastwood had been able to land bit parts in such forgettable films as *Revenge of the Creature* (1955), *Francis in the Navy* (1955), and *The First Traveling Saleslady* (1956).

Other important roles in the series were Pete Nolan, directly below Favor and Yates in the chain of command on the drive, played well by character actor-singer Sheb Wooley, and Wishbone, the cantankerous, comic cook, a *tour de force* for veteran character actor Paul Brinegar, who had played a similar role in Warren's *Cattle Empire*.

Most of the stories used during the first six seasons involved "incidents" that occurred along the drives as the drovers encountered interesting characters of various types usually played by guest stars such as Peter Lorre, Mercedes McCambridge, Ed Wynn, Burgess Meredith, Brian Donlevy, or Gary Merrill. Each became caught up in some way with the drive, providing ample opportunity for both character development and physical action.

The show was enormously popular with viewers during the first five seasons and was ranked as high as sixth in 1960–61. When the TV cowboy craze began to die as public taste shifted from Westerns to situation comedies in the early 1960s, only the giants of the genre such as *Gunsmoke* and *Bonanza* were able to survive.

Prior to the series' final season, CBS and Eric Fleming parted company and Clint Eastwood was "promoted" to trail boss. Rowdy Yates became the lead character. Other changes were also made in the supporting cast, and *Rawhide*'s former popularity never returned. Nevertheless, *Rawhide* made a significant mark on the world of television Westerns. Only three, *Gunsmoke*, *Bonanza*, and *The Virginian* ran longer and the series is still doing well in syndication. *Rawhide* came as close as any TV Western to evoking the same grit and realism found in the better Western movies.

The number of new television Westerns began to decline after the 1958 season, but not without a struggle. Twelve series made their debuts in 1959. The best and most successful was *Bonanza*, the only one to survive longer than three seasons. *Bonanza* remained on prime-time television until 1973 and has been in syndication all over the world ever since.

Set in the vicinity of Virginia City, Nevada, during the Civil War period soon after the discovery of the fabulous Comstock Silver Lode, *Bonanza* was the story of a prosperous family of ranchers. Widower Ben Cartwright, patriarch of the all-male clan and owner of the one-hundred-thousand-acre Ponderosa Ranch, had three sons by three different wives. Adam, the oldest of the half-brothers, was the most serious, thoughtful, and balanced, and the likely successor to his father as manager of the sprawling Cartwright holdings. Hoss, the middle son, was a mountain of a man who was as gentle as he was huge, sensitive, naive, and, at times, not particularly bright. Little Joe was the youngest, most impulsive, and most romantic of the Cartwrights.

*Bonanza* differed from the majority of television Westerns in that it emphasized the bonds of affection between four strong men. Although constantly engaging in family scrapes, father and sons clung together to protect the family name and the family property from corrupt and thieving outsiders. As owners of the largest ranch in the area, the members of the Cartwright clan were required to make frequent business trips to neighboring communities and take an intense interest in any local project or occurrence that might affect them. Such a broad format permitted a wide variety of plots and the opportunity for guest stars to be featured in most episodes.

The series had another distinction. It was the first network Western to be televised in color. The great expanse of gorgeous outdoor scenery utilized in the show was probably the most significant single factor in stimulating the early sale of color television sets.

NBC wanted established stars for *Bonanza*, but the program's creator, David Dortort, insisted that the show would make its own stars. Of the four leads, all but Michael Landon were unknowns. Lorne Greene, who played Ben, had once been the main announcer for the Canadian Broadcasting Company. He had done some film work in supporting roles, *The Silver Chalice* (1954), *Peyton Place* (1957), *The Buccaneer* (1958), but had never even ridden a horse. Dortort cast him in the series after seeing him in an episode of *Wagon Train*.

Most of Pernell Roberts's previous acting experience was on the New York stage. He had done some television work, including several small roles on *Gunsmoke*, but he seemed right at home as Adam until

Lorne Greene as Ben
Cartwright in *Bonanza*.
*Stephen Sally*

he tired of the role and left the series in 1965. Dan Blocker, who played
Hoss until his sudden death in 1972, was a former Texas schoolteacher
who once had worked with Dortort on an episode of another TV Western, *The Restless Gun*. Michael Landon gained some notoriety in the
title role of *I Was a Teenage Werewolf* (1957), but it was his numerous
appearances in supporting parts on other television shows such as
*Gunsmoke* that prepared him for his role as Little Joe.

More than any other Western series with continuing characters,
except *Wyatt Earp*, *Bonanza* relied on historical events and characters
to develop its story lines. Especially during the first several seasons,
references to the Civil War, statehood for Nevada, and the discovery of
the Comstock Lode were common and appearances by figures such as
Samuel Clemens, Lotta Crabtree, Julia Bulette, and Cochise were
frequent.

The problem with this device was that many of these events could not have taken place within the purported time frame of the stories. Consequently scriptwriters often resorted to "time compression." The most glaring example of this type of historical distortion could be found in the map which appeared in every opening sequence, then caught on fire and disintegrated to reveal the Cartwrights riding into the foreground. The map also hung behind Ben's desk in the huge ranch house. Although most of the distances shown were grossly inaccurate, this was not particularly unusual in most early maps of that type. However, one of the locations on Ben's map, the town of Reno, was not named until May 1868, yet many of the incidents occurring in the stories took place considerably before that period.[27]

This was not the only error in the series. In several episodes, Ben refers to events that happened in Virginia City fifteen to twenty years earlier, but that town was not established until after the discovery of the Comstock Lode in 1859. When *Bonanza* supposedly took place, Virginia City was depicted as a stable town with a lengthy history. During the community's early years, however, the look of the town was quite crude with a few permanent buildings and about four hundred people "camped" there.[28] TV historian Richard K. Tharp points out this inconsistency in the series quite bluntly:

> Where was the boisterous mining town, the center of a mining industry that produced forty million dollars worth of bullion between the years 1860 and 1864? For that matter, where were the miners? For a series supposedly based on the Comstock Lode, there was a dearth of miners.... and all of this was watched over by one lonely sheriff, with a deputy or two....[29]

To most viewers these historical inaccuracies apparently mattered little and after a somewhat slow beginning, *Bonanza* became the most watched television program of any genre during the 1960s. It reached number seventeen in the Nielsen ratings during its second season, zoomed to second during the third year, and held the number one position from 1964–67. The show never left the Top Twenty until its final season when it was canceled after experiencing the death of one of its most popular leads (Dan Blocker) and a shift from its familiar Sunday evening time slot.

Some sixteen Westerns were attempted in the three years following the debut of *Bonanza*, but only one managed to capture the public's fancy. *The Virginian* was television's first weekly "movie" with each program running ninety minutes. The series was loosely based on

Owen Wister's 1901 novel that twice previously had been brought successfully to life on the screen. The first starred Gary Cooper in 1929 and the second featured Joel McCrea in 1946. The stories centered around the Shiloh Ranch near Medicine Bow in Wyoming Territory owned by Judge Henry Garth. The title character was a mysterious drifter with no name, a man everyone respected, but no one really knew, who became ranch foreman.

The theme of the show, set in the 1880s, was that a century-old way of life on the Western frontier was being slowly eroded by the "civilizing" encroachment of the East. This change was not easily accepted by the rough pioneers of the prairie and *The Virginian* realistically depicted these clashing cultures. Only the Virginian himself refused to be broken or moved by this conflict, becoming, in fact, a kind of antihero, a man more interested in preserving the past than in submitting to inevitable change.

The ninety-minute series used a core of continuing cast members, but the extra length provided the time for the stories to develop and for guest stars such as Jack Warden, George C. Scott, Bette Davis, and Robert Redford to deliver highly credible performances. *The Virginian* was closer to an anthology of Western films than a regular Western TV series. The show's ratings indicated that viewers accepted feature-length television shows and enjoyed seeing movies on TV.

James Drury, who had gained experience in such Westerns as *Gunsmoke*, starred in the title role. The wild, young cowhand, Trampas, was "reformed" from the villain's role he had been given in Wister's novel, and, as played by Doug McClure, a veteran of TV's detective drama *Checkmate*, became one of the most popular continuing characters in the show. Star power and dramatic respectability was given the series by casting the experienced and well-known actor Lee J. Cobb as Judge Garth, until he left the show in 1966. Ownership of the ranch changed hands several times during the eight years that *The Virginian* aired, including a one-year stint by John McIntire, who had also ridden in to rescue *Wagon Train* after the death of Ward Bond. During the last season the program was retitled *The Men From Shiloh* and the historical period was moved forward by about ten years.

The series made Neilsen's Top Twenty-Five during its second year on the air and remained there until 1969. *The Men from Shiloh* ranked number eighteen during the program's final season.

There was a dearth of new Western hits between 1962 and 1965. Only Walt Disney's *Daniel Boone* was modestly successful and this was simply a re-working of their earlier winner, *Davy Crockett*, even down to its star, Fess Parker.

Two Westerns of note—out of a total of seven—premiered in 1965 (*The Big Valley* and *The Wild Wild West*). The first of these was significant because the major character in the series was a woman. Barbara Stanwyck was cast as Victoria Barkley, matriarch of the Barkley clan, who ran the sprawling Barkley ranch in California's San Joaquin Valley in the 1870s.

Experienced and adept from years of appearing in a wide variety of film roles, Stanwyck had given some of her best performances in Westerns (*Annie Oakley*, 1935; *Union Pacific*, 1939; *California*, 1947; *Cattle Queen of Montana*, 1955; *The Maverick Queen*, 1956; *Forty Guns*, 1957). Describing her role as "an old broad who combines elegance with guts," she expressed great pride that *The Big Valley* was the first (and only adult) Western featuring a woman. In a *New York Times* interview Stanwyck pointed out, "Some producers think women did nothing in those days except keep house and have children. But if you read your history they did a lot more than that. They were *in* cattle drives. They were *there*.[30]

It should be pointed out that by 1965 women were treated by television producers as domestic consumers who were vital members of the viewing audience. Furthermore, successful TV Westerns such as *Wagon Train*, *Rawhide*, *Bonanza*, and *The Virginian* had prominently featured female guest stars on a regular basis.

What was truly unique about Stanwyck's role was the strength and domination of the character. Most of the women in television Westerns had appeared in secondary roles as barmaids, farmers' wives, or damsels in distress. Although *Annie Oakley* was an exception, the heroine in that series was actually cast in a masculine, tomboyish mold.

In the adult Western of the late 1950s and 1960s, the "bad girl," a woman who used her sexuality to advance herself in society, had appeared from time to time. In the opinion of Ralph Brauer, the only woman in a TV Western that came close to being "normal" was Kitty Russell of *Gunsmoke*. She was "more independent and less submissive" than the typical virtuous heroine and, "yet not as scheming as the bad girl."[31] Victoria Barkley brought Western women full-cycle. She was a heroine with feminine characteristics and the inner strength of a man—a female Ben Cartwright.

Stories on *The Big Valley* were built around the widowed matriarch, her four adult offspring, and their continual struggle against the lawless elements of the Old West. Populated with such evil characters as murderers, bank robbers, Mexican revolutionaries, and con men, the action-filled program also used major guest stars in featured roles.

Stanwyck, who appeared in all but seven of the 112 episodes produced, remained *The Big Valley*'s strongest appeal during its four seasons. In 1966, following the series's first season, Stanwyck won an Emmy as "Outstanding Actress in a Dramatic Series" and received an additional nomination in that category in each of the next two seasons. Nevertheless, with Westerns declining in popularity and with weak Nielsen figures, the program was canceled in 1969.

*The Wild Wild West* was the product of a unique combination of an espionage thriller and a Western adventure based on the unlikely premise of two U.S. government spies in the American West of the 1870s. The series, a creation of Michael Garrison, owed more to such James Bond clones as *The Man from U.N.C.L.E.* than to earlier TV Westerns, although the two leading characters resembled the flippant Maverick brothers. The major difference between *The Wild Wild West* and earlier Westerns was its incredible "comic-book style violence."

The series contained much of the gadgetry associated with spy programs, but in an embryonic form. Instead of the technological wonders of U.N.C.L.E., the agents used primitive explosives and carried plenty of hidden devices in their unending struggle against villains who commonly resembled Jules Verne-type scientists. President Ulysses S. Grant personally assigned special agents James T. West and Artemus Gordon to the Western frontier to undermine or expose the attempts of various radical, revolutionary, or criminal groups to take over the country.

The two agents were actually superheroes in the traditional mold with a few modern gimmicks, such as the special three-car train in which they traveled, thrown in. West, handsome and athletic, was a master at all forms of self-defense and weaponry and at some point in every episode he dispatched at least five thugs simultaneously with impeccable style. The role was tailor-made for Robert Conrad who had gained television experience as Tom Lopaka in the moderately popular *Hawaiian Eye* series. Conrad kept himself in excellent physical condition and performed most of his own stunts.

Gordon was a master of disguises and dialects. The role was played with skill and charm by Ross Martin, a Polish-born American whose

Robert Conrad as James
T. West in *The Wild Wild
West. Art Fernandez*

prior acting experience included radio (in the soap opera *Janice Gray*),
the Broadway stage (in *Hazel Flagg*), films (in *Conquest of Space*, 1955,
and *Experiment in Terror*, 1962), and television (in *Mr. Lucky* and on
the charades game show, *Stump the Stars*). On the show Martin convincingly passed as everything from a drunken Portuguese fisherman
to a dignified German baron with the aid of a special eight-piece plastic
nose that he himself had designed.[32]

One problem *The Wild Wild West* faced was the criticism of the
PTA and other educational groups who objected to the show's extensive
use of sadistic violence. It seemed that every villain on the series
delighted in conjuring up methods of torture for the heroic West. West
survived a great variety of ingenious traps, and the series outlived the
storm of objections these exploits produced.[33]

Gently spoofing both Westerns and spy shows at the same time, the
series developed especially offbeat and intriguing stories. Conrad and

Martin used light banter in the face of danger to raise the series above what some considered a ridiculous premise to become a solid, entertaining hybrid and a CBS Friday night fixture for four seasons.

Two encore film versions of the series were presented, including a ninety-minute version on May 9, 1978, entitled *The Wild Wild West Revisited* and a split two-hour version on October 7 and 8, 1980, entitled *More Wild Wild West*. Both sequels concentrated on comedy rather than adventure. The reverse was true in the original episodes with tongue-in-cheek humor clearly secondary to the action.

*The Wild Wild West* reached Nielsen's Top Twenty-Five only once after placing twenty-third during its first season, but was successfully syndicated for many years. Without a doubt the series expanded the creative limits of the TV Western.

In 1966, seven new Western series made their appearance on the home screen, but as opposition to the war in Vietnam increased, interest in the violence and bloodshed that was such an integral ingredient of most TV Westerns declined.[34]

Only one series out of some twenty with a Western setting which debuted between 1966 and 1985 was successful in attracting viewers. By some standards, that one successful program, *Little House on the Prairie*, would not even be considered a Western. It was set in the American West during the 1870s, but it did not have the other usual trappings associated with Westerns. There were no cowboys or Indians in the stories and the town of Walnut Grove, Minnesota, where the Ingalls family lived, did not have a saloon.

The series, based on the *Little House on the Prairie* stories of Laura Ingalls Wilder, owed more to *The Waltons* than it did to other television Westerns. Presenting an incredibly sentimental view of the trials and tribulations of a homesteader family struggling to make a living on a small farm on the frontier, episodes presented character studies of individual family members and their friends in time of crisis. They were usually told from the perspective of the second-oldest daughter Laura (Melissa Gilbert). The plots dealt with the family's constant struggle against natural disasters and ruined crops as well as their dealings with other members of the little community in which they lived. Adapting to the changing demands of life during an uncertain period of American history, the Ingalls also faced difficult personal crises, such as the sudden blindness of their oldest daughter Mary.

The program played down violence, presenting it as the exceptional rather than the commonplace experience of family life in the Old

West. The series was given a strong boost by Michael Landon who had gained great popularity in the role of Little Joe on *Bonanza*. Landon not only produced and directed most of the episodes, he played the lead role of Charles Ingalls, the young father and struggling homesteader who was loved by his family and respected by his fellow pioneers.

The judicious combination of sentimentality and realism made the series one of NBC's most popular television programs of the 1970s. *Little House on the Prarie* jumped into the Top Twenty within weeks of its premiere and remained there, reaching seventh in 1977–78, until its final season in 1982.

One can conclude from even this brief examination of the television Western, that the genre as a whole derived much of its "inspiration" from the B Western and radio Westerns. Several shows, however, made significant innovations including the derivation of a Western hero from historical research (*The Life and Legend of Wyatt Earp*); the development of the Western anti-hero (*Have Gun, Will Travel* and *Wanted: Dead or Alive*); the use of satire in Westerns (*Maverick*); the utilization of guest stars in featured roles (*Wagon Train* was the first); the verification of actual conditions for greater authenticity (*Rawhide*); the emphasis on family relationships within the Western drama (first, *The Rifleman*, then *Bonanza*); the employment of James Bond gadgetry in a Western setting (*The Wild Wild West*); and the creation of a heroic Western female lead (*The Big Valley*), all landmarks in the evolution of the television Western.

Except for programs being rerun in syndication, the Western virtually disappeared from the home screen in the early 1980s. The reasons are many. There were too many Westerns with too many gimmicks trying too hard to be all things to all viewers. Too many plots seemed too familiar. Too few rising young stars were interested in gambling their careers on a dying genre. And, did the Western any longer relate to our complex urban society?

The venerable Walt Disney Productions, with such moderately successful juvenile TV Westerns to their credit as *Davy Crockett*, *Daniel Boone*, and *Zorro*, developed *Wildside* which premiered in March 1985. The show focused on five businessmen in a frontier town who turn into an elite law enforcement unit whenever evildoers threaten their community.

The cinematography was creative in utilizing close-up, slow-motion, and stop-action techniques. The characters were interesting— one expertly used knives to disarm villains, another was proficient with a rope, while a third specialized in explosives. The stories were innovative—a phony Buffalo Bill brings a complete Wild West Show to Wildside, renegade British soldiers claiming to be members of the Light Brigade terrorize the community, fortune seekers are lured to a coal mine and forced to become slave laborers. The casting was strong—Howard E. Rollins, Jr., who had won recognition in such films as *Ragtime* (1981) and *A Soldier's Story* (1984) became one of the few continuing black characters in a television Western.

Yet *Wildside* lasted only six weeks. The ratings were dismal, but could ABC have expected better? It was scheduled opposite the number one show on TV, *The Bill Cosby Show* and the well-established and popular *Magnum, P.I.* Lovers of television Westerns can only hope that Clint Eastwood's recent revival of the Western film will convince the networks that there is still a significant place on the home screen for that unique literary creation, the Western hero.

NOTES

1. Tim Brooks and Earle Marsh, *The Complete Directory to Prime Time Network TV Shows, 1946–Present* (New York: 1979). All data concerning the A.C. Nielsen Company ratings is taken from Appendix 3, "Top-Rated Programs by Season," pp. 802–10.

2. Quoted in Mario DeMarco, *Hopalong Cassidy: Knight of the West* (privately printed, 1983), p. 100.

3. David Rothel, *Who Was That Masked Man? The Story of the Lone Ranger* (New York, 1976), p. 86.

4. Gary H. Grossman, *Saturday Morning TV* (New York: 1981), p. 191.

5. Ibid., p. 186.

6. Ibid., p. 192.

7. Ibid., p. 321.

8. Don Miller, *Hollywood Corral* (New York, 1976), p. 242.

9. Ralph Brauer, *The Horse, the Gun and the Piece of Property: Changing Images of the TV Western* (Bowling Green, Ohio, 1975), p. 42.

10. J. Fred MacDonald, *Television and the Red Menance: the Video Road to Vietnam* (New York, 1985), p. 140.

11. Quoted in Ibid., pp. 141–42.

12. Brauer, *The Horse*, p. 55.

13. Harry Castleman and Walter J. Podrazik, *Watching TV: Four Decades of American Television* (New York, 1982), p. 104.

14. Quoted in Jeff Roven, *The Great Television Series* (New York, 1977) p. 46.

15. Kristine Fredricksson, "Gunsmoke: Twenty-Year Videography, Part I," *The Journal of Popular Film and Television* (Spring, 1984), p. 16.

16. Quoted in Roven, *Great Television Series*, pp. 51–52.

17. Brooks and Marsh, *Complete Directory*, p. 664.

18. Quoted in Roven, *Great Television Series*, p. 52.

19. Richard F. Tharp, "The World According to Pappy," *Reruns, the Magazine of Television History* 3 and 4 (November 1982), pp. 6–7.

20. Quoted in Castleman and Podrazik, *Watching TV*, p. 116.

21. Quoted in Roven, *Great Television Series*, p. 52.

22. Ibid., p. 53.

23. Ibid., p. 61.

24. Richard K. Tharp, "Rawhide, Part 1," *Reruns, the Magazine of Television History* (April, 1981) p. 6.

25. Ibid., p. 6.

26. *Rawhide*, Episode 9, March 6, 1959, ("Incident of the Town in Terror").

27. Richard K. Tharp, "Bonanza, Part 1," *Reruns, the Magazine of Television History* (April, 1982) p. 7.

28. Ibid., p. 7.

29. Ibid., p. 7.

30. Quoted in Jerry Vermilye, *Barbara Stanwyck* (New York, 1975), p. 135.

31. Brauer, *The Horse*, pp. 189–90.

32. Robert Reed and Richard K. Tharp, "The Wild Wild West, Part 1," *Reruns, the Magazine of Television History* (October, 1980), p. 12.

33. Ibid., p. 12.

34. John H. Lenihan, *Showdown: Confronting Modern America in the Western Film* (Urbana, Ill., 1980), Chap. 3.

# APPENDIX

# TV Westerns (1948–85)

by Gary A. Yoggy

| | | | |
|---|---|---|---|
| *Action in the Afternoon* | 1953–54 | CBS | J |
| *The Adventures of Champion* | 1955–56 | CBS | J |
| *The Adventures of Jim Bowie* | 1956–58 | ABC | A |
| *The Adventures of Kit Carson* | 1956 | SYN | J |
| *The Adventures of Rin-Tin-Tin** | 1952–55 | ABC, CBS | J |
| *The Alaskans* | 1959–60 | ABC | A |
| *Alias Smith and Jones* | 1971–73 | ABC | A |
| *Annie Oakley* | 1954–59 | ABC | J |
| *The Barbary Coast* | 1975–76 | ABC | A |
| *Bat Masterson* | 1958–61 | NBC | A |
| *Bearcats* | 1971 | CBS | A |
| *Best of the West* | 1981–82 | ABC | A |
| *The Big Valley* | 1965–69 | ABC | A |
| *Black Saddle* | 1959–60 | NBC | A |
| *Bonanza* | 1959–73 | NBC | A |
| *Boots and Saddles* | 1957–58 | SYN | A |
| *Born to the Wind* | 1982 | NBC | A |
| *Branded* | 1965–66 | NBC | A |
| *Brave Eagle* | 1955–56 | CBS | J |
| *Bret Maverick* | 1981–82 | NBC | A |
| *Broken Arrow* | 1956–58 | ABC | A |
| *Bronco* | 1959–60 | ABC | A |
| *Buckskin* | 1958–59 | NBC | J |
| *Buffalo Bill, Jr.* | 1955 | SYN | J |
| *Cade's Country* | 1971–72 | CBS | A |
| *The Californians* | 1957–59 | NBC | A |
| *Cheyenne* | 1955–63 | ABC | A |
| *The Chisholms* | 1979–80 | CBS | A |
| *Cimarron City* | 1958–59 | NBC | A |
| *Cimarron Strip* | 1967–68 | CBS | A |
| *The Cisco Kid** | 1950–56 | SYN | J |
| *Colt Forty-Five* | 1957–61 | ABC | A |
| *Cowboy G-Men* | 1952–53 | SYN | J |
| *The Cowboys* | 1974 | ABC | A |
| *Custer* | 1967 | ABC | A |

\*     Episodes in author's personal collection
\*\*   Also broadcast on radio
A = Adult
J = Juvenile

| | | | |
|---|---|---|---|
| *The Dakotas* | 1963 | ABC | A |
| *Daniel Boone* | 1964–70 | NBC | J |
| *Davy Crockett* | 1954–55 | ABC | J |
| *Death Valley Days*** | 1952–72 | SYN | A |
| *The Deputy* | 1959–61 | NBC | A |
| *Destry* | 1964 | ABC | A |
| *Dirty Sally* | 1974 | CBS | A |
| *Dundee and the Culhane* | 1967 | CBS | A |
| *Dusty's Trail* | 1973 | SYN | A |
| *Empire* | 1962–65 | NBC | A |
| *F Troop* | 1965–67 | ABC | A |
| *Father Murphy* | 1981–82 | NBC | A |
| *Frontier* | 1955–56 | NBC | A |
| *Frontier Circus* | 1961–62 | CBS | A |
| *Fury* | 1955–66 | NBC | J |
| *The Gabby Hayes Show* | 1950–51 | NBC | J |
| *The Gene Autry Show*** | 1950–56 | CBS | J |
| *The Gray Ghost* | 1957 | SYN | A |
| *Gunshy* | 1983 | CBS | A |
| *The Guns of Will Sonnett* | 1967–69 | ABC | A |
| *Gunslinger* | 1961 | CBS | A |
| *Gunsmoke*** | 1955–75 | CBS | A |
| *Have Gun, Will Travel*** | 1957–63 | CBS | A |
| *Hawkeye and the Last of the Mohicans* | 1957–58 | SYN | A |
| *Hec Ramsey* | 1972–74 | NBC | A |
| *Here Come The Brides* | 1968–70 | ABC | A |
| *The High Chaparral* | 1967–71 | NBC | A |
| *Hondo* | 1967 | ABC | A |
| *Hopalong Cassidy*** | 1949–55 | SYN | J |
| *Hotel de Paree* | 1959–60 | CBS | A |
| *How the West Was Won* | 1978–79 | ABC | A |
| *Iron Horse* | 1966–68 | ABC | A |
| *Jefferson Drum* | 1958–59 | NBC | A |
| *Johnny Ringo* | 1959–60 | CBS | A |
| *Judge Roy Bean* | 1956–57 | SYN | A |
| *Klondike* | 1960–61 | NBC | A |
| *Kodiak* | 1974 | ABC | A |
| *Kung Fu* | 1972–75 | ABC | A |
| *Lancer* | 1968–70 | CBS | A |
| *Laramie* | 1959–63 | NBC | A |
| *Laredo* | 1965–67 | NBC | A |
| *Lash of the West* | 1953 | SYN | J |
| *Law of the Plainsman* | 1959–62 | NBC | A |
| *Lawman* | 1958–62 | ABC | A |
| *The Legend of Jesse James* | 1965–66 | ABC | A |
| *The Life and Legend of Wyatt Earp* | 1955–61 | ABC | A |
| *The Life and Times of Grizzly Adams* | 1977–78 | NBC | A |

| | | | |
|---|---|---|---|
| *Little House on the Prairie | 1974–83 | NBC | A |
| *The Lone Ranger** | 1949–57 | ABC, CBS | J |
| The Loner | 1965–66 | CBS | A |
| MacKenzie's Raiders | 1958–59 | SYN | A |
| A Man Called Shenandoah | 1965–66 | ABC | A |
| The Man from Blackhawk | 1959–60 | ABC | A |
| Man of the West | 1958–59 | SYN | A |
| The Man Without a Gun | 1958–59 | SYN | A |
| The Marshal of Gunsight Pass | 1950 | ABC | J |
| *Maverick | 1957–62 | ABC | A |
| The Men from Shiloh | 1970–71 | NBC | A |
| The Monroes | 1966–67 | ABC | A |
| My Friend Flicka | 1957–66 | ABC, CBS, NBC | J |
| Nakia | 1974 | ABC | A |
| The New Land | 1974 | ABC | A |
| Nichols | 1971–72 | NBC | A |
| The Nine Lives of Elfego Baca | 1958–59 | ABC | A |
| Northwest Passage | 1958–59 | NBC | A |
| The Oregon Trail | 1977 | NBC | A |
| The Outcasts | 1968–69 | ABC | A |
| The Outlaws | 1960–62 | NBC | A |
| The Overland Trail | 1960 | SYN | A |
| Pistols 'n Petticoats | 1966–67 | CBS | A |
| Pony Express | 1960–61 | SYN | A |
| The Quest | 1976 | NBC | A |
| *The Range Rider | 1952–53 | SYN | J |
| Rango | 1967 | ABC | A |
| *Rawhide | 1959–66 | CBS | A |
| RCMP | 1960 | SYN | A |
| The Rebel | 1959–62 | ABC, NBC | A |
| Red Ryder** | 1956–57 | SYN | J |
| Redigo | 1963 | NBC | A |
| Renfrew of the Royal Mounted** | 1953 | SYN | J |
| The Restless Gun | 1957–59 | NBC | A |
| *The Rifleman | 1958–63 | ABC | A |
| Riverboat | 1959–61 | NBC | A |
| The Road West | 1966–67 | NBC | A |
| Rough Riders | 1958–59 | ABC | A |
| The Rounders | 1966–67 | ABC | A |
| The Rousters | 1983–84 | NBC | A |
| *The Roy Rogers Show** | 1951–62 | NBC, CBS | J |
| The Saga of Andy Burnette | 1957 | SYN | J |
| Sara | 1976 | CBS | A |
| Saturday Roundup | 1951 | NBC | A |
| *Sergeant Preston of The Yukon** | 1955–58 | CBS | J |
| Seven Brides for Seven Brothers | 1982–83 | CBS | A |
| Shane | 1966 | ABC | A |

| | | | |
|---|---|---|---|
| *The Sheriff of Cochise* | 1956–60 | SYN | A |
| *Shotgun Slade* | 1959–61 | SYN | A |
| *Sky King** | 1951–66 | NBC, ABC, CBS | J |
| *Stagecoach West* | 1960–61 | ABC | A |
| *State Trooper* | 1957 | SYN | A |
| *Steve Donovan, Western Marshal* | 1955–56 | SYN | A |
| *Stoney Burke* | 1962–63 | ABC | A |
| *Stories of the Century* | 1956–58 | SYN | A |
| *Sugarfoot* | 1957–61 | ABC | A |
| *Tales of the Plainsman* | 1959 | SYN | A |
| *Tales of The Texas Rangers** | 1955–59 | ABC | A |
| *Tales of Wells Fargo* | 1957–62 | NBC | A |
| *The Tall Man* | 1960–62 | NBC | A |
| *Tate* | 1960 | NBC | A |
| *Temple Houston* | 1963–64 | NBC | A |
| *The Texan* | 1958–60 | CBS | A |
| *Texas John Slaughter* | 1958–59 | ABC | A |
| *The Tim McCoy Show* | 1951 | SYN | A |
| *Tomahawk* | 1957–58 | SYN | A |
| *Tombstone Territory* | 1957–59 | ABC | A |
| *Trackdown* | 1957–59 | CBS | A |
| *The Travels of Jamie McPheeters* | 1963–64 | ABC | A |
| *Twenty-Six Men* | 1957–59 | SYN | A |
| *Two Faces West* | 1961–62 | SYN | A |
| *Union Pacific* | 1958–59 | SYN | A |
| *The Virginian* | 1962–70 | NBC | A |
| *Wagon Train* | 1957–65 | NBC, ABC | A |
| *Wanted: Dead or Alive* | 1958–61 | CBS | A |
| *The Westerner* | 1960 | NBC | A |
| *Whiplash* | 1961–62 | SYN | A |
| *Whispering Smith* | 1961 | NBC | A |
| *Wichita Town* | 1959–60 | NBC | A |
| *The Wide Country* | 1962–63 | NBC | A |
| *Wild Bill Hickok** | 1951–58 | CBS, ABC | J |
| *Wildside* | 1985 | ABC | A |
| *The Wild Wild West* | 1965–69 | CBS | A |
| *Wrangler* | 1960 | NBC | A |
| *Yancy Derringer* | 1958–59 | CBS | A |
| *The Yellow Rose* | 1983–84 | NBC | A |
| *Young Dan'l Boone* | 1977 | CBS | J |
| *Young Maverick* | 1979–80 | NBC | A |
| *The Zane Grey Theatre** | 1956–62 | CBS | A |
| *Zorro* | 1957–59 | ABC | J |
| *Zorro and Son* | 1983 | CBS | A |

# CONTRIBUTORS

**Michael K. Schoenecke** is Assistant Professor of English at Texas Tech University, Lubbock, Texas, where he teaches film studies and popular culture. He has published on film studies and American Literature, and he will be editing a book on film adaptation which will be published in 1986.

**Ray White's** interest in Western films originated in the Saturday afternoon "shoot 'em ups" that he saw as a child in Luling, Texas. As a teacher of United States frontier history at Ball State University he made comparisons of the mythic Hollywood Westerns and historical reality. Eventually, he developed a course on history of the low-budget Western, which he uses as a device to teach social and cultural history. He has presented papers on the Western at meetings of the Western History and Popular Culture associations and has published in *The Indiana Media Journal, The History Teacher, Indiana Library Journal, Under Western Skies*, and *Favorite Westerns*. He holds a Ph.D. in history from the University of Texas at Austin.

**John H. Lenihan** is Associate Professor of History at Texas A&M University in Bryan, Texas, where he specializes in American cultural-intellectual history and film. He is the author of *Showdown: Confronting Modern America in the Western Film*, published by the University of Illinois Press.

**Stephen Tatum** teaches American literature and American studies courses in the English department at the University of Utah. He has published articles on Western American literature, history, and film in such journals as *Western American Literature, Western Historical Quarterly*, and *The Journal of Popular Film and Television*. His book *Inventing Billy the Kid: Visions of the Outlaw in America 1881–1981* (University of New Mexico Press, 1982) is now available in paperback. His interest in the West and the Western began with his childhood viewing of the numerous television Westerns, faltered somewhat during the Nixon presidency, and became a central focus after spending a year in Australia working on cattle stations in Queensland. He is working now on a book-length study of the historiography of the fur trade.

**Ray Merlock** was born in Pittsburgh, Pennsylvania, and became interested in Westerns at an early age. Preparation for this essay began with listening to the *Melody Ranch* radio show, watching Gene Autry television episodes, and collecting Autry comics. His Ph.D. dissertation, completed in 1981, is entitled "From Flintlock to Forty-Five: James Fenimore Cooper and the Popular Western Tradition in Fiction and Film." Presently he is a Visiting Professor at

Clemson University. His publications center on the Western, film, and popular culture. For six years an instructor of film studies at the University of Oklahoma, he was also involved in advertising, public relations, and film scripting for the Modern Volunteer Army project with US Army HQ Recruiting Command.

**Archie P. McDonald** is Regent's Professor of History at Stephen F. Austin State University, Nacogdoches, Texas. He is the author of a number of books, monographs, and articles, including *Texas: All Hail the Mighty State, Travis,* and *Make Me A Map of the Valley,* voted as one of the best 100 books on the Civil War by *Civil War Times Illustrated.* His favorite subjects are Texas and John Wayne, and he teaches a popular history class using John Wayne films. In 1986 he will publish two more books to commemorate the Texas Sesquicentennial.

A native Texan, **Don B. Graham** was born in 1940. He holds B.A. and M.A. degrees from North Texas State University and a Ph.D. from the University of Texas, where he is currently Associate Professor of English. Graham's publications include many articles and the following books: *The Fiction of Frank Norris: The Aesthetic Context* published by the University of Missouri Press and co-edited with William T. Pilkington; *Western Movies* published by the University of New Mexico Press; edited, *Critical Essays on Frank Norris,* published by G. K. Hall; *Cowboys and Cadillacs: How Hollywood Looks at Texas* published by the Texas Monthly Press; and co-edited with James W. Lee and William T. Pilkington, *The Texas Literary Tradition,* published by the University of Texas Press. Graham is writing a biography on Audie Murphy. A collection of short stories edited by Graham, *South by Southwest: Twenty-four Stories from Modern Texas,* will be published in Spring 1986 by University of Texas Press.

**Michael E. Welsh** is a member of the faculty of the History Department of the University of New Mexico. His research interests are the U.S. Southwest, American Indian history, and the modern West. He has published several articles on Western history, including one on early Western film companies for *Journal of the West.* He is the author of *A Mission in the Desert: The Albuquerque District, U. S. Army Corps of Engineers, 1935–85.*

**Richard C. Robertson** taught history at the University of Mississippi and Auburn University in Montgomery, where he was Director of the Alabama Humanities Resource Center. He presently lives in St. Louis, Missouri.

**Jim Miller** is the author of ten original Western novels, six of which form the "Colt Revolver Novels." Miller is a thirteen-year United States Army veteran. He lives in Aurora, Colorado, with his wife and two children. The only fancy degree he has ever received was that of "Storyteller," which he claims to have gotten from Rocky Mountain College, an institute originated some time ago by the Mountain Men in the area in which he lives.

**Sandra Kay Schackel** is a doctoral candidate at the University of New Mexico where she is specializing in the American West with a special interest in Women's History. She is also assistant editor of the *New Mexico Historical Review* and has published in the *Journal of the West, El Palacio*, and has a chapter on Hispanic and Indian women in *New Mexico Women*.

**Gary A. Yoggy** is Professor of History at Corning Community College in Corning, New York, and Lecturer in History at Elmira College in Elmira, New York. He holds a B.A. in History from the University of Michigan and a M.A. in History from Syracuse University. Professor Yoggy developed and teaches a course on the history and culture of the American West. His special interest is radio and television Westerns and he has extensive collections of each.

*Editor:* Jane Rodman
*Book designer:* Matthew Williamson
*Jacket designer:* Matthew Williamson
*Production coordinator:* Harriet Curry
*Typeface:* Century Schoolbook
*Typesetter:* Modern Type & Design, Inc.
*Printer:* Thomson-Shore

**Archie P. McDonald** is Regent's Professor History at Stephen F. Austin State University. He is the author of a number of books, monographs, and articles, including *Texas: All Hail the Mighty State* and *Make Me a Map of the Valley.*